Invisible Parade

THE FICTION OF FLANNERY O'CONNOR

Miles Orvell

Since her death in 1964, Flannery O'Connor's two novels and more than twenty short stories have continued to attract readers. Her work has been the subject of growing critical interest (*The Complete Stories* won the 1972 National Book Award), but there is no published study offering a balanced treatment of her work with the scholarly depth and perception of Orvell's present book.

The author has three related aims in this study: to "place" O'Connor's writings, to elucidate them, and to evaluate them. He examines the distinctive symbolic and comic qualities of her work and places her, because of her concern with the mystery of man's life, in the American romance tradition of Poe, Hawthorne, and Melville.

Orvell explores possible formative influences on O'Connor, stressing the claim her Catholic faith had on her imagination. He supports this assertion with original research on previously unexamined book reviews

Continued on back flap

INVISIBLE

PARADE

INVISIBLE PARADE

The Fiction of Flannery O'Connor

MILES ORVELL

TEMPLE UNIVERSITY PRESS

Philadelphia

TEMPLE UNIVERSITY PRESS, PHILADELPHIA 19122

© 1972 by Temple University
All rights reserved. Published 1972
Printed in the United States of America

International Standard Book Number: 0-87722-023-9

Library of Congress Catalog Card Number 72-91132

In Memory of

SAMUEL ORVELL

CONTENTS

PREFACE

THIS study of Flannery O'Connor's fiction has three related aims: to "place" the writings, to elucidate them, and to evaluate them. Chapter 1—the longest—is devoted to the first of these, and there I try to define some of the chief qualities of O'Connor's fiction and to view these qualities from a number of perspectives in an effort to establish certain contexts—historical and contemporary— within which her achievement can be placed. The following chapters discuss the two novels and selected short stories in greater detail, giving attention as well to the distinguishing patterns in her imagination. Along the way, some particular judgments are proposed, but I have left to the last chapter a discussion of the larger question of how the author's Christian viewpoint may affect the reader's response —a question that must be raised in any evaluation of her works. Finally, I use the late, reworked version of O'Connor's first story— concerned, as it is, with things final—as the basis for a concluding perspective.

Any critical approach must be appropriate to its subject, and I note here my own assumption in this regard. Flannery O'Connor wrote stories and novels that are exceedingly (sometimes excessively) well made: each of her works has a "central meaning and design," and it was her habit, as she wrote, "to take great pains to control every excess, everything that does not contribute to this central meaning and design."[1] Because of this control, the texture of her fiction is denser than it at first seems; life means in O'Connor, and means intensely. To find a comparable effect, one must turn to works in the allegorical mode, where "every experience has a greater possible value than the hero can himself detect," as Edwin Honig has written.[2] The result of such a texture is that the burden of detection falls on the reader, and there is usually more going on than can be taken in on a casual reading. Thus, if my discussion turns, at times, to levels of meaning, it is because O'Connor wrote with precisely such "levels" in mind.[3]

I have therefore not hesitated to accord the fiction close scrutiny: at times, by emphasizing the line of a plot, at other times by taking apart the work and putting it together again in order better to reveal the imaginative patterns underlying it. "The form of a story," O'Connor wrote, "gives it meaning which any other form would change, and unless the student is able, in some degree, to apprehend the form, he will never apprehend anything else about the work. . . ."[4] My effort, then, has been to avoid talking about the "abstract meaning" of her fiction, but to talk, instead, about what O'Connor called the "experienced meaning"—which I have taken to mean the reader's perception of the complex interaction of drama and metaphor, emotion and idea, that shapes the central design.

During the fifteen or so years that she published regularly, O'Connor produced two novels and some twenty stories; it is not a large body of works, but it has continued to fascinate readers and critics. Any critic, I suppose, is chary of taking his own responses as representative, and he may be doubly cautious if he has marked the following caveat from his subject. "No matter how favorable all the critics in New York City may be, they are an unreliable lot, as incapable now as on the day they were born of interpreting Southern literature to the world."[5] Having spent the first twenty years of my own life in New York City, I cannot, alas, claim complete immunity from that dictum; facing South, I can only turn the other cheek.

ACKNOWLEDGMENTS

IT is a pleasure to acknowledge here my gratitude to several persons who have aided and abetted me in this undertaking. Mr. Leo Zuber of Decatur, Georgia, was extremely helpful in making certain materials available, and most patient in answering my queries about the book review column of *The Bulletin* (a Georgia Catholic weekly), which he edited for several years. I am happy also to thank Mr. and Mrs. James Tate for their encouragement and hospitality, and Mrs. Regina O'Connor, for her kindness, during my visit to Milledgeville, Georgia.

The libraries of the Georgia State College at Milledgeville and of the University of Georgia at Athens provided some of the materials for this study. I would like to thank their staffs for their courteous assistance.

I began this work as a doctoral dissertation under the direction of Professors Robert Kiely and Joel Porte of Harvard University. I am glad to thank them for their patient and sensitive criticism of it. I also note with gratitude my debt to Professor Robert Fitzgerald of Harvard University, who read sections of this study and whose criticism and generous encouragement I have much appreciated. Finally, I must thank Professor Mary Cohen of Temple University for her close reading of the final draft and her many helpful suggestions.

A NOTE ON EDITIONS USED

I have incorporated page references into the text (in parentheses following quote) wherever possible, using the following editions of Flannery O'Connor's works:

Everything That Rises Must Converge. New York: Farrar, Straus & Giroux, 1965. [Containing the following stories: "Everything That Rises Must Converge," "Greenleaf," "A View of the Woods," "The Enduring Chill," "The Comforts of Home," "The Lame Shall Enter First," "Revelation," "Parker's Back," "Judgement Day."]

A Good Man Is Hard to Find and Other Stories. New York: Harcourt, Brace & Co., 1955. [Containing the following stories: "A Good Man Is Hard to Find," "The River," "The Life You Save May Be Your Own," "A Stroke of Good Fortune," "A Temple of the Holy Ghost," "The Artificial Nigger," "A Circle in the Fire," "A Late Encounter with the Enemy," "Good Country People," "The Displaced Person."]

The Violent Bear It Away. New York: Farrar, Straus & Cudahy, 1960.

Wise Blood. 2d edition. With an Introduction by the Author. New York: Farrar, Straus & Cudahy, 1962.

When I initially quote from a text, I indicate in a footnote the volume used; for subsequent quotations (especially from the stories), the reader may find it convenient to ascertain the proper volume by using the above list.

After this study was completed, Robert Giroux brought out *Flannery O'Connor: The Complete Stories* (New York: Farrar, Straus & Giroux, 1971). It contains not only the contents of O'Connor's two previously published books of stories, but also the hitherto uncollected fiction—stories written for her Master's thesis at the University of Iowa (some of which were published during her early career and some only posthumously by her literary executor, Robert Fitzgerald), and also the stories that were later reworked into the novels *Wise Blood* and *The Violent Bear It Away.* (See Appendix 1.) When dealing with this previously uncollected material I have added to my original references—for the convenience of the reader—the corresponding pages in *The Complete Stories.* I should say, however, that where there are minor discrepancies between the original text and the posthumously published text (mostly matters of punctuation), I have adhered to the original.

"When you get well," [his mother] said, "I think it would be nice if you wrote a book about down here. We need another good book like *Gone With the Wind.*"

He could feel the muscles in his stomach begin to tighten.

FLANNERY O'CONNOR, "The Enduring Chill"

1

DEFINING CONTEXTS AND QUALITIES

THE best place to begin a study of Flannery O'Connor's fiction seemed to be the O'Connor farm itself, where Flannery had lived and written during the last thirteen years of her life. So I visited there with a couple who had been her friends for many years and who were kind enough to show me around the place they had visited frequently in the past. We turned off the red clay road at the sign "Andalusia," and followed the long driveway up to the white farmhouse. (Mrs. O'Connor, Flannery's mother, ran the farm still, but lived in the town of Milledgeville, a few miles away.) It was drizzling lightly and there was a vague mist about the place, and in the late afternoon the green of the meadows and trees surrounding the house seemed a greeny hue indeed, even for June. I noticed that the farm still had a sizable population of peafowl—cocks and hens— and while the cocks were reluctant to spread their tails, they did startle me with their eerie hooting from perches in the trees. And not only peafowl were there: several guinea hens awkwardly tilted by, along with some birds we found difficult to identify—indefinable hybrids, grotesques (the word inevitably came to mind), such as

Flannery O'Connor liked to raise—and, mutatis mutandis, write about. There were fruit trees too growing around the house, heavy with several varieties of pears and things unknown to me. What brave old world was this, what Eden?

Near the white farmhouse stands an unpainted wooden house where an old black woman, Louise, has lived for years, helping to take care of the farm. We walked over there and said hello to Louise and her guests, who were four young sisters, between the ages of three and nine, who looked like four different ages of the same person. They lived close by. The youngest was most shy, but they were all shy; they said nothing, but they smiled the most captivating smiles, and clung to each other like captives. I had not brought my camera for nothing: three clicks. We talked a bit more (with Louise —the children still mum) and were about to continue our walk when my hostess turned to her husband and me and asked if we might have some change in our pockets for the children. It was clearly a natural and affectionate gesture, and my first feeling was one of embarrassment, as if I'd been caught walking out of a restaurant, having forgotten to pay. I quickly fished in my pocket and then stopped dead. Where had this happened before?

Of course: the ending of "Everything That Rises Must Converge," where Julian's mother, Mrs. Chestny, alights from the bus and hurriedly offers a shiny penny to the Negro boy who is so cute—only to have called down upon her, as a responding gesture, a thunderous clout from the boy's mother—" 'He don't take nobody's pennies!' "[1] —a clout that launches Mrs. Chestny into death and her son into tragedy. Not fifty yards from where we were now standing, that story had been written, and as I offered the silver to the children, I felt, uneasily, that O'Connor's ghost was still presiding over the spot— amused, perhaps appallingly amused, that life was once more imitating art. But no, not quite. The children accepted the money shyly but gratefully; Louise, who didn't know exactly how old she was, was still, by appearances, old enough not to be part of the new South; and besides, she had no pocketbook, no weapon of any sort around her. We moved off and had a look at the peacocks.

At this time, four years after Flannery O'Connor's death, Milledgeville and surrounding Baldwin County, Georgia, had a population of about 45,000, the town alone more than 14,000. A circular issued by the Chamber of Commerce listed almost ninety clubs and organizations, among them the American Legion, Colonial Dames, Woman's Missionary Union, Future Farmers of America, Milledgeville Garden Club, Concern, Milledgeville Little Theatre, United Daughters of the Confederacy, and the Optimist Club. There were thirty-nine churches.

How did O'Connor get those stories out of this land?

No easy question to answer. But at least one observation pressed itself out of the afternoon: she got, it would seem, beyond the surface of life by going beyond what "usually" happens; her penetration was in her devising, in her plots, in that unsuspected moment that comes in almost every story when something surprising happens, when the tone changes from that of comedy and satire to something quite other—when an offhand gesture inadvertently ignites a bombshell. The reader reaches the conclusions of her fictions like a dumb witness. Often, indeed, the fictional situation seems set up so that he is precisely that—a dumb witness to some terrible accident; he has had the experience—he is sure of that—but has he got the meaning?

Another thing he is sure of: long or short, these are stories O'Connor wrote. Hardly one is a "sketch with an essay woven through it, or an essay with a sketch woven through it, or an editorial with a character in it, or a case history with a moral, or some other mongrel thing," as O'Connor herself defined what a story isn't.[2] Something happens in these works to disturb the world the characters live in and, in that disturbance, to reveal some new, some foreign knowledge.

When I left the farm and, later that week, the town of Milledgeville, I had seen some of the "materials" for O'Connor's fiction; or rather, the fiction had opened my eyes to the surface of this world— to the landscape, the manners of the people, to things that every Southerner has lived with and takes for granted but that can surprise a Northerner: there are signs, crudely lettered, nailed at odd angles to the trees along the road, proclaiming that "Jesus saves"; whether or not the South is, as O'Connor liked to say, Christ-haunted, it does seem haunted by the Christ-haunted. And yet I felt that however much one became familiar with the materials of O'Connor's fiction (and I had of course only scratched the more hospitable surfaces), one could hardly claim a "familiarity" with those disturbing stories she hatched out at Andalusia. Oh, one might find the seed of "The Displaced Person" in the refugees who came to live nearby one year, but the strange and awful conclusion to that story, where the farm woman acquiesces in the death of the Pole, is of a world apart.

Or is it?

The Matter of the South

A critical definition of O'Connor's world might well start with a look at a few of the stories that deal overtly with the matter of the South. "Somewhere is better than anywhere,"[3] O'Connor wrote, and, with one or two exceptions, somewhere was of course the South. Her illness (O'Connor became a victim of disseminated lupus in her mid-twenties) kept her pretty much confined to the Milledgeville farm, but she drew strength from that rustification. "The fiction writer finds in time, if not at once," she wrote, "that he cannot proceed at all if he cuts himself off from the sights and sounds that have developed a life of their own in his senses."[4] O'Connor seems indeed to have found this out at once, for in "The Barber," a story written for her master's thesis (1947) at the University of Iowa Writer's Workshop, she captures, with a mimetic fidelity that rivals Mark Twain, the native accents and mentality, the local raw material in its unique shape, that have always supplied strength to American writing. The story is centered on the inevitable barber shop political debate between liberal and conservative. The barber, at one point, relates the following episode in the election campaign of his own favorite, Hawk, who is described reacting in public to the charge by his opponents that he is a demagogue.

> "Demagogue!" the barber slapped his knee and whooped. "That's what Hawk said!" he howled. "Ain't that a shot! 'Folks,' he says, 'them Mother Hubbards says I'm a demagogue.' Then he rears back and says sort of soft-like, 'Am I a demagogue, you people?' And they yells, 'Naw, Hawk, you ain't no demagogue!' And he comes forward shouting 'Oh yeah I am, I'm the best damn demagogue in this state!' And you should hear them people roar! Whew!"[5]

The issue in Hawk's election (one presumes he won) was the Negro, and, as one might expect of a writer with a sharp eye on native materials, O'Connor peopled much of her later fiction with Negro characters. One story that is especially interesting to consider for its similar reliance on "Southern" materials is "Everything That Rises Must Converge" (1961), mentioned earlier. In it, O'Connor returns to the subject of white attitudes toward the Negro, but also uses black characters effectively in the dramatic development of the situation. The conflict, however, is not between a razor-tongued barber and his lathered customer but between a mother and son. The old lady, Mrs. Chestny, recalls her "darky" nurse, Caroline, with nostalgic fondness but feels now, with the onset of unfamiliar integration, that "'they [blacks] should rise, yes, but on their own side of the fence.'" (7) She is on her way to an evening reducing class at the local Y, and insists that her son accompany her on the journey there and back, in view of the new and dangerous civil rights legislation, which allows Negroes access to public transportation. As she enters the temporarily all-white bus, she utters with vast satisfaction and relief, "'I see we have the bus to ourselves.'" (10) Her son Julian, a college graduate and typewriter salesman with a dubious future as a writer before him, is O'Connor's version of the liberal intellectual; it is his fervent desire, on the bus ride, to teach his mother a lesson about race relations, to correct her antique notions of white superiority, and to force her to see the new demands of a changing era.

The situation on the bus, then, while more abstract in its contrivance than, for example, Faulkner's dealings with race relations, uses a setting of an everyday familiarity to expose feelings hidden beneath the surface of our daily lives. So familiar, in fact, is the setting for the story that one can observe a coincidental use of it in a meditation on the adjustments of the Southerner to the race "question" written by James Dickey, "Notes on the Decline of Outrage." Dickey observes that, for the Southerner, buses "have been transformed into small, uncomfortable rolling arenas wherein the forces hidden for a hundred years in the structure of his society threaten to break loose and play themselves out each time a bus pulls away from a corner." Dickey's essay provides a fascinating parallel with the O'Connor story. The Southerner enters the bus prepared, as usual, to sit "perhaps next to a thin man in a flowered sports shirt and steel-rimmed glasses."

But suddenly he realizes that quite another thing is now possible. Seized by a desperate logic and a daring he cannot and does not want to account for, he walks past this man and on into the section occupied by Negroes. As he passes the last of the whites he has a powerful sense of pure transgression which gives way immediately to a kind of guilty clandestine joy even more powerful. It is the sense of crossing a boundary beyond which there will be no going back, and it has all the exhilaration and fear, all the intimations of possibility and danger that might be occasioned by passing a real frontier into a strange land, perhaps even into the country of an enemy.

. . . [He] slides into the seat beside the plump man and his son [both Negroes]. . . . He realizes only too well his intense self-consciousness about the meaning of his gesture; for it is purely that. At the same time, through an awesome silence, he hears his mind repeat every cliché about Negroes he has ever heard: "Would you want one living next door to you?"[6]

There follow thoughts about the meaning of the post-Civil War South, about collecting relics of the Civil War, about the strengths of the Negroes, about industrialism, and so forth. Meanwhile, the Southerner is making tentative contact with the man and his son and—the law providing the occasion and opportunity for knowing the Negro—he resolves to go further in this direction.

The behavior of the man on Dickey's bus embodies almost exactly what Julian, on O'Connor's bus, would like to think his own behavior exemplifies. But what is so interesting about the Dickey essay with regard to "Everything That Rises Must Converge" is not so much the fortuitous similarities between the two pieces but rather the significant differences. For where Dickey writes from a point of view sympathetic with the effort of growth and comprehension that is required of the white Southerner in adjusting to the new South, O'Connor writes with a clearly ironic detachment from that effort. And yet it would not be correct to say that the purpose of the story is to undermine the young Julian's pro-Negro sentiments and vindicate his mother's anachronistic attitude. As firmly rooted as the story is in the exacerbations of race relations in the South, it nevertheless is designed to render an experience on still another level.

Midway through the story a Negro woman enters the bus with her child, whom Mrs. Chestny finds adorable (as she finds most Negro children). Julian wishes that something might happen to punish his mother for her attitude toward adult Negroes, and something does: when they get off the bus (as I have already noted), his mother offers the child a shiny penny from her pocketbook, and, in return, gets from the boy's mother a pocketbook swung in her face. She is knocked down, violently stunned, and (a masterful stroke) seems to regress to her secure childhood, calling, indeed, for her old "darky" nurse, Caroline. Julian, however, is even more deeply stunned, it turns out. For when he discovers that she has not merely been taught a lesson she deserved but may be dying, his feelings of disdain and hatred toward her violently reverse themselves, and he realizes for the first time his profound dependence on her. He runs down the street shouting for help, and the story concludes: "The tide of darkness seemed to sweep him back to her, postponing from moment to moment his entry into the world of guilt and sorrow." (23)

When we look closely at the structure of the story we discover that Julian is not simply, as one critic has put it, "a comic character lesser writers would treat as tragic: the alienated intellectual."[7] O'Connor's characterization is more complex than that statement would suggest, and furnishes a carefully designed counterpoint to the mother. For both pride themselves on knowing who they are. The mother recalls her descent from the Godhighs (one of O'Connor's many wonderfully explicit, comic names) and lives with the innocent security that she is still, somehow, a divine being, though now in exile. In that sudden intrusion of an unexpected violence on her life, when the abstraction "Negro" is powerfully individualized, the habit of success and self-assurance is broken, and Mrs. Chestny pathetically regresses to her childhood Eden. Julian, on his part, prides himself on knowing that he lives, truly and tragically, in a fallen world. But the luxury of his torment and martyrdom (he has been comically compared, by O'Connor, to Saint Sebastian) and his presumptuous certainty of himself—of knowing "who he is"—are suddenly overturned by the sight of his mother. In his discovery of the truly tragic, the truly tormenting, he discovers that he has in fact been ignorant of the possibility of tragedy.

Reinforcing Julian's ironic reversal is the reader's knowledge of a particular deception the young man has indulged himself in. While he has outwardly scorned his mother's dream of her grandfather's house, that house has in fact been the focus of all his secret longings, and appears regularly in his own dreams—not in its present condition ("Negroes were living in it") but "as his mother had known it." (7) "He would stand on the wide porch, listening to the rustle of oak leaves, then wander through the high-ceilinged hall into the parlor that opened onto it and gaze at the worn rugs and faded draperies." (7–8) But his attachment to the house is not as fatal to Julian as his failure to admit that attachment and to assess its value to him in the world he is forced to live in. Instead, he has let it divide his consciousness of reality, producing a rent in his person—a longing for the past, on the one side, and a forced embrace of the future, on the other. Through this rent he falls at the end of the story—into a fearful present.

It would be a mistake, then, to read Flannery O'Connor on a chiefly political or social level. Her concern was less with uncovering the tensions in race relations, less with the Southerner's adjustments to the modern world, than with uncovering the self-deceptions and evasions that keep us from recognizing our identities in a context rather larger than the immediately contemporary one. Julian's entry at the end of "Everything That Rises Must Converge" is thus not into the world of the rising Negro, or even into a world without his mother, but, rather, in the abstractly moral language with which the story concludes, "into the world of guilt and sorrow." (23)

A similar use of the materials of the South to supply the dramatic texture of O'Connor's writings can be observed in "A Late Encounter with the Enemy" (1953). And a self-deception about the significance of the past also defines the particular blindness of the protagonist of this earlier story; but, in contrast to the final tone of tragic irony O'Connor applies to Julian, General Sash is subjected to a comic irony throughout "A Late Encounter." Although the antebellum South survives in several other stories through the symbol of the plantation house (in addition to "Everything That Rises," see "A Good Man Is Hard to Find"), this is the only story by O'Connor to deal explicitly with that obsessive subject of so many Southern writers—the Civil War. Alfred Kazin has written that it is the special intelligence of some Southern writers (he names O'Connor as an example) to "find the present meaningful because they find the past so."[8] "A Late Encounter" makes that point negatively, by revealing an aged Civil War veteran who finds the present meaningless because he finds the past so.

The grandparent-grandchild relationship which is present in so many of O'Connor's stories is also the basis of this story, but in a particularly grotesque shape. The opening lines establish the pair and the plot: "General Sash was a hundred and four years old. He lived with his granddaughter, Sally Poker Sash, who was sixty-two years old and who prayed every night on her knees that he would live until her graduation from college. The General didn't give two slaps for her graduation but he never doubted he would live for it."[9] He does. Just. Death comes to the ancient as he is seated honorifically on the stage of the college's auditorium almost at the precise moment that his sexagenarian granddaughter finally receives her diploma. The narrative line of the story moves deliberately toward that event with a comic ease that gradually grows taut with tension, only to be pointedly released again at the end.

To his granddaughter, Sash is the embalmed symbol of her family's greatness, and she wants him at her graduation in order to show the merely common townsfolk " 'what all was behind her.' " (156) To the public, Sash is the last living representative of the South's glorious past, and O'Connor wonderfully undermines that image by revealing that in fact General Tennessee Flintrock Sash's name was George Poker Sash and that he had been only a major. His more elevated name, rank, and uniform were issued by a public relations expert for a Hollywood film on the Civil War, who "honored" Sash at the film's premiere in Atlanta. The General himself has no use at all for history, whether romanticized or not. "The past and the future were the same thing to him, one forgotten and the other not remembered; he had no more notion of dying than a cat." (161) With anachronistic lustiness, Sash lives in the present; and he associates with "life" the color and verve of "floats full of Miss Americas . . . and Miss Queen Cotton Products" as opposed to a "procession full of schoolteachers," which was "about as deadly as the River Styx to his way of thinking." (155) The parade and the procession become key metaphors in the story.

As Sash sits on the stage during the graduation ceremonies, it is not a parade but a procession that comes toward him, and he is irritated. A speech maker intones, " 'If we forget our past . . . we won't remember our future and it will be as well for we won't have one.' " (165–66) And yet, as the speaker recites the meaningless words of Chickamauga, Shiloh, Johnston, Lee, and as the music eats away at Sash's head, the words and the renewed procession come at him fast.

> He felt that he was running backwards and the words were coming at him like musket fire, just escaping him but getting nearer and nearer. . . . As the music swelled toward him, the entire past opened up on him out of nowhere and he felt his body riddled in a hundred places with sharp stabs of pain and he fell down, returning a curse

for every hit. . . . the black procession was almost on him. He recognized it, for it had been dogging all his days. He made such a desperate effort to see over it and find out what comes after the past that his hand clenched the sword until the blade touched bone. (167)

It is a wonderfully effective passage of interior narration, fusing external impressions with the tenor of meaning that has ironically run throughout the story, the whole rendered with a perfect rhythm. It is Sash's last stand against time, history, the past, death. And he loses, overwhelmed by his submerged consciousness of the inescapable past. Almost the only words he had uttered on the graduation day were "'God damm every goddam thing to hell.'" (163) It is therefore as a striking coda to this refrain that Sash dies trying to grasp some half-perceived sight of things which miserably eludes him.

The reader's own encounter with the late General Sash concludes on a note of wry humor: after the ceremony is finished, the Boy Scout John Wesley, Sally Poker's nephew, wheels the Southern Tithonus out of the hall, oblivious to any change in his condition. "That crafty scout had bumped him out the back way and rolled him at high speed down a flagstone path and was waiting now, with the corpse, in the long line at the Coca-Cola machine." (168) The irony of that passage cuts two ways: necessarily the image of the general's pell-mell exit strips him of any dignity or grandeur he might have held in the eyes of the public or, for that matter, in the eyes of the reader. But the irony works as well against "the public," who have made of Sash the object of a factitious mythology, and who, as they queue up for the native drink of Georgia, are oblivious to the presence of death among them.

It would be easy, however, to oversimplify O'Connor's attitude toward the meaning of the Civil War in the South merely from the example of "A Late Encounter." Or at least let it be observed that while the worst exploitation of the relics of that battle is satirized by the writer, the point of the story is not that the remembrance of the war is necessarily a meaningless ritual but, rather, that if it is only a meaningless ritual in self-glorification or if it is driven from the consciousness of the South as it is driven from old Sash's mind, then it will rise like a specter again and demand battle in some other shape. Thus it would be well to observe O'Connor's reference to Walker Percy's remark that the reason there were so many good

Southern writers was " 'Because we lost the War.' " And she goes on: "He didn't mean by that simply that a lost war makes good subject matter. What he was saying was that we have had our Fall. We have gone into the modern world with an inburnt knowledge of human limitations and with a sense of mystery which could not have developed in our first state of innocence—as it has not sufficiently developed in the rest of our country."[10]

The notion is of course not original with O'Connor. Andrew Lytle, for example, has written of the depth of perception that came out of the loss of the Civil War: only the South knows, writes Lytle, "the meaning of defeat, that is, the nature of the world."[11] And, in a study of the historical dimension of Southern literature, Louis Rubin quotes Allen Tate's assertion that the memory of the Civil War gave to the Southerner entering World War I a "double focus, a looking two ways, which gave a special dimension to the writings of our school." And out of this perspective, Tate says, out of this "backward glance . . . [came] the Southern renascence, a literature conscious of the past in the present."[12] Carrying these perceptions to their logical conclusion, Rubin observes that the image of change is at the core of Southern literature: "Molded by the past, tempered by the present, the literature of the South is truly a historical literature."[13]

However true in general this observation may be, it is doubtful whether it can be applied to Flannery O'Connor; for despite her agreement with these other writers on the effect of the Civil War on the Southern imagination, hers is not truly "a historical fiction." And yet it is certainly true that the image of change is evident: we have observed already the use of social upheaval in the dramatization of "Everything That Rises Must Converge"; and we could add to that the delineation of the characters in "Greenleaf" according to their altering social classes and the key role that change in social status plays in "Revelation." And too, one could add the even more decisive part that change plays in "A View of the Woods," where a conflict over the transformation of the countryside by the force of "progress" seems to be at the heart of the drama.

Yet a closer look at "A View of the Woods," which seems at first the dramatization of an orthodox agrarian imagination, will reveal the precise degree to which O'Connor's interests lay in historical change. The principal conflict in this tale is between old man Fortune and his granddaughter Mary Fortune Pitts. And the issue that divides the two is Fortune's insistence that a gas station be built directly in front of the house where the Pitts family—and the old man himself—live. The effect of this construction, which is part of Fortune's larger plan to bring progress to the rural area, would be not only to do away with the "lawn" where Mr. Pitts grazes his cows but also to block the view from the house of the woods across the road. Notwithstanding little Mary's vehement objections to his plan, the old man settles the deal with Tilman, a local entrepreneur; but Fortune has been so riled by his favorite grandchild's refusal to second his desires that he feels he must teach her a lesson and—for the first time in his life—he takes her out in the woods to beat her. Only *she* wins; the old man is licked.[14]

If this were, indeed, merely an agrarian tale, then one might well agree with Stanley Edgar Hyman, who felt that this is where the story should properly end and that O'Connor erred in extending it beyond comic irony to a violent ending—in which Fortune gains the upper hand with little Mary and, in blind rage, cracks her skull against a rock, only to stagger off to the construction site, where he is surrounded by monstrous visions of the huge yellow excavation machinery.[15] In fact, however, the actual ending would seem entirely justified if one has picked up along the way the larger, enveloping significance of the tale.

For what Fortune himself is blind to is the emotional and figurative connotations of the view of the woods which would be cut off by the gas station. " 'There's not a thing over there but the woods,' " he says to Mary uncomprehendingly.[16] He stares repeatedly at the woods trying to see what is not there, until one time around twilight, when

> the gaunt trunks appeared to be raised in a pool of red light that gushed from the almost hidden sun setting behind them. The old man stared for some time, as if for a prolonged instant he were caught up out of the rattle of everything that led to the future and were held there in the midst of an uncomfortable mystery that he had not apprehended before. He saw it, in his hallucination, as if someone were wounded behind the woods and the trees were bathed in blood. (71)

Clearly what the language demands in this passage is a recognition of the presence of mystery in the view: old Fortune has had a momentary glimpse of it, and the imagery of wounds and blood suggests more concretely to the reader the metaphorical presence of Christ. In the context of the whole story, the woods become a kind of spiritual touchstone, comparable to the use O'Connor makes of the peacock in "The Displaced Person." And what the vision of mystery comes down to at these times is a kind of seeing that fuses spiritual and aesthetic qualities in a perception of gratuitous beauty, apparent inutility, and ostensible absurdity—a perception in some ways analogous, one presumes, to the perception of the value of Christ's sacrifice. Put another way, what Fortune has been blind to is the final identity of nature as physical matter and nature as sacrament. (*Wise Blood* and *The Violent Bear It Away* also assert this identity.)

And that is why, for O'Connor's Georgian Babbitt, the violence of that ending is required: not as a punishment for old Fortune but as a dramatization of his spiritual condition—and as a prerequisite to his final insight. For what the master builder sees as he stumbles convulsively toward the water in his effort to escape the ugly pines surrounding him is a vision of salvation from which he is sickeningly excluded.

> . . . the whole lake opened up before him, riding majestically in little corrugated folds toward his feet. He realized suddenly that he could not swim. . . . On both sides of him he saw that the gaunt trees had thickened into mysterious dark files that were marching across the water and away into the distance. He looked around desperately for someone to help him but the place was deserted except for one huge yellow monster which sat to the side, as stationary as he was, gorging itself on clay. (81)

If a vision of grace is denied Fortune, if the mystery that opens up to him at the end includes a tragic discovery of his own evil (he is identified with the clay-eating monster), then one might also extend the theological meaning of the story and say that the land the old man seeks to destroy in his dreams is a kind of Edenic paradise, and that the process he has set in motion under the name of progress is the Fall. This sort of reading seems reinforced, moreover, by the descriptions of the executant (in a Southern revival) of that fate which brought death into the world (along with the labor of tilling the soil): the businessman Tilman. His present establishment, a store selling practically everything, is framed on either side by a "field of old used-car bodies" and, in back, "so as not to depress his dance-hall customers, a line of tombstones and monuments." (67)

Tilman himself is described in language which unmistakably defines his serpentine function of destroyer. "He sat habitually with his arms folded on the counter and his insignificant head weaving snake-fashion above them. He had a triangular-shaped face with the point at the bottom. . . . His eyes were green and very narrow and his tongue was always exposed in his partly opened mouth." (76) O'Connor's tongue, one might add, would seem to be partly in cheek as she designates with relish his theological role.

In reading "A View of the Woods" in this manner, it must be stressed that the theological level implicit in it does not cancel the issue of whether or not Fortune should be building a gas station qua gas station on a site that will block a view of the woods qua woods. Rather, what O'Connor liked to call the "anagogical level" is there to be discovered in the story, and grows out of a naturalistic reading of it.

One would certainly not want to underestimate O'Connor's very real feelings about the South and about historical change in themselves. Her conservatism was strong but not unthinking. "The anguish that most of us have observed for some time now has been caused not by the fact that the South is alienated from the rest of the country, but by the fact that it is not alienated enough, that every day we are getting more and more like the rest of the country, that we are being forced out not only of our many sins, but of our few virtues."[17] She even went so far as to say that the Southern writer who would leave the South, leave the cohesion of his community, would do so "at great peril to that balance between principle and fact, between judgment and observation, which is so necessary to maintain if fiction is to be true."[18] And yet, as that last statement suggests, it was what the South could afford her as a writer that was so crucial. And even those stories that deal explicitly with Southern materials (the ones discussed above) derive their values and shaping spirit not so much from the concerns of time and history, of social manners and human—merely human—dignity but, rather, from a sense of the mystery of human life.

What O'Connor added when she said that the special privilege of Southerners derived from the sense of the Fall gained from the loss of the Civil War was that "not every lost war would have this effect on every society, but we were doubly blessed, not only in our Fall, but in having a means to interpret it. Behind our own history, deepening it at every point, has been another history. Mencken called the South the Bible Belt, in scorn and thus in incredible innocence."[19] So, in considering O'Connor a Southern writer, one must add, as she always did, that, for the Christian writer, one's "country" is more than just the sod underfoot; it is also what she liked to call one's "true country . . . what is eternal and absolute."[20] It would be well at this point, then, to consider in more detail the contours of O'Connor's Christian belief and her conception of herself as a Christian writer.

The Shape of Belief

Assessing the state of contemporary fiction in 1954, Gore Vidal wrote: "The sense of man not being king of creation (nor even the work of a king of creation) is the burden, directly and indirectly, of modern literature. For the writer there is no reality for man except in his relations with his own kind." And he went on to note with ironic detachment the existence of some few writers, like Graham Greene and Evelyn Waugh, who have "accepted some huge fantasy wherein . . . death is life and the doings of human beings . . . are of much consequence to some brooding source of creation who dispenses his justice along strictly party lines at the end of a gloomy day."[21] He did not mention the as yet little-known Flannery O'Connor in this odd group. Yet three years later, in 1957, Granville Hicks would bring out a collection of essays by contemporary American novelists called, in defiance of any rumors of a moribund fiction, *The Living Novel*, and to it O'Connor contributed a piece called "The Fiction Writer and His Country," which, in the context of essays by Saul Bellow, Ralph Ellison, Herbert Gold, Wright Morris, and others, must have struck the reader, as it would doubtless have struck Vidal, as something of an anomaly. "I am no disbeliever in spiritual purpose and no vague believer," O'Connor declared forthrightly. "I see from the standpoint of Christian orthodoxy. This means that for me the meaning of life is centered in our Redemption by Christ and what I see in the world I see in its relation to that."[22]

In short, O'Connor was fully aware that her beliefs as a Catholic set her apart from most writers of her time—and from most readers.

And yet the fact that many who read O'Connor for the first time—
and I am speaking here mainly of the short stories—are not aware of
the author's reigning beliefs points not merely to the sometimes elusive quality of her fiction but, more importantly, to her commitment
to the demands of fiction. In fact, it is precisely when the "true
country" exercises untoward suzerainty over the "countryside" that
her intentions tend to be obvious and hence her effects diminished.
Her best works (and all of her writings on the art of fiction) reveal a
constantly felt tension between the pull of reality and the pull of
Reality, between surface and depth, between fact and mystery. "St.
Gregory wrote that every time the sacred text describes a fact, it
reveals a mystery. This is what the fiction writer, on his lesser level,
hopes to do."[23]

The word "mystery" is of course the key word in O'Connor's critical vocabulary, and I have used it before. It is at the heart of her
Catholic belief, as it is at the heart of her view of human life. And
yet, by definition, it is a word which cannot be precisely, noetically
defined: in essence, mystery is what is finally unknowable. But from
her use of the word one can at least infer something of its significance
for the writer herself. The following instance seems most revealing.
Fiction, O'Connor wrote, ". . . leaves us, like Job, with a renewed
sense of mystery."[24] What is the "mystery" God's servant feels at the
end of Job? Partly, it would seem to result from a new recognition
of his rightful place in the universe, and it is evoked by the fact of
God's power as set forth by the author of the scripture. "Canst thou
draw out leviathan with an hook? or his tongue with a cord which
thou lettest down?" God asks. And, with the addition of fact to
fact, the conclusion for Job is inescapable: "Wherefore I abhor myself,
and repent in dust and ashes." But Job's abasement is ultimately
followed by his exaltation. "So the Lord blessed the latter end of
Job more than his beginning." Failure and exaltation; death and
redemption. The mystery of this rhythm of human life is, for O'Connor, the mystery of Christianity—though of course with the quali-
fication that, for the Christian, God's grace is embodied in the person
of Christ, who is therefore the agent of redemption.

It may be useful to place this sense of mystery within the context of O'Connor's broader intellectual engagement with Catholicism

throughout her life. Apart from her formal essays and talks on the role of the Catholic novelist,[25] the most fertile ground to explore in determining the nature of O'Connor's commitment is the set of book reviews she wrote at regular intervals from about 1956 to 1963 for the weekly journal of the Catholic Diocese of Georgia.[26] The books reviewed range from editions of the Bible to Church history and saints' lives, from theology and the philosophies of religion and history to discussions of the life of the Catholic in the modern world. Indeed, what may be surprising is that, with the exception of some reviews of such Catholic novelists as J. F. Powers, Caroline Gordon, and Paul Horgan, O'Connor seems to have preferred a diet of nonfiction.

Because O'Connor addressed herself to a sympathetic audience, it becomes possible to draw from these reviews, with greater refinement than is permitted from her more public essays, a fairly distinct picture of her underlying viewpoint. What emerges from her remarks, which were designed to provide a guide to current books for the lay readership, is an orthodoxy one might describe as socially conservative and culturally enlightened. Thus, in her confrontations with the increasing literature of engagement, of social activisim within the Church, she conservatively asserts the need for a basic humility and perspective of the whole solidly grounded in a sense of the inevitable imperfection of life. On the other hand, her frequent effort is to pull the mass of laymen out of the slough of complacency and mediocrity that, she felt, popular Catholic culture in America breeds, and to force an engagement with the real world and an appreciation for the art of the twentieth century.

The same sense of a balance between fact and mystery that she demands from fiction informs her discussions of faith; thus, for example, where a writer under consideration asserts the importance of reason in the modern Catholic viewpoint and the need to take into account the facts of science and evolution, O'Connor will counter with the importance of revelation, affirming as well the essentially mystical nature of the religious experience; and when her subject emphasizes faith or feeling, O'Connor will assert the importance of reason. (In the light of her fierce satire of such rationalists as Rayber in *The Violent Bear It Away* and Sheppard in "The Lame Shall Enter First," one would not, perhaps, have expected that latter assertion. But then again, it is a synthesis of reason and faith, not a denial of faith, that elicits her happiest support, as in a favorable review of Jacques Maritain's neo-Thomist *The Range of Reason*.)[27]

It is not surprising, then, that she greatly admired Teilhard de Chardin; and she would seem to have circumvented the Church's disapproval of him by declaring that the Jesuit-geologist's lifelong effort to "fit his knowledge of evolution into the pattern of his faith in Christ . . . is the work of neither scientist nor theologian, but of poet and mystic."[28] She wrote in another review that "it is doubtful if any Christian of this century can be fully aware of his religion until he has reseen it in the cosmic light which Teilhard has cast upon it."[29] What was also tremendously appealing in Teilhard's vision was the central element (so crucial for her aesthetics) that matter is penetrated by spirit: "The discovery that we owe to Teilhard is that vocation of spirit is visible, concrete, and of absorbing interest."[30]

Baron von Hügel's awareness of the ideal unity (achieved through the admitted tension) of the flesh and the spirit made him, as well, an important figure for O'Connor. Thus, for example, in a review of *Letters from Baron Friedrich von Hügel to a Niece*, O'Connor cites approvingly von Hügel's admonition to his niece not to let the fascination of grace "deaden the expressions of nature and thereby 'lose the material for Grace to work on.'" "'How thin and abstract,'" she quotes von Hügel as writing, "'or how strained and unattractive, the religion of most women becomes, owing to this their elimination of religion's materials and divinely intended tensions!'"[31] This same consciousness of the material base of the spirit is what she picks out for notice in a review of Romano Guardini's *Freedom, Grace, and Destiny*, quoting the author's lamentation that "'the believer no longer stands with his faith amid the concrete, actual world, and he no longer rediscovers that world by his faith.'"[32]

What is perhaps most interesting in these reviews is the consistent strain of emotional austerity that colors O'Connor's conception of divine reality. When she is dealing with paragons of the religious life, or with Christ himself, it is the pain and self-denial that are the expenses of spiritual greatness, the terrible severity and majesty of God, that O'Connor emphasizes. A review of *Two Portraits of St. Therese of Lisieux*, by Etienne Robo, for example, is the occasion for O'Connor to decry the sentimentalized "edifying" images of St. Therese that have been fabricated by the convents, and to celebrate Father Robo's uncovering of the "real saint in her very human and terrible greatness."[33] A similar impulse is behind her assertion, in another review, that our present superficial image of Christ is far inferior to the image held in the Middle Ages of a Lord who was a "stern and majestic Pantacrator, not . . . a smiling Jesus with a bleeding heart." The medieval images, she wrote, were "adequate to the realities they stood for," and were able to "hold up under the assaults given to belief. Today the idea of religion of large numbers of Catholics re-main[s] trapped at the magical stage by static and superficial images which neither mind nor stomach can any longer take."[34] And one can add to these affirmations of a hard, masculine image of Christ O'Connor's remark, in an essay likewise intended for a Catholic audi-ence, "As Catholics we are interested in man's reaction to grace, but we should not be so prone to ignore how very divisive grace is; we should not so often forget that it cuts with the sword Christ said He came to bring."[35]

It is essential to bear in mind these feelings when reading O'Con-nor, for otherwise much becomes either inexplicable or liable to an unwarranted ironic reading. Just because this conception of a severe, all-demanding, terrible Lord and a grace that divides man from man is alien not only to modern humanism but to much religious thought today, O'Connor's fiction takes on the appearance of violent irony—hence the frequent early misreadings of Wise Blood and The Violent Bear It Away, for example, as works that portrayed their heroes' progress toward God as an ironic self-deception. In the context of O'Connor's faith, these heroes seem quite other than comic-epic self-deceivers, and a speech such as old Tarwater's in the latter novel becomes a harsh but genuine statement of a strong current in her fiction.

> "The Lord is preparing a prophet with fire in his hand and eye and the prophet is moving toward the city with his warning. The prophet is coming with the Lord's message. 'Go warn the children of God,' saith the Lord, 'of the terrible speed of justice.' Who will be left? Who will be left when the Lord's mercy strikes?"[36]

And too, the self-punishing asceticism of Hazel Motes in Wise Blood must be read as a sign not of his defeat and failure to attain

God but of his failure not to attain God. For a passage like the following by O'Connor on *The Life of St. Catherine of Siena*, by Raymond of Capua, clarifies retrospectively the attitude that lay behind the conception of Hazel.

> What emerges most profoundly is that all the saint's actions were conformed to a Reality of which the ordinary man is not aware. If the reader can once realize the strength and power of Catherine's vision, the scourgings and other self-punishments become understandable. Conversely, it is only from these penances that the vision can be surmised and vouched for.[37]

Scourgings? Self-punishments? Penances? In assessing O'Connor's underlying viewpoint, one must, I think, make allowance for a certain temperamental affinity with Jansenism. The images of Christian experience informing the stories and, most obviously, the longer *Wise Blood* and *The Violent Bear It Away* emerge from a moralism and severity akin to that sect, which held, in the words of the authoritative *New Catholic Encyclopedia*

> that humanity had to be kept in check by penitential rigor. . . . They looked upon Jesus as a severe and inscrutable redeemer. . . . They ranged themselves against the humanistic spirit of the times, which seemed to glorify man at God's expense. . . . Jansenism effected a divorce between the flesh and the spirit, between the sensible and the spiritual, that was disintegrating to moral equilibrium. . . . [It affirmed] a profound sense of mystery, a simplicity of worship.[38]

Without going so far as to call O'Connor a latter-day Jansenist, we may ask whether the polarities of Teilhard de Chardin and Catherine of Siena can meet in a single field of vision. Are we dealing with a world where matter is penetrated by spirit and evolves toward spirit or a world where the flesh is burned clean by divine reality? With a balance of grace and nature, reason and faith, or with an all-devouring Lord who divides the flesh from the spirit by the sword of his grace?

Indeed, we seem to have uncovered at the heart of Flannery O'Connor's sensibility something of a paradox, if not an inconsistency. And yet if we look back again to the example of Job which was used to define the sense of mystery inherent in nature—if we look back at Job in this context—that same paradox seems to be lurking: Job, standing before the power of God in created nature, is penetrated by a sense of mystery. At the same time, Job abhors his own flesh made painful and abominable. And out of this seeming paradox comes Job's sanctification. But in the person of Christ, the paradox flourishes. The Word made flesh glorifies the flesh; the flesh crucified is a testament to the Word.

In a sense, the two sides of the paradox divide between them the sources of O'Connor's peculiar power as a writer: on the one side, the mystery of the Word made flesh is the basis of her aesthetic energy, defining, almost, the process of symbolism in her works. And, on the other side, the mystery of the flesh crucified is the emotional crux of her writings, for the discovery of the mystery of reality—whether in the shape of grace or exclusion from grace—is always painful for her characters and almost always violent.

Art as Incarnation

The way in which these paradoxical elements of O'Connor's vision shape the fiction can be illustrated by "Greenleaf" (1956). What happens in the story is that a woman is gored to death by a bull. Put another way, what happens is that a woman experiences the intrusion of a sense of mystery upon her life at the moment of her death. In the process by which the bull comes to symbolize something more mysterious than a dumb beast, one can see the operation of O'Connor's aesthetic habit of endowing the flesh with a spiritual significance; while in the agony of the woman's death, one can see an accession to mystery through the painful annihilation of the flesh. The tone of the story, meanwhile, is governed by a carefully modulated comic control, whereby seemingly gratuitous violence is subsumed under a vision of order.

The protagonist, Mrs. May, is a hard-headed, hard-beset woman who runs a farm; her greatest fear in life is that her property will eventually devolve upon the Greenleafs (Mr. Greenleaf is a hired hand on the farm)—that they, and not her own sons, will prosper and endure. Mrs. Greenleaf is a woman obsessed with Jesus and, as a figure of abstract misery, she is a foil to the complacent Mrs. May. Although the former doesn't play an active role in the plot, her presence is felt throughout, with a force deriving from Mrs. May's memory of their chance encounter once in the woods, when she had come across the woman in the midst of her usual exercise of prayer healing.

> Every day [Mrs. Greenleaf] cut all the morbid stories out of the newspaper—the accounts of women who had been raped and criminals who had escaped and children who had been burned and of train wrecks and plane crashes and the divorces of movie stars. She took these to the woods and dug a hole and buried them and then she fell on the ground over them and mumbled and groaned for an hour or so, moving her huge arms back and forth under her and out again and finally just lying down flat and, Mrs. May suspected, going to sleep in the dirt.[39]

It is a comic scene, deliberately so, but, as it develops, the grotesque agony of Mrs. Greenleaf's devotion, her Job-like self-abasement, takes on the quality of an authentic backwoods devotion. "Her face was a patchwork of dirt and tears and her small eyes, the color of two field peas, were red-rimmed and swollen, but her expression was as composed as a bulldog's. She swayed back and forth on her hands and knees and groaned, 'Jesus, Jesus.'" (31) In its down-to-earth suffering and self-humiliation, it is an image of devotion that looks back to Hazel Motes's ascetic rituals in *Wise Blood* and forward to young Tarwater's image of his own fated destiny in *The Violent Bear It Away*, to follow the "bleeding stinking mad shadow of Jesus." (91)

Mrs. May's own puritanical notion of religion is somewhat different—a scrubbed and laundered Sunday morning—and O'Connor cannot resist a mocking tone in describing it. "She thought the word, Jesus, should be kept inside the church building like other words inside the bedroom." (31) And her presumptuous complacency is brought out on a still larger scale later on in the story, when, with ironic foreshadowing, she is made to imagine crying out to her sons, "'You'll find out one of these days, you'll find out what *Reality* is when it's too late!'" (35) The particular manner of Mrs. May's own discovery of "*Reality*" is of course the true subject of the story. But how do you make the goring of a woman by a bull a spiritual event?

What we are involved in, in answering that question, is the process of symbolism itself as Flannery O'Connor understood it. And that process is, for the reader, a discovery of the meaning latent in a given object or action, a meaning which grows out of the pattern of imagery and the tone of the fiction in such a way that a judgment may be made as to its moral significance. The writer's problem, she wrote, "is really how to make the concrete work double time for him. . . . The fiction writer states as little as possible. The reader makes [the] connection from things he is shown. He may not even know that he makes the connection, but the connection is there nevertheless and it has its effect on him."[40] The accretion of symbolic meaning around the naked object, the metamorphosis of reality into Reality, is, one might say, the literary equivalent of the incarnation of the Word in the flesh. Indeed, O'Connor said as much herself on one occasion, when she called fiction "an incarnational art."[41]

From the first advent of the stray bull on Mrs. May's farm, that lady has been trying to persuade Mr. Greenleaf to get rid of it; finally, she has determined to make him shoot the animal, which, she has learned, is the unwanted property of Mr. Greenleaf's upwardly mobile twin boys. Accordingly, Mrs. May and her assistant (the latter all unwilling) seek it in the pastures, and, as Mr. Greenleaf disappears into the woods after the bull, Mrs. May sits down on her car fender to wait for him. As the sun beats down on her, she experiences a feeling of great tiredness, in which the meaning of her years of work comes before her: "Before any kind of judgement seat, she would be able to say: I've worked, I have not wallowed." (51) The proud exemplar of the Protestant work ethic imagines Mrs. Greenleaf, by contrast, "flat on the ground, asleep over her holeful of clippings" (51), and she recalls saying to Mr. Greenleaf: " 'I'm afraid your wife has let religion warp her. . . . Everything in moderation, you know.' " (51) She thinks of Mr. Greenleaf: perhaps he has been gored by the bull. And the irony of that catastrophe pleases her—"as if she had hit on the perfect ending for a story she was telling her friends." (51–52) In a moment, however, we move from Mrs. May's ironic viewpoint—herself the superior onlooker—to a description (still through her eyes) of the bull's charge toward her; but the ironic vantage point shifts to the reader.

> [The bull] was crossing the pasture toward her at a slow gallop, a gay almost rocking gait as if he were overjoyed to find her again. . . . She stared at the violent black streak bounding toward her as if she had no sense of distance, as if she could not decide at once what his intention was, and the bull had buried his head in her lap, like a wild tormented lover, before her expression changed. One of his horns

sank until it pierced her heart and the other curved around her side
and held her in an unbreakable grip. She continued to stare straight
ahead but the entire scene in front of her had changed—the tree line
was a dark wound in a world that was nothing but sky—and she had
the look of a person whose sight has been suddenly restored but who
finds the light unbearable. . . .

[As the story ends, Mrs. May] did not hear the shots but she felt
the quake in the huge body as it sank, pulling her forward on its
head, so that she seemed, when Mr. Greenleaf reached her, to be bent
over whispering some last discovery into the animal's ear. (52–53)

It is a shocking climax, but what adds to our surprise is the amo-
rous language in which it is described. And yet, the "wild tormented
lover" who joyously sinks his horns into her chest has been courting
Mrs. May throughout the story; and the imputation of a conscious
design in his final charge has the curious effect of increasing the sense
of an inescapable, painful destiny, of placing the violence within an
ordered framework. Moreover, the fancifulness of that last figure
("she seemed . . . to be bent over whispering some last discovery into
the animal's ear")—as if Mrs. May is at last reciprocating her lover's
demands—heightens this effect; so that, despite the horrible image
of a woman impaled on the horns of a dying beast, one also feels
that this is a "happy" ending: the persistent suitor has at last gained
his mark.

The metaphorical significance of the bull is first intimated early
in the story through Mrs. May's first half-understood dream: sleeping, she hears it eating the shrubbery outside her window—eating
through her house, her boys, herself—"eating everything but the
Greenleafs." (25) The bull's alliance with the Greenleafs (and with
Jesus) is subsequently reinforced when Mrs. May remembers Mrs.
Greenleaf groaning, "'Jesus! Jesus!'" and the sound of it is "so
piercing that she felt as if some violent unleashed force had broken
out of the ground and was charging toward her." (30–31) Mrs.
Greenleaf's own groaning receptivity to the violence is made clear
when she shrieks, "'Oh Jesus, stab me in the heart!'" (31) All of
this of course ironically foreshadows the final scene, as does another
of Mrs. May's oneiric experiences—one that connects the animal's
bulletlike charge from the tree line with the greater yet equally
inevitable cosmic movement of the sun, which she imagines racing
down the hill toward her (see 47). And one begins to piece together
some of the imagery of the death scene itself: "the dark wound" of

the tree line (suggesting Christ's wound), the sight that is "restored" to Mrs. May.

In short, what O'Connor is dramatizing in "Greenleaf" is an image of the discovery of the mystery of Reality, and the language in which that discovery is portrayed suggests an association with the coming of Christ to the unsuspecting Mrs. May. Does Christ come like a bull? Does he gore those he saves? Not literally, of course, but in the sense that his coming is, presumably, an agony and, at the same time, a lover's embrace. What makes "Greenleaf" convincing, finally, is the rich psychological dimension of the characterization: the various dreams, half-perceptions, fears, and anticipations of Mrs. May validate, it seems to me, the possibility of the theological meaning.

It is not enough, in other words, to simply let the *reader* make the necessary connections: the character must himself in some manner comprehend or half-comprehend the experience. This is not so, I think, in certain other stories by O'Connor—for example, "The River," "The Enduring Chill," and "Revelation." In these latter tales, there is insufficient psychological preparation for the concluding apocalypse. Rather, a theological experience seems to be imposed by the author on the characters in a way that may make acceptable allegory but unacceptable "realistic" fiction.[42]

O'Connor's best tales usually cannot be reduced to some specific theological formula—that would be to do less than justice to the weight of complexity they bear. Rather, they culminate in an image that is true dramatically, psychologically, and morally. With O'Connor, as with other writers of firm belief (Dante, for example), the unassailable dramatic image is closer to the vision than any doctrinal equivalent. Just this was meant by Romano Guardini (whose unsentimental theology O'Connor admired) when he wrote apropos of St. John's verse, "and behold, a door standing open in heaven" (Apoc. 4:1):

> The intellect may attempt to express in concepts and sentences all that the image "door" implies; but such concepts are mere props to the essential, not more. The truth is the other way around: it is the image that is the reality; the mind can only attempt to plumb it. The image is richer than the thought; hence the act by which we comprehend an image, gazing, is richer, more profound, vital and storeyed than the thought.[43]

In O'Connor's best fiction too, it is "the image that is the reality."

In addition to "Greenleaf," the posthumously published "Parker's Back" offers an especially transparent illustration of this imagination. For the figure of Parker embodies in its purest shape the O'Connor paradox: his own tattooed flesh incarnates the wonder and mystery of the world and finally is engraved with the image of Jesus himself; and that same flesh suffers a mock crucifixion at the hands of Parker's harridan wife: the Word is made flesh, and the flesh is crucified.

Despite the comic tone of "Parker's Back," one can see in it what is almost the defining emotion of O'Connor's fiction: the shock and pain that attend the birth into mystery. Such is the emotion, not only in "Greenleaf" and the two novels but in such stories as "A Good Man Is Hard to Find," "A Circle in the Fire," "The Artificial Nigger," "A View of the Woods," "The Comforts of Home," and "Everything That Rises Must Converge." It is also the concluding emotion in "The Enduring Chill," which, though dramatically forced, expresses the point succinctly when the hero sees "that for the rest of his days, frail, racked, but enduring, he would live in the face of a purifying terror."[44]

And if one may add a further paradox, it must be noted that while the representation and communication of heightened feeling are at the heart of O'Connor's imaginative writings, it seems also to have been her habit as a Catholic personally *not* to trust emotion. Thus she could write to a friend who had converted to Catholicism from Protestantism, "Having been a Protestant, you may have the feeling that you must feel you believe; perhaps feeling belief is not always an illusion but I imagine it is most of the time." Yet what she then added qualifies her distrust significantly. "But I can understand the feeling of pain on going to Communion and it seems a more reliable feeling than joy."[45] It is a telling remark, I think, and suggests much about her intellectual and emotional temper.

In defining the nature of O'Connor's belief and the correlative processes of her art, I have assumed an integrity and individuality in her writings that may, at this point, be conveniently sharpened and placed in some broader context. It would be silly to try to define what a "Catholic writer" is, and to measure O'Connor's art by that standard, but it would be useful, perhaps, to note certain attributes that she shares with other writers who are by habit and conviction Catholic. I will rely for that purpose on Conor Cruise O'Brien's excellent study of eight European writers (Mauriac, Bernanos, Greene, O'Faoláin, Waugh, Péguy, Claudel, and Bloy), *Maria Cross: Imaginative Patterns in a Group of Modern Catholic Writers*. In many ways, O'Connor may be classed with these writers. Most obviously, the sense of pain that we have discovered in O'Connor finds its parallel in the current of suffering that runs throughout O'Brien's Catholic writers, providing for them the ground for a solidarity of feeling among men of a class or a nation; and what O'Brien says of those eight writers seems particularly applicable to O'Connor—that this sense of a suffering community of men "can ascend to a majestic and vividly present conception of the community of all mankind."[46] In other respects too, O'Connor shares the attributes of the Catholic temper proposed by O'Brien: in her sense of nostalgia for an idealized past; and in her sense of exile from the present age of science and rationalism, of bourgeois culture. A sense of the discrepancy between the present age and the imagined ideal provides the source of the critical and satirical energy that is present in all of these writers—and not least vividly in O'Connor.

Though she did not write directly of the common passions of men and women, O'Connor would seem, in addition, to share with these other Catholic writers certain assumptions about the nature of passion. One cannot be very precise in making such judgments, but O'Brien's observation of the identity of repressed sex and violence in the European Catholic imagination finds a certain resonance in the story we have just discussed, "Greenleaf," and also, as we shall see, in "Good Country People" and "The Comforts of Home." It is perhaps odd that O'Connor—a woman—should share certain other assumptions with the group O'Brien considers (all men): thus the sometimes explicit identification of woman with the Cross noted by O'Brien will be equally visible in the psychology of Hazel Motes and, in different ways, in that of Thomas ("The Comforts of Home") and Parker. Moreover, the analogy of Christ's Passion and sexual passion that O'Brien remarks, particularly in Claudel and Mauriac, is of course made explicit in Mrs. Greenleaf's turbulent devotions and Mrs. May's excruciating death.

O'Connor's imagination does, then, work in ways that suggest a characteristic "Catholic" sensibility, if we use the term inductively. Yet several distinguishing features must be noted. One must say, for example, that O'Connor's imagination was purer than that of the various European writers O'Brien discusses—less vivid in its imaginings of evil, less carnal, less corrupt. The South did give her a sense of the Fall, as noted earlier, and she was not in any case "innocent"; but it would be hard to concur in John Hawkes's advocacy of the devil as artistic inspiration in her works—although the Gidian doctrine of the "collaboration of the demon" is convincingly observed by O'Brien in certain of *his* subjects.[47] Put another way, what is distinctive in O'Connor is her strong belief in the efficacy of faith and in the operation of grace in our lives. This, together with her less realistic texture, results in a fiction quite different in tone and color from that of her European spiritual kin. Most significantly, her faith governs the typical recurring shapes of her plots, as we shall see in subsequent chapters.

The point of these comparisons is of course not invidiously to judge the respective merits of Flannery O'Connor as against other Catholic writers but merely to distinguish the quality of the former's imagination when set beside writers whose works and goals she might herself, in many cases, applaud. So much is true also when O'Connor is compared with certain other American Catholic writers. What sets O'Connor apart from her countrymen, like an ax amid a collection of manicure scissors, are the extremes of violence and comedy in her imagination. Thus while she wrote that as "a born Catholic . . . death has always been a brother to my imagination,"[48] it is the style, the manner, the context of death that are important. J. F. Powers, for example, in "Lions, Harts, Leaping Does" may have sent Didymus's soul on its way to "the snowy arms of God" in a canary, but O'Connor would have turned the canary into a fierce bird with depending icicles and aimed its terrifying beak at the Father's heart (see, for example, "The Enduring Chill"). Katherine Anne Porter may have shown us the soteriological "Jilting of Granny Weatherall" in a subtly ironic stream of consciousness ending with the extinction of a lamp light, but O'Connor would have put the pinpoint of light at the end of a long tunnel and had her protagonist reach it (his is a different fate) by walking barefoot on rocks (as she does, mutatis mutandis, in *Wise Blood*). Similarly, though she acknowledged her debt to Caroline Gordon's criticism and advice, O'Connor's techniques are typically more extravagant than Miss Gordon's. For example, in the latter's *The Malefactors*, a novel of conversion O'Connor admired, a bull may be kept on the scene throughout as a vaguely phallic, mysterious stage prop, but the conversion itself is brought about by a dream the protagonist has; we have seen already in "Greenleaf" what O'Connor did with the bull.

We must soon reach the limit of these comparisons, however, a limit O'Connor herself saw clearly. She was wary, she said, of "Catholic discussions of novels by Catholics" which forget that "the eye sees what it has been given to see by concrete circumstances, and the imagination reproduces what, by some related gift, it is able to make live."[49] O'Connor's relationship to the Church was by no means uneasy, but neither was it without a certain tension—one might almost say ambivalence. Thus while she would often affirm the imaginative freedom accorded the Catholic writer who would see with the eyes of the Church, she would at other times imply that the eyes were her own and that the Church merely supplied a congenial pair of glasses. When the two views were brought together, they might easily issue in what some might benignly call a paradox and others a casting of empiricism to the winds of doctrine. "The fiction writer is an observer, first, last, and always, but he cannot be an adequate observer unless he is free from uncertainty about what he sees."[50]

O'Connor and the American Romance Tradition

Leaving aside the imprimaturs of doctrine and Church, we may yet find a meaningful context for O'Connor's writings, one that she indeed construed for herself. It will not of course be in the mainstream of twentieth-century writing, but one can infer from her strictures of modern fiction her own implicit standards. "In twentieth-century fiction," she wrote, "it increasingly happens that a meaningless, absurd world impinges upon the sacred consciousness of author or character; author and character seldom now go out to explore and penetrate a world in which the sacred is reflected."[51]

"Explore and penetrate"—what is meant is not, necessarily, any literal movement of a character into any literally unknown seas so much as the movement of consciousness into a sphere of undiscovered reality, a figurative penetration which will not ignore the workings of the mind—not by any means—but, rather, will present a character's sudden awareness of what O'Connor would argue is the ultimate nature of reality. In fact, one might almost say, the distinction she is drawing is not so much between the "impingement" of a world upon consciousness as opposed to a "penetration" of the world, as between the impingement of a "meaningless, absurd world" upon a character as opposed to the penetration of a "sacred" world.

In any case, the metaphors of exploration and penetration suggest the tradition in which O'Connor may most comfortably be located (and in which she often located herself), and that is the tradition of the American romance. *Moby Dick* comes to mind, as does *The Narrative of Arthur Gordon Pym*, or "Young Goodman Brown," or "My Kinsman, Major Molineux"—all works that portray a discovery of the nature of reality through metaphors of the journey, the quest, the movement of a character into the unknown world. And something like the same tensions between literal and symbolic level, between realism and allegory, something like the same tendencies toward phantasmagoric distortion and apocalyptic poetry that can be observed in Melville, Poe, and Hawthorne—all can be seen also in O'Connor. "Hawthorne knew his own problems and perhaps anticipated ours," she wrote, "when he said that he did not write novels, he wrote romances."[52]

At the same time, however, it will not do to exaggerate either the similarities between O'Connor and these nineteenth-century romancers or, indeed, those earlier writers' similarities among themselves: some discriminations and illustrations are necessary.

The amplitude of Melville's imagination—his effort to embrace through an encyclopedic accumulation of detail the fullness of existence—is of course alien to O'Connor's spare, selective literary procedures, but Melville's metaphysical passion is one the Southerner quite definitely shares. And if we set aside *Moby Dick* and look, instead, at the shorter tale *Benito Cereno*, the similarity of intention can be grasped. Thus the reader's unsuspecting view of Benito's ship as seen through Captain Delano's eyes is utterly transformed in the discovery that things are not what they seem: that the slave Babo is the deus absconditus in that microcosm. And Benito's own discovered insight into the dark mystery of reality is one that is shared by many an O'Connor character in his discovery of evil—for example, Mrs. McIntyre in "The Displaced Person" or Thomas in "The Comforts of Home." But while Melville's is an essentially narrative strategy, using the resources of irony and point of view, O'Connor's strategy is more typically dramatic. (Robert Lowell's theatrical adaptation of the Melville story in *The Old Glory* trilogy comes closer to the impact of O'Connor's fiction: when the black slave-king utters, of his race, "The future is with us," Lowell's Captain Delano declares in answer, firing his pistol, "This is your future." With its logic of violence, the climax recalls the end of O'Connor's "A Good Man Is Hard to Find.")

In spite of this difference, it must be said that Melville's satiric genius comes closest of the nineteenth-century writers to serving as a model for O'Connor's style; *The Confidence Man*, especially, seems written with the same mordantly comic irony that O'Connor would bring to her fiction (this description of Onnie Jay Holy in *Wise Blood* is strikingly like some of Melville's trompe-l'oeil sketches of the disguised confidence man: "He looked like an ex-preacher turned cowboy, or an ex-cowboy turned mortician. He was not handsome but under his smile, there was an honest look that fitted into his face like a set of false teeth"),[53] and from a similar satiric norm of Christianity—a viewpoint, however, that is willed in Melville and willingly espoused in O'Connor. In fact, what finally divides the two writers is O'Connor's certainty and Melville's search. The mystery O'Connor uncovers, grounded in her firm faith, took a darkly divided Manichean shape in Melville—the dark and light sides of the tortoise in *The Encantadas*—and, finally, one must settle on the following passage (which may deliberately echo Hawthorne's journal description of Melville on his visit to England) to draw the line between them. "And there is another type of modern man," O'Connor wrote, "who can neither believe nor contain himself in unbelief and who searches desperately, feeling about in all experiences for the lost God."[54]

The blackness of darkness that Melville discovered in Hawthorne and which finds its source of Puritanic gloom in the human heart's Original—and ongoing—Sin is a darkness that is most importantly at the center of O'Connor's conception of man. "I write 'tales' in the sense Hawthorne wrote tales," she told an interviewer. "I'm interested in the old Adam. He just talks southern because I do."[55] And we will have occasion to observe later that certain scenes in O'Connor dramatize this discovery of the Fall in ways strikingly similar to scenes in Hawthorne. Time and again in the lives of O'Connor's characters there is a moment at the edge of a precipice—a moment like that in the Roman Forum in Hawthorne's *Marble Faun* when the chasm opens almost underfoot. And what Miriam says on that occasion in Hawthorne's romance neatly sums up the metaphoric significance of that chasm and of its pervasiveness.

> "I fancy," remarked Miriam, "that every person takes a peep into it in moments of gloom and despondency; that is to say, in his moments of deepest insight. . . . The chasm was merely one of the orifices of that pit of blackness that lies beneath us, everywhere. The firmest substance of human happiness is but a thin crust spread over it, with just reality enough to bear up the illusive stage-scenery amid which we tread."

And she adds, with characteristic Hawthornian subtlety, " 'It needs no earthquake to open the chasm, a footstep, a little heavier than ordinary, will serve. . . .' "[56] It was not precisely in Hawthorne's own footsteps that O'Connor followed, however, for her tread was of course broader and heavier, her dramatic climaxes more sudden and violent.

What is also at work in both Hawthorne and O'Connor is a metamorphic imagination: the image of Richard Digby turned to stone is, one might say, simply the reverse metamorphosis of Mrs. Turpin in O'Connor's "Revelation" gazing into the "very heart of mystery" (into a pig parlor, in fact), "like a monumental statue coming to life."[57] But where Hawthorne is frankly allegorical, O'Connor discovers a metaphor for the motions of grace. Where Hawthorne deliberately violates the decorum of realism in his fantastic symbolism, O'Connor stays within the limits of a realistic fiction, inducing in her characters a dreamlike vision or, more characteristically, leaving them on the brink of some insight into mystery through the impact of a naturalistic violent action. Where she does resort to grotesque symbolism, as, say, in Hulga Hopewell's wooden leg ("Good Country People"), the symbol gains a psychologically meaningful dimension while still remaining a literal wooden leg, and does not undergo the allegorical transformation that occurs, for example, in Hawthorne's "The Birthmark," where Georgiana's handlike blemish shocks the obsessed Aylmer "as being the visible mark of earthly imperfection." (2:48) So that while Georgiana, quite fittingly for the moral of Hawthorne's story, suffers death with the removal of her birthmark, the Bible salesman who steals Hulga's leg leaves her quite simply suffering. Where O'Connor does found a story on an allegorical symbol, as in "The River," the result is an inferior tale: Bevel's drowning may be in the "River of Life," but the story fails to convince us that the little boy has done anything but unfortunately confuse a literal meaning and a symbolic meaning; the atmosphere of the story is not "liberated" sufficiently (in the way Hawthorne's is) to accommodate the allegory.

Hawthorne's tales differ from those of O'Connor in still another revealing way. The moral allegory of the New Englander induces chiefly the pleasure of ironic contemplation; Hawthorne's tales are subtle, and demand a reflection from the reader that will often, to his surprise, turn into its mirror image upon further reflection; but characteristically they end in an allegorical emblem or allegorical scene that brings the tale to a complex stasis. With O'Connor, however, the specific effect is, in her best tales, one of surprise, if not shock. The reader is not asked to question the relationship between art and life, between dream and reality, but, rather, is drawn into the realistic texture of the story, caught up in the emotions of the characters and delivered over, finally, to a violent conclusion. The first effect of her fiction, then, is emotional rather than contemplative, although, to be sure, for the experience to take hold, contemplation is an essential afterthought.

To Melville, discovery means piercing through the veneer of appearances to the dark mystery at the heart of things; to Hawthorne, it means uncovering the abyss at our feet or the evil in the isolated heart; to Poe, discovery means transcending the limitations of the material earth in a vision of supernatural wonder. And because the structure of O'Connor's imagination bears, I think, closest resemblance to that of the Southern-bred Poe, the difference between the two may throw into relief O'Connor's peculiar qualities. Let me first establish the parallel.[58]

Perhaps the most theatrical of Poe's transcendent visions is the one that concludes *The Narrative of Arthur Gordon Pym*, when, as Pym floats in his little bark through a sea of milky-white liquid, there suddenly looms up before his eyes a vast white curtain; as the curtain parts, he and his companions rush into an embracing cataract, "where a chasm threw itself open to receive us. But there arose in our pathway a shrouded human figure, very far larger in its proportions than any dweller among men. And the hue of the skin of the figure was of the perfect whiteness of the snow."[59] There are many things surprising about this conclusion, not least of which is that it follows a strictly realistic account of Pym's adventures up to this point, at which literal meaning breaks down and gives way to a purposely vague, dreamlike vision, clothed in a syntax at once mellifluous and analytic. And, as the reader feels vaguely cheated, left out, the only clue Poe gives, aside from a subtly ambiguous concluding "note," is in the deliberately anapestic last line, which insinuates that descriptive prose has here passed into visionary poetry. But even on this superficial level of observation, one detects in *Pym* a resemblance to the structure of O'Connor's tales. For in the best of them too, naturalistic observation, culminating in decisive, violent action, gives way to a visionary conclusion. And too, O'Connor's conclusions strike us with a force that is at first hardly definable.

The pattern of *Pym* is one that recurs in Poe and calls for a word more of explanation. Thus, for example, the reader will recall "MS. Found in a Bottle" and "Descent into the Maelström"—tales which likewise submit their heroes to some final, horrendous, ultimate vision. And too, there is the same vehicle used to progress to the absolute: the small wooden vessel—barrel or boat. Poe is always going somewhere, always discovering something, be it horror or horrible beauty or beauty. The pattern behind the efforts at transcendence that obsess Poe was systematically, if not transparently, expounded by the poet in his philosophical "Art-Product," "Romance," or "Poem" (Poe called it all three), *Eureka*. What it describes is, briefly, a three-phase vision of the cosmos: the world begins in concentrated Godhead; it then diffuses and fills the universe with created matter (the phase we live in); and, in the final phase, all matter contracts again into the "Spirit Divine," to begin the cycle over again. Human life exists in the expansion stage, Poe imagined, and it is the constant effort of man to regain, in the last stage, the unity of the "Heart Divine."

But this ultimate unity may be gained only through death. "The Colloquy of Monos and Una" is indeed an account of just such a death and redemption: the decay of the body, the awakening of the soul's "sixth sense," and the ecstatic apperception of "the majestic novelty of the Life Eternal" (4:200) are described by Monos to his love, Una, in great detail. The climax of his narration comes when, from his moldering coffin, the "dead" man senses the descent of his own beloved's coffin (surely the most macabre mise-en-scène for a dialogue ever imagined). What "The Colloquy" makes plain is that those boats Poe is always traveling in (as, indeed, is suggested by one of the nightmares of *Pym*) are in fact coffins; and the ultimate vision that comes to his characters when they reach the center of the maelström, or the great opening chasm, is a vision of the transcendence of matter and of unity with the Godhead—on the brink of death. Or, as he put it in "Mesmeric Revelation": "There are two bodies—the rudimental and the complete; corresponding with the two conditions of the worm and the butterfly. What we call 'death,' is but the painful metamorphosis. Our present incarnation is progressive, preparatory, temporary. Our future is perfected, ultimate, immortal. The ultimate life is the full design." (5:250) The coffin is also the cocoon.

The relevance of all this to Flannery O'Connor may now become clear. For her imaginative realization of her Christian faith is strikingly close to Poe's cosmology. For her too, life is the imperfect state; for her too, the completion of life is in death at the great Judgement Day when a union with God will be perfected. And in her works too, coffins abound—in *Wise Blood*, in *The Violent Bear It Away*, and, most explicitly, in "Judgement Day," where, from his life of exile in New York City, Tanner dreams of arriving home in the South in a coffin. And one can extend the parallel even further or, rather, backward. Where Poe posits a state of union before life, O'Connor imagines, for some of her characters, a state of innocence in a mythical childhood. And where Poe envisions, in "To Helen," going *back* to a vision of perfection and glory and grandeur, so does O'Connor: repeatedly her protagonists will hold in their minds an image of perfection as it existed in the past, one that is usually associated with a containing structure—the house that is the first "cocoon." Thus, for example, in *Wise Blood*, Hazel's Eastrod home is the emotional and theological focus of his life—from it he starts out, and to it (symbolically) he returns. Tarwater too, in *The Violent*, leaves and returns to his Powderhead home. The grandmother who is graced with death at the end of "A Good Man Is Hard to Find" likewise dreams of an old plantation house as the center of all that is good and long since gone. And, as previously mentioned, in "Everything That Rises Must Converge," both Julian and his mother envision the ancestral house as a focus of yearning, as an unfallen state.

Yet here an important distinction must be made: for O'Connor, in every case where the mystery is experienced, it is through an act of God, through grace. That Christian agency is absent in Poe, where, whether it be accident of nature or force of will that leads to the rebirth into the transcendent, it is never an act of divine intervention and, seemingly, it is without moral overtones.

This last point is an interesting one, for if we examine the processes of Poe's tales we find them to reside in an almost amoral, almost abstract dramatization of his cosmology. O'Connor may have asserted that the essence of her art was "a reasonable use of the unreasonable,"[60] but in the word "unreasonable" is implicit the power of the Christian mystery: the source of order in a world of good and evil lies in the "unreasonable" sacrifice of Christ. But in Poe, the unreasonable is truly unreasonable. Situations are set up which his characters must endure for the mere interest of endurance. His focus is on the *psychological* reactions of his characters in extreme situations, rather than, as with O'Connor, on the moral and theological meaning of extreme situations. With O'Connor, matter is penetrated with mystery and transformed by mystery. With Poe, matter is matter and mystery is mystery—the gulf between Israfel and the earthly poet is unbridgeable. There is no divine incarnation.

We have said that for Poe death is the means of passage from one state to another, and, to be sure, death comes at the moment of insight for many of O'Connor's characters. But, and I emphasize the point, for Poe death is *passage* from matter to a transcendence of matter, while for O'Connor the soul is itself metamorphosed through descending grace. Poe's is a transcendent, whereas O'Connor's is a metamorphic, imagination. Hence, while in both writers the tale builds to a single climax and a singleness of effect, in Poe that effect is abstract, amoral, and sensational; in O'Connor (while it is often sensational) that impact is grounded in a controlled transformation of naturalistic surface into theological mystery.

The sharp division in Poe's sensibility is reflected in the sharp separation of styles into which his tales fall. Leaving aside the quite distinct tales of ratiocination (a reasonable use of the reasonable?), one can group the fiction into those stories which are rooted in the supernatural (and which we have been considering) and those which are humorous in their intentions. No one has suggested an ancillary Bacon to Poe's Shakespeare, and, quite naturally, these humorous tales reflect the sensibility (and, as Marie Bonaparte has suggested, the latent psychology) of the man as much as his horror tales do. (One might observe that when the supernatural descends from the realm of the transcendent to that of the mundane, it becomes the "odd," and, to be sure, there is a tale of comic wonders called "The Angel of the Odd.") Nevertheless, the point is that Poe's intentions in these tales are not serious—at least not as serious, cosmologically, as in his tales of the supernatural. Poe did not, in short, fuse, in his imagination, the comic and the serious modes. And that of course is the most significant difference between O'Connor and Poe. For as the Catholic writer fused in her metamorphic imagination the Word and the flesh, so did she fuse in her style the comic and the gravely serious.

If in this discussion I have seemed to emphasize differences in O'Connor's relationship to the major writers in the American romance tradition, let me, in concluding this section, call the reader back to the underlying similarities. For O'Connor possesses, in common with Melville, Hawthorne, and Poe, the metaphysical and artistic habit of discovery—of penetrating beyond the surface of life to some hidden reality. What she successfully brought to the romance tradition was her Catholic vision, and therein lies the difference. So that while she shares with Melville a search for ultimate meaning, she does not share his uncertainty; while she shares with Hawthorne an awareness of the potency of Original Sin, she does not share his gloom; and while she shares with Poe a transcendent visionary imagination, she does not share his bifurcated sensibility. In short, her roots are in the nineteenth-century romance tradition, but she carries that tradition into the twentieth century and gives it the spiritual cast of her Catholic faith.

Prophets and Failed Prophets

Some of the most striking of Flannery O'Connor's characters may also be related to the romance tradition in America. For one of the distinguishing features of that tradition (shared, I might add, with fiction springing from the gothic romance strain in England) is a tendency toward the grotesque in characterization. The reasons for this are consistent with the main intentions of the romance. For if, as has been suggested, the tendency of works in this tradition has been not to portray with mimetic fidelity the manners and social surfaces of everyday life but, rather, to uncover at the heart of reality a sense of mystery, then the grotesque figure becomes the Ulysses of this terra incognita. He is a figure who is in some way distorted from the shape of normality—whether by a physical deformity (Ahab) or by a consuming intellectual (Usher), metaphysical (Pierre), moral (Ethan Brand, the veiled minister), or emotional (Bartleby) passion; and his discovery often takes a violent shape—destructive of himself or of others.

And it was well that O'Connor had this tradition, for it would help her to solve what would be her chief literary problem—how to embody not necessarily the grand ungodly quester but the godly ungrand one, the man whose distortion signifies that God, through his grace, is alive in him. W. H. Auden put the problem this way.

> The Incarnation, the coming of Christ in the form of a servant who cannot be recognized by the eye of flesh and blood, but only by the eye of faith, puts an end to all claims of the imagination to be the faculty which decides what is truly sacred and what is profane. A pagan god can appear on earth in disguise but, so long as he wears his disguise, no man is expected to recognize him nor can. But Christ appears looking just like any other man, yet claims that He is the Way, the Truth and the Life, and that no man can come to God the Father except through Him. The contradiction between the profane appearance and the sacred assertion is impassible [sic] to the imagination.[61]

O'Connor solved the problem by portraying the man of Christ in a form unlike any other man and by projecting this inner upheaval of the soul not only in a wild look but in wild and violent action. (And sometimes an image of divine intervention would have no human shape at all: the "Greenleaf" bull, the icicled bird of "The Enduring Chill," the tattoo on "Parker's Back.") The effects may not always have been what she intended for some of her readers—"My vocation," she wrote to a friend, "seems to be to scare nice old ladies"[62]— but, given the proper allowance for irony, she succeeded admirably well.

The major figures of her long fictions, Hazel Motes (*Wise Blood*) and the Tarwaters (*The Violent*), succeed precisely by virtue of this wildness and eccentricity in their appearance and actions. O'Connor called them "prophet freaks" and they are just that, associated in her mind with the Old Testament prophets who "were seen by their contemporaries as inspired men," in communication with the divine

—"an Isaiah walking naked as a warning to Egypt, an Hosea ago-
nizing over his prostitute wife or an Ezekiel baking his bread over
dung to symbolize the destruction to come."[63] In addition, however,
O'Connor's prophets are men in whose lives the conversion is the
central drama. And hence the New Testament of Christ's salvation
provides the theological energy. One crucial difference, however,
between O'Connor's prophet freaks and those of the Scriptures is
that where the precursors "were seen by their contemporaries as
inspired men," the modern heirs are seen by their contemporaries
as madmen.

O'Connor's closeness to both the Old and the New Testaments
helps to explain an interesting difference between her attitude toward
the grotesque prophet and the attitude of Hawthorne toward a strikingly similar character of his own. For one story by the latter that
cannot resist comparison with Flannery O'Connor is "The Man of
Adamant." Subtitled "An Apologue," it concerns the retreat of old
Richard Digby—"the gloomiest and most intolerant of a stern brotherhood" (3:564)—into the mountains, there to escape the abomina-
tion and ruin that will befall, he thinks, the " 'horrible perversity of
this generation.' " (3:564) Secreting himself in a calcifying cave,
Digby devotes himself to reading the Scriptures; but, Hawthorne
says, "he made continual mistakes in what he read, converting all
that was gracious and merciful to denunciations of vengeance and
unutterable woe on every created being but himself." (3:570) He is
"visited" in his retreat by Mary Goffe, a quondam convert who
loves Digby and who pleads, " 'Come back to thy fellow-men; for
they need thee, Richard, and thou hast tenfold need of them.' "
(3:569) But he refuses; the petrifying atmosphere of the cave reinforces the old man's already calcified arteries, until finally Digby
turns to patently allegorical stone. He is discovered, Hawthorne concludes, "in the attitude of repelling the whole race of mortals,—not
from heaven,—but from the horrible loneliness of his dark, cold
sepulchre!" (3:573)

How close a resemblance Digby bears to so many of O'Connor's
pivotal characters—Hazel Motes's grandfather, old Tarwater, Rufus
Johnson's father (gone with a remnant to the hills)—those "prophet
freaks" who, she wrote, "seem to carry an invisible burden and to fix
us with eyes that remind us that we all bear some heavy responsibility
whose nature we have forgotten. They see what we do not. They are

prophetic figures, the result of outrage and not of geniality."[64] The extremes of backwoods Southern fundamentalism and New England Puritan orthodoxy seem to meet in these grotesque figures of O'Connor and Hawthorne.

But do they, in fact, meet? Not quite. For what is an emblem of evil to Hawthorne is an emblem of good to O'Connor. This is not to say that the Southern writer would necessarily have accorded faith to old Richard Digby but, rather, that she would—and did—see in her own representations of the alien, self-appointed prophet not an image of sin and error but an image of divine favor. When, by contrast, O'Connor chose to represent arrogance and proud alienation from the truth, she did so in the figures of the intellectual, the would-be writer (shades of Miles Coverdale?), or—a character Hawthorne could not know—the smugly complacent middle-class woman for whom religion is, precisely, a social occasion. It is true that, like Hawthorne, she portrayed the separation of heart from head (the synecdochic Mr. Head in "The Artificial Nigger" is a notable example), but the values of the heart, or of the soul, did not mean for O'Connor, as they did for Hawthorne, communion with one's fellow but, rather, communion with God. And her works are full of images of isolation which are also images of positive spiritual value—the rustic sanctuary of the Heads in "The Artificial Nigger," for example, or the Powderhead retreat of the Tarwaters, or the last-ditch withdrawal from society by Hazel Motes at the end of Wise Blood.

And it is interesting to observe that where Protestant Hawthorne, in, for example, The Marble Faun, portrays the solace of Communion in the Catholic Church, Catholic O'Connor dramatizes the epitome of the religious life in figures of radical Protestantism. Perhaps they are both responding to the respective pressures of their differing backgrounds in this: the isolation bred by the ideals of individualism in Puritan New England producing in the alienated Hawthorne an image of needed brotherhood, and the pressures of the social unit of the Church producing in O'Connor an image of individualistic faith. Also relevant of course is O'Connor's own explanation of why she chose to write chiefly about Protestants and to ignore—with the exception of a Catholic priest here and there ("The Displaced Person," "The Enduring Chill")—the life of the Church. In a letter written to a friend in a religious order, she declared that the only difference between Catholic fanatics and Protestant fanatics is that "if you are a Catholic and have this intensity of belief you join the convent and are heard no more; whereas if you are a Protestant and have it, there is no convent for you to join and you go about the world getting into all sorts of trouble and drawing the wrath of people who don't believe anything much at all down on your head." And she went on, "This is one reason why I can write about Protestant believers better than Catholic believers—because they express their belief in diverse kinds of dramatic action which is obvious enough for me to catch."[65]

But what is perhaps most telling in distinguishing Hawthorne from O'Connor is what she then went on to say: "When you leave a man alone with his Bible and the Holy Ghost inspires him, he's going to be a Catholic one way or another, even though he knows nothing about the visible Church. His kind of Christianity may not be socially desirable, but it will be real in the sight of God. If I set myself to write about a socially desirable Christianity, all the life would go out of what I do."[66] In short, behind O'Connor's assertion that the Protestant prophet offers better material for fiction is a belief that the Holy Ghost and not the devil will finally be the source of inspiration. Behind Hawthorne's "The Man of Adamant" is the conviction that it is the devil who will triumph. And it is in accord with these beliefs that the tone of Hawthorne's fiction is tragically ironic and the characteristic tone of O'Connor's is comically ironic. The Old Adam may offer some resistance in O'Connor's world, but the redemptive force of grace is stronger; in Hawthorne's world, the Old Adam remains adamant.

In accounting for the provenance of these prophets, it seems relevant to note as well their historical authenticity in American life. As early as 1835, de Tocqueville observed that "here and there in the midst of American society you meet with men full of a fanatical and almost wild spiritualism which hardly exists in Europe."[67] The reasons for such "religious insanity," as de Tocqueville judged it, have doubtless changed over the years, but the strain seems to have survived into the twentieth century. (Indeed, it is curious to observe the marked resurgence of intense fundamentalism, some eight years after O'Connor's death, among the young, although a sense of community seems at least as appealing to the more recent sects as the faith itself.) The South, particularly, has been a perennial seedbed of religious enthusiasm, and O'Connor's witnessing of the more striking forms must surely have quickened her interest in the available literary precedents for grotesque characterization.

I have been using the overused word "grotesque" in this discussion for want of a better one, and also because O'Connor herself used it. In fact, she used the word in a way that might be confusing: to designate not only those characters whose distortion signified some good (the prophets we have been discussing) but also those whose distortion was meant to suggest some evil. For there is another type of character closely related to the heroes of the long fictions, and that is the prophet freak, who (the will being free) does *not* undergo a conversion experience. Of this latter type are the man who calls himself The Misfit in "A Good Man Is Hard to Find," the trio of destructive youths in "A Circle in the Fire," and Rufus Johnson in "The Lame Shall Enter First." These characters are likewise somewhat mad, and their madness is born of frustration and anguish. Possessed by a sense of the vast importance of redemption, or of a dream of salvation and paradise, they are yet unpossessed of grace. And they commit acts of wanton violence or acts of murder in accordance with their austere conviction of their sinful nature. Sometimes, especially with Rufus, one feels that such perversity is a requirement of the logic of damnation—a damned character is by definition evil—and this somewhat diminishes his force as a fictional character. But in the example of The Misfit, obedience to the logic of damnation is carried to such a grotesque extremity—accompanied, moreover, by final frustration—that his acts of brutal murder seem the acts of a living character and take on an imaginative logic of their own.

This latter use of grotesque exaggeration is entirely characteristic of O'Connor's moral stance as a writer, and because it resembles, but is importantly distinct from, the general sense of the term "grotesque" in modern literature, some clarification is essential. For the modern grotesque is typically a more pitiable and a more representative figure than O'Connor's or than the nineteenth century's version. Seldom does he achieve the complexly tragic stature of Poe's mad scholar-poets; of Hawthorne's Ethan Brand, or minister with the black veil, or Aylmer; of Melville's Pierre. Instead, the pages of a work like *Winesburg, Ohio* are filled with the frustrated, the lonely, the obsessed—characters who are not tragically grotesque but pathetically grotesque, and of a putative universal dimension. Thus Sherwood Anderson could write in a letter to Kenneth Davenport in 1937:

> You speak of the characters in my stories being grotesque. Are you quite sure you are not grotesque, speaking in these terms? I am quite sure I am. It seems to me that in speaking of literary characters you are making some queer separation between people in stories and people in life. I rather think that modern life, and, in fact, any life wherein most people are compelled to be driven by the profit motive makes it impossible for all of us to be anything but grotesque.[68]

Carson McCullers might be another in whom the romance tradition has become the vehicle not of a tragic view of life but (and I use the word with no pejorative sense intended) a sentimental view of life: her characters live in a world where loneliness is inevitable, and they appeal to our "tender emotions." The isolation of a character like dumb Singer in *The Heart Is a Lonely Hunter* becomes grotesquely heightened in later works, like *The Ballad of the Sad Café*, where physical deformity becomes an emblem of inescapable exclusion and where even the world from which the deformed are excluded is deformed. The limping young lady of Tennessee Williams's *The Glass Menagerie*, Laura, is still another example of the pathetically grotesque, for whom no possibility exists save a withdrawal into the slightly mad, hermetically sealed world of her frangible animals. One can, it is true, find a superficial resemblance between the physically deformed in McCullers's or Williams's world and a character like wooden-legged Hulga Hopewell in "Good Country People," but the grotesques of the former are objects of our compassion, whereas O'Connor's are not only ill-favored but often unregenerate, and hence the objects of ironic satire.

What is behind these differences between O'Connor and these other writers, as the author herself made clear in an essay on "Some Aspects of the Grotesque in Southern Fiction," is the difference between compassion and austere judgment.

> It's considered an absolute necessity these days for writers to have compassion. Compassion is a word that sounds good in anybody's mouth and which no book jacket can do without. It is a quality which no one can put his finger on in any exact critical sense, so it is always safe for anybody to use. Usually I think what is meant by it is

that the writer excuses all human weakness because human weakness is human. The kind of hazy compassion demanded of the writer now makes it difficult for him to be anti-anything. Certainly when the grotesque is used in a legitimate way, the intellectual and moral judgments implicit in it will have the ascendency over feeling."[69]

O'Connor herself never had any trouble in expressing the ascendency of "moral judgments" over "hazy compassion," and the sureness of her judgment underlies both her strengths and her weaknesses as a writer. At its best, it made possible a brilliant comic satire when dealing with human limitations—as with Hulga and the portraits of the sturdy, hardheaded farm women (grotesques of the practical virtues) in "Good Country People," "The Life You Save May Be Your Own," "A Circle in the Fire," "The Displaced Person," "Greenleaf," and "Revelation." At its worst, however, a disturbing uncertainty of tone pervades her characterizations of some male parents in the fiction (Rayber in *The Violent Bear It Away*, for example, and Sheppard in "The Lame Shall Enter First"), who are self-styled intellectuals and humanists but are overstylized to the point of caricature. The frank caricature of Enoch in *Wise Blood*, by contrast, is sucessful because he is given not the slightest loincloth of credibility and so elicits not a whit of compassion.

The equivalent of O'Connor's own compassion for the grotesque is visible in a story atypical for its absence of violence and for its consistent use of a single narrative viewpoint, "A Temple of the Holy Ghost." What the story describes is a little girl's encounter with the notion of the body (and the story is notable for the abundance of corporeal imagery it contains). The chief focus of the little girl's consciousness is a carnival freak, part man part woman, whom she learns about from her visiting cousins, who saw, and were unpleasantly shocked by, the sight. But the words of the freak, as the cousins relate them to the child, sink into her consciousness—" 'God made me thisaway and if you laugh He may strike you the same way. . . . God made me thisaway and I don't dispute hit. . . . God done this to me and I praise Him' "[70]—until, at the end of the story, she inwardly experiences (there is no violence in "A Temple") the mystery of the Incarnation in a vision of the sun as "a huge red ball like an elevated Host drenched in blood." (101) The Word made flesh makes a temple of even the most grotesque of bodies.

Such is O'Connor's compassion: if you will, a theological compassion. But what is interesting is that, in "A Temple of the Holy Ghost" at least, there seems to be a tension between this consciously directed, consciously symbolized feeling and the more spontaneous attributes of her art. Thus toward the end of the story, as the point about the compassionate dwelling of God in potentially every man is being clinched, there intrudes a comic description of one of the characters that tends (unintentionally, I think) to undercut the point of the story and hence to evoke an uncertain response from the reader: on the way home from the convent school where the child and her mother have deposited the cousins, the little girl, sitting in the back seat gazes at the back of the driver's head—"The child observed three folds of fat in the back of his neck and noted that his ears were pointed almost like a pig's." (100) If we can laugh at Alonzo, why can't we laugh at the sideshow freak?

In short, where there is not the pressure of a "meaning" to be unequivocally conveyed, it seems to have been natural to O'Connor's imagination to regard grotesquerie with a cool, comic, detached eye. Even as a child, she tells us in her essay on raising peacocks, "The King of the Birds," she had an eye for the rara avis: ". . . I began to collect chickens. What had been only a mild interest became a passion, a quest. I had to have more and more chickens. I favored those with one green eye and one orange or with overlong necks and crooked combs. I wanted one with three legs or three wings but nothing in that line turned up. . . . I could sew in a fashion and I began to make clothes for chickens."[71] And this fascination with the comic grotesque was reflected in her early literary tastes as well, for, as she told an interviewer once: "Many years ago I read a volume of 'The Humorous Stories of Edgar Allan Poe,' and I think that started me thinking of a writing career. . . . And I'm sure Gogol influenced me."[72] "The Man Who Was Used Up," the man who becomes "The Nose"—such apparently were her early delights, and they would foster her naturally satirical habits.

The Comic Balance

The techniques of satire are most successful in O'Connor when they are used to support a consistently comic, ironic characterization. Such is the case in her handling of certain would-be intellectuals, like Asbury in "The Enduring Chill," Julian in "Everything That Rises Must Converge," and Calhoun in "The Partridge Festival." In these stories, there seems little conflict between final intention and comic treatment. For example, in the last-named, O'Connor effectively uses contrasting speech patterns to deflate the overblown rhetoric of the cynical young hero (Calhoun), who scorns the town azalea festival and its paraphernalia.

> "I see you've paid your tribute to the god," [Calhoun] said.
> The boy did not seem to get the significance of this.
> "The badge," Calhoun said, "the badge."
> The boy looked down at it and then back at Calhoun. . . .
> "Are you enjoying the festive spirit?" Calhoun asked.
> "All these doings?" the boy said.[73]

And in "The Enduring Chill," not only the rhetoric of the hero ("He had failed his God, Art, but he had been a faithful servant and Art was sending him Death." [103]), but his histrionic gestures as well are handled with a deft and chilling irony. Thus, for example, as Asbury nears what he takes to be his death, he imagines a final fulfilling communion with the Negroes who work on his mother's farm, and accordingly he orders his mother to bring in Randall and Morgan, "preparing himself for the encounter as a religious man might prepare himself for the last sacrament." (110) The scene that follows is one of O'Connor's finest, though it depends on comic caricatures of the two Negroes.

> The two of them came in grinning and shuffled to the side of the bed. They stood there, Randall in front and Morgan behind. "You sho do look well," Randall said. "You looks very well."
> "You looks well," the other one said. "Yessuh, you looks fine."
> "I ain't ever seen you looking so well before," Randall said.
> "Yes, doesn't he look well?" his mother said. "I think he looks just fine."
> "Yessuh," Randall said, "I speck you ain't even sick." (110)

Face to face with them, Asbury can think of saying only, "I'm going to die."

> Then with relief he remembered that they were going to smoke together. He reached for the package on the table and held it out to Randall, forgetting to shake out the cigarettes.
> The Negro took the package and put it in his pocket. "I thank you," he said. "I certainly do prechate it." (111)

And then he must give the other Negro a package too! The communion of kindred spirits disintegrates as Randall and Morgan argue over cold remedies and Asbury calls for his mother to remove his guests; with a spinning head he sinks into sleep. "He knew now there would be no significant experience before he died." (112)

A similar ironic deflation of the protagonist's desire for an unholy communion in "Everything That Rises Must Converge" also employs a Negro figure, but this time he has a human shape free from caricature. Thus when a "large Negro . . . well dressed" (12) and carrying a briefcase, gets on the bus, Julian wants to converse meaningfully with him on "art or politics" (13), but the man remains entrenched behind his newspaper. Finally, Julian has a conversation opener.

> "Do you have a light?" he asked the Negro.
> Without looking away from his paper, the man reached in his pocket and handed him a packet of matches.
> "Thanks," Julian said. For a moment he held the matches foolishly. A NO SMOKING sign looked down upon him from over the door. This alone would not have deterred him; he had no cigarettes. He had quit smoking some months before because he could not afford it. "Sorry," he muttered and handed back the matches. The Negro lowered the paper and gave him an annoyed look. He took the matches and raised the paper again. (13)

Such is the fate of Julian's hollow liberalism: his gesture, ironically, has the effect of seeming a deliberate annoyance of the Negro.

On such occasions, O'Connor is masterful in her use of the nuances of manners and class differences, making her points with precision and understatement. She is equally impressive in her sense of timing, as in this scene from *Wise Blood*, in which Enoch Emery is in the greasy Paris Diner, reading the outside sheet of another customer's newspaper.

> The man lowered the paper and looked at him. Enoch smiled. The man raised the paper again. "Could I borrow some part of your paper that you ain't studying?" Enoch asked. The man lowered it again and stared at him; he had muddy unflinching eyes. He leafed deliberately through the paper and shook out the sheet with the comic strips and handed it to Enoch. (193)

It is a comedy of insult worthy of W. C. Fields, whom O'Connor relished greatly.[74]

The mention of Fields suggests another characteristic of O'Connor's comedy—its cinematic quality. With the sharp focus of a camera eye, she will isolate details and shift our attention to create a terse comic effect—as in this scene, also from *Wise Blood*, where Hazel Motes, his faith in his car as yet unshaken, looks on as a one-armed mechanic tries to fix it.

> [The mechanic] looked for a long time under the hood while Haze stood by, but he didn't touch anything. After a while he shut it and blew his nose.
> "What's wrong in there?" Haze asked in an agitated voice. "It's a good car, ain't it?"
> The man didn't answer him. He sat down on the ground and eased under the Essex. He wore hightop shoes and gray socks. He stayed under the car a long time. . . . [Hazel saw that] he wasn't doing anything. He was just lying there, looking up, as if he were contemplating; his good arm was folded on his chest. (125–26)

After getting a push, Hazel finally starts the car, meeting the mechanic down the road.

> "I told you this car would get me anywhere I wanted to go," Haze said sourly.
> "Some things," the man said, "'ll get some folks somewheres," and he turned the truck up the highway. (127)

The visual images are precise and laconic. As laconic as the last line of dialogue, where O'Connor's country fixer seems to echo the dry talk of the waterfall leaper Sam Patch, who is quoted by Constance Rourke as saying, "Some things can be done as well as others."

As these scenes suggest, one cannot always point to a crucial thematic relevance for O'Connor's comedy, and, indeed, how tiresome if one could! Some of her most brilliant moments seem to exist for the sheer delight of the humor itself, as, for example, when old Fortune in "A View of the Woods" is looking for his granddaughter after she has disappeared from in front of a country store, and comes across a Negro boy, "drinking a purple drink . . . sitting on the ground with his back against the sweating ice cooler." (68) Fortune asks him,

> "Where did that little girl go to, boy?" . . .
> "I ain't seen nair little girl," the boy said.

The old man irritably fished in his pocket and handed him a nickel and said, "A pretty little girl in a yeller cotton dress."

"If you speakin about a stout chile look lak you," the boy said, "she gone off in a truck with a white man." (68)

It goes without saying that such a passage also implies a good deal about the limits of social custom and about the instrumentality of language.

O'Connor habitually fleshes out her characters by isolating the telling idiosyncrasy, the individual habit or manner of speaking, whether it is, as with several of her farm women, an addiction to vapid banality, or, as with Mr. Shortley in "The Displaced Person," a little trick he acquired years ago when he courted Mrs. Shortley, a trick that "drove her wild every time he did it": Mr. Shortley, "without appearing to give the feat any consideration, lifted the cigarette stub with the sharp end of his tongue, drew it into his mouth, closed his lips tightly, rose, stepped out, gave his wife a good round appreciative stare, and spit the smoldering butt into the grass."[75] And there is the characteristic physical detail too, as in this superbly pointed passage from *Wise Blood*.

[Enoch] was exhausted and he had to lean against Walgreen's window and cool off. Sweat crept down his back and provoked him to itch so that in just a few minutes he appeared to be working his way across the glass by his muscles, against a background of alarm clocks, toilet waters, candies, sanitary pads, fountain pens, and pocket flashlights, displayed in all colors to twice his height. (135)

Doubtless the texture of Flannery O'Connor's world owes something to Nathanael West, whom she read with enthusiasm during her formative years. Here, for example, is a passage from *Day of the Locust*.

On the corner of La Huerta Road was a miniature Rhine castle with tarpaper turrets pierced for archers. Next to it was a little highly colored shack with domes and minarets out of the *Arabian Nights*.

With her equally sharp eye for the grotesque in everyday life, O'Connor might have written that passage. But one draws the line between the two writers by noting that O'Connor would not have continued it as West does.

> Both houses were comic, but he didn't laugh. Their desire to startle was so eager and guileless.
>   It is hard to laugh at the need for beauty and romance, no matter how tasteless, even horrible, the results of that need are. But it is easy to sigh. Few things are sadder than the truly monstrous.[76]

It is the difference, again, between austere judgment and what O'Connor might regard as "hazy compassion."

O'Connor was susceptible to West's influence, it would seem, because she saw in him not a kindred spirit but a kindred artist. West confirmed in her what was there almost from the beginning—the odd, comic look of her world. One finds it, rudimentarily, in her early fiction; one finds it even in the cartoons she drew for her college publications, which are graphic analogues of the fiction. The figures in these drawings are obvious caricatures of young people—college students—and they are extraordinarily, humorously, ugly figures. Body types are extremes of skinny and fat; clothes are sharply stylized, dumpy and disheveled; noses are pulled out to sharp points beyond the rest of the face. These figures are caught frozen in some grotesque version of everyday activity—a girl standing on her head, another sawing violently at a violin, and another crouching over a botanical specimen form one grouping for a yearbook sketch. In another, a clumsy girl is tripping over a sailor as they "dance" under the watchful eyes of two grim ancient chaperones: it is captioned "Having a wonderful time."[77]

These cartoons are not sidesplitting, but they seem to foreshadow recurrent subjects in the fiction; as, for example, the one portraying an exceptionally ugly girl sitting alone on the sidelines of a dance floor, and gesturing sardonically toward the ungainly dancing couples, and saying "Oh, well, I can always be a Ph.D." Hulga-Joy ("Good Country People") and the Wellesley College girl of "Revelation" are her cousins. Another cartoon with more potential than humor forecasts the insults and puns of the fiction when one girl says to another as they stare at an obese WAVE walking by with "Mess" on her sleeve (the school was a training center during the war), "Aw quit trying to tell me that thing means she's a MESSENGER. I'm not so dumb." And what is particularly notable is that in all of the drawings, as in the fiction, these grotesque figures stand out from the page in a barely suggested space; there is little detail of background.

Robert Fitzgerald has observed that she was an admirer of George Price's cartoons, which are indeed strikingly similar to O'Connor's not only in the style of drawing but in certain basic attitudes toward life as well.[78] Price uses a stark line, angularly distorting his figures; his background is spare. And his humor thrives on the incongruity between pretense and actuality, with a pointed satire of human foibles. Often there is a certain incongruous but harmless violence in his cartoons as well, as, for example, when a man blows up a TV set in order to eliminate a panel show on the screen.

Others of Price's cartoons seem more directly analogous with O'Connor's fiction and might possibly have provided a situation or two for her to work with: a park scene displays a collection of grotesques—a hairy man, a hunchback, a bloated woman, and so forth; an old man sits at the window of a city apartment, with his doctor saying: "What he needs is a change of scene. Why don't you move him to some other window?" (compare "The Geranium" and "Judgement Day"); a member of a Salvation Army street band steps forward and says, "When I get done, Sister Tilton will tell you how she was saved—from a thirty-foot python"; a boy goes out into the street with a soapbox as his mother says, "Take good care of it, son —it belonged to your father" (compare Wise Blood, The Violent Bear It Away); an irate zoo attendant kicks a surprised peacock into the air, as another attendant says to a third person, "Riley always said he couldn't stand their damned strutting" (compare "The Displaced Person," "King of the Birds"); two men look at a half man half woman and ask him/her, "My friend and I want you to settle a little argument" (compare "A Temple of the Holy Ghost").

Naturally, any comparison between Price's cartoons and O'Connor's fiction goes only so far: the cartoons strike us as isolated moments, brief insights that can be quickly passed over; whereas in the fiction, comic incongruity, satire, grotesquerie are embedded in a meaningful context, and serve the purposes of a complex literary experience. Much the same contrast can be made between the writings of O'Connor and the broadly drawn figures of Erskine Caldwell. For while the reader of Tobacco Road, for example, will find a considerable number of coincidences between that work and O'Connor's novels, he soon discovers the difference: Jeeter always wears a "droop-ing black hat" on his head, but it has none of the symbolic overtones of a Hazel Motes's or a Tarwater's hat; Bessie and Dude may buy a car and go preaching and praying all over the country, but it is a far cry from Hazel Motes's car and gospel; Jeeter may have left explicit instructions for his burial, but they leave no impact on anyone the way old Tarwater's do on Tarwater; no-nose Bessie may be as unap-pealing a sexual figure as Leora Watts, but Dude succumbs eagerly to her, whereas Hazel spends a night of restless nightmares with Leora. In short, the cartoonlike figures in Caldwell (who was at first cited by reviewers as a predecessor of O'Connor in the so-called Southern gothic school) are just that—cartoon figures; they lack complexity, and they lack a significant context.

Nevertheless, both Caldwell and O'Connor are heirs to the popu-lar tradition of native American humor that was so strong in the nineteenth century, and whose richness lay in "the freshness and originality of character incidental to a new country," as one of its Canadian practitioners, Thomas Chandler Haliburton, put it.[79]

Surely this humorous tradition (more exactly, the various threads of Down East, Southwestern, and tall-tale humor) is a major force behind O'Connor's writing, along with the romance tradition dis-cussed earlier. Faulkner had already shown what might be done with these two characteristic native forms of expression; but it was equally Flannery O'Connor's genius to synthesize the two currents, thereby giving a unique shape to her Christian faith. And whether before or after the fact, she was quite conscious of the co-mingling.[80]

Some such explanation must supplement my earlier account of the group of characters who are probably O'Connor's strangest: The Mis-fit ("A Good Man Is Hard to Find"), Tom Shiftlet ("The Life You Save May Be Your Own"), and Manley Pointer ("Good Country People"). For they seem born out of a fusion of, on one side, the familiar comic folk hero (the drifter, the jack-of-all-trades, mean Sut Lovingood, crafty Simon Suggs) and, on the other side, the meta-physical restlessness of an Ethan Brand or a Bartleby.[81]

And too, such an explanation helps account for what is most diffi-cult to define in O'Connor's fiction: the peculiar blend of comic violence and mysterious shock that concludes a story like "A View of the Woods," already discussed in another context. Here are some excerpts from the fight scene between old man Fortune and nine-year-old Mary Pitts Fortune which occurs toward the end of the story.

> She was on him so quickly that he could not have recalled which blow he felt first, whether the weight of her whole solid body or the jabs of her feet or the pummeling of her fist on his chest. He flailed the belt in the air, not knowing where to hit but trying to get her off him until he could decide where to get a grip on her. . . .
> He caught his knee and danced on one foot and a rain of blows fell on his stomach. He felt five claws in the flesh of his upper arm where she was hanging from while her feet mechanically battered his knees and her free fist pounded him again and again in the chest. Then with horror, he saw her face rise up in front of his, teeth exposed, and he roared like a bull as she bit the side of his jaw. . . . (79)

Beside this scene let me place a passage from "The Fight," a story in A. B. Longstreet's *Georgia Scenes* (1835). (Longstreet, incidentally, first began publishing his sketches in a Milledgeville paper.) The combatants in the Longstreet sketch, Bill and Bob, are, like Fortune and Mary Pitts, long-time pals, and they have been brought to battle by a perverse mutual acquaintance (Ransy Sniffle). It looks as if Bill has won, the narrator tells us.

> I deemed it impossible for any human being to withstand for five seconds the loss of blood which issued from Bob's ear, cheek, nose, and finger, accompanied with such blows as he was receiving. Still he maintained the conflict, and gave blow for blow with considerable effect. But the blows of each became slower and weaker after the first three or four; and it became obvious that Bill wanted the room which Bob's finger occupied for breathing. He would therefore, probably, in a short time, have let it go, had not Bob anticipated his politeness by jerking away his hand, and making him a present of the finger. He now seized Bill again, and brought him to his knees, but he recovered. . . . A third effort, however, brought him down, and Bob on top of him. These efforts seemed to exhaust the little remaining strength of both; and they lay, Bill undermost and Bob across his breast, motionless, and panting for breath. After a short pause, Bob gathered his hand full of dirt and sand, and was in the act of grinding it in his adversary's eyes, when Bill cried "ENOUGH!"[82]

The extravagant violence of the Georgia "Scene"—exaggerated (one hopes) to achieve a peculiar effect of horror and humor—survives intact in O'Connor. What has changed, however, is the narrative voice: Longstreet remains (or tries to remain) detached from the scene, enveloping it in a buffer of polite language, while O'Connor brings the reader into the midst of the action through her use of point of view and a vivid economy of language. But a further and more significant difference is that where Longstreet draws a tidy frame around his violent scene—such things "are a disgrace to [the] community"—O'Connor carries the reader from comic horror on through to a final culmination of real horror (Fortune ends by killing his granddaughter) and then opens up the ending still more by showing the deepening impact of the act upon the old man himself. I am not sure whether Longstreet succeeds in overcoming the violence of his sketch by his frame, but I am sure that O'Connor succeeds, as she desired, in not overcoming that violence.[83]

This shift from a comic violence to the shock of a tragic irony is one that can be seen in other tales besides "A View of the Woods." One thinks, for example, of "Everything That Rises Must Converge," or of "The Comforts of Home," or of "Judgement Day." Yet in some other tales by O'Connor, violence seems to exist side by side with a kind of grimly comic, ironic detachment that is sustained through to the end of the tale. This is the case with "A Good Man Is Hard to Find," with "A Late Encounter with the Enemy," and with "Greenleaf." One of the most interesting examples of this effect is the death scene in *Wise Blood*. Such a scene is at some remove from the world of Longstreet's Southwestern humor, with its exuberant comic brutality: the violence of a scene like the following is colder, more austere than the violence of the nineteenth-century humorists, and yet withal there is a stylized comic quality to it. Hazel has left Mrs. Flood's rooming house to wander in the rain. The latter has asked the police to retrieve the wayward ascetic on the grounds that he has not paid the rent.

> Two days later, two young policemen cruising in a squad car found him lying in a drainage ditch near an abandoned construction project. The driver drew the squad car up to the edge of the ditch and looked into it for some time. "Ain't we been looking for a blind one?" he asked.
>
> The other one consulted a pad. "Blind and got a blue suit and ain't paid his rent," he said.
>
> "Yonder he is," the first one said, and pointed into the ditch. The other moved up closer and looked out of the window too.

"His suit ain't blue," he said.

"Yes it is blue," the first one said. "Quit pushing up so close to me. Get out and I'll show you it's blue." . . .

"It might have uster been blue," the fatter one admitted.

"You reckon he's daid?" the first one asked.

"Ast him," the other said.

"No, he ain't daid. He's moving."

"Maybe he's just unconscious," the fatter one said, taking out his new billy. They watched him for a few seconds. His hand was moving along the edge of the ditch as if it were hunting something to grip. He asked them in a hoarse whisper where he was and if it was day or night.

"It's day," the thinner one said, looking at the sky. "We got to take you back to pay your rent."

"I want to go on where I'm going," the blind man said.

"You got to pay your rent first," the policeman said. "Ever' bit of it!"

The other, perceiving that he was conscious, hit him over the head with his new billy. "We don't want to have no trouble with him," he said. "You take his feet."

He died in the squad car but they didn't notice. . . . (229–31)

What gives this scene its strange beauty is the coldly objective tone O'Connor sustains; the author is nowhere present, save in the pervasive irony of the dramatic dialogue. And the comic effect of that dialogue and of the darkly innocent actions of the policemen coolly contrasts with the understated sufferings of the dying Hazel. And—what is so perfect—even in his death, Motes is slightly absurd. He has been an absurd figure throughout the novel, but the quality of that absurdity has deepened: no longer amusing, he is now a frankly disturbing character, and yet one whom we are asked not to pity but to wonder at. Our response is similar to the one we entertain toward Tanner in "Judgement Day," who is likewise a comic figure but one who at the same time astonishes us with his world-disdaining faith: "IF FOUND DEAD SHIP EXPRESS COLLECT TO COLEMAN PARRUM, CORINTH, GEORGIA. . . . COLEMAN SELL MY BELONGINGS AND PAY THE FREIGHT ON ME & THE UNDERTAKER. ANYTHING LEFT OVER YOU CAN KEEP," Tanner writes on a note to be attached to his person in his homeward-bound coffin.[84] And of course he fully intends to be alive— to leap out of that coffin and shout, "Judgement Day!"

This sort of coffin humor may have its precedents in the many examples of resiliency in the face of pain and death that mark Amer-

ica's native humor, but how much more resonant is O'Connor's handling of such moments than is, say, Poe's treatment of a situation
which is in other respects similar to the one in "Judgement Day."
Consider the horror, but especially the undercutting humor, of this
monologue from Poe's "Loss of Breath," where the narrator has been
buried alive—but not for long. "I knocked off . . . the lid of my coffin, and stepped out. The place was dreadfully dreary and damp, and
I became troubled with *ennui*. By way of amusement, I felt my way
among the numerous coffins ranged in order around. I lifted them
down, one by one, and breaking open their lids, busied myself in
speculations about the mortality within." (2:161) Poe's handling of
life-after-death is here farcical by intention, and has a nervous edge
as well. But O'Connor brings to the classic gothic scene a typically
cold and warm quality, an unnerving austerity and terrible pathos.

In short, O'Connor is mistress of the mixed effect. This is not to
say that the effects mixed are always of the same kind (Hazel Motes's
death is quite different from Tanner's in "Judgement Day," and both
are different from the death of the grandmother in "A Good Man Is
Hard to Find") but what remains characteristic is a certain incongruity between style and subject, a kind of impassivity in the face of
the extraordinary. In some ways this quality recalls a characteristically
medieval effect and if, indeed, the art of the middle ages did inspire
O'Connor, it is possible that she came by it via Nathanael West,
whose influence on her has already been noted. This passage from
West's *Day of the Locust* neatly describes the mixed effect and also
locates the tradition. Apropos of a character's narration of a fantastic
story, West writes, "Although the events she described were miracu-
lous, her description of them was realistic. The effect was similar to
that obtained by the artists of the Middle Ages, who, when doing a
subject like the raising of Lazarus from the dead or Christ walking
on water, were careful to keep all the details intensely realistic."[85]
In O'Connor, this incongruity between subject and treatment is often
right at the edge of comedy, as in the death scene from *Wise Blood*.

I do not wish to assert that Flannery O'Connor was an anachro-
nism, but the imagination that could conceive of a policeman hitting
the barely conscious Hazel Motes over the head with his billy club
while coolly uttering, "We don't want to have no trouble with
him," may indeed seem the product of a world view that is in some

respects, at least, medieval.[86] Insofar as it suggests the seeing of things under the aspect of eternity, J. L. Styan's description of medieval Christian life as "one of optimism," inviting "a certain contempt for the sufferings of common existence," is suggestively close to O'Connor. "For the devout Christian," Styan continues, "happiness lay in the next world. Thus poverty, bad weather, bad crops, bad wives or hate, cruelty, murder and crucifixion were part of the divine comedy. In a divine order of things the incongruity of man's baseness and stupidity was part of the sacred pattern."[87]

One further aspect of O'Connor's comedy should be observed, and that is its occasionally Jansenist cast. I have noted earlier her temperamental affinity with Jansenism, and that same awareness— hers "was a narrow vision, but deep," as Allen Tate has put it; "unworldly, but aware of human depravity as only a good Jansenist can be"[88]—seems to shape her comic representations of sexuality and of the relationships between a man and a woman. Actually, such relationships are extremely rare in the fiction (on the periphery of her tales, one finds a veritable graveyard of divorced and deceased marital partners): the serious configuration is that of parent or grandparent and offspring. Where marriage is portrayed—as in "The River" or The Violent Bear It Away—it is often the object of caustic satire; at other times, as in "Parker's Back," or "Revelation," or "The Displaced Person" (the Shortleys), there is no trace of sexuality in the comic relationship between the sexes.

And when nakedness or sex is present in O'Connor, it is always funny, often nervously so. It is the kind of humor that makes one think one is peeking blasphemously around the side of the mirror into which D. H. Lawrence stared, with sacred reverence, at the sexual act. And, to be sure, some very funny moments result from O'Connor's posture; as for example, when Enoch Emery in Wise Blood describes how he prayed to Jesus to help him get rid of his guardian, and how Jesus showed him the way. "'I got up one morning at just daylight and I went in her room without my pants on and pulled the sheet off her and giver a heart attact. Then I went back to my daddy and we ain't seen hide of her since.'" (48) Or there is this passage from the same book, when Hazel is being seduced by Sabbath Lily; it is sexual comedy, but Henry Miller is in another room.

> "Listen," she said. . . . "from the minute I set eyes on you I said to myself, that's what I got to have, just give me some of him! I said look at those pee-can eyes and go crazy, girl! That innocent look don't hide a thing, he's just pure filthy right down to the guts, like me. The only difference is I like being that way and he don't. Yes sir!" she said. "I like being that way, and I can teach you how to like it. Don't you want to learn how to like it?"
>
> He turned his head slightly and just over his shoulder he saw a pinched homely little face with bright green eyes and a grin. "Yeah," he said with no change in his stony expression, "I want to." . . .
>
> "Come on! Make haste," she said, knocking his back with her knee. . . .
>
> She was breathing very quickly. "Take off your hat, king of the beasts," she said gruffly and her hand came up behind his head and snatched the hat off and sent it flying across the room in the dark. (169–70)

Other stories one might look at in this context are "A Stroke of Good Fortune," where a dubious comedy is made out of a woman's fear of the pain and aging that attend childbirth, and the much better "Good Country People," where ugly Hulga, on the verge of breaking down her defense against men and giving herself at last to a suitor, finds herself relinquishing instead, all unwillingly, her wooden leg. It could be a painful scene, but in O'Connor's hands it is timed to comic perfection, and with a biting edge of irony—turned against the girl. "Human laughter is intimately linked with the accident of an ancient Fall, of a debasement both physical and moral," as Baudelaire observed.[89] With O'Connor, that is often the case.

In fact, a passage from one of O'Connor's earliest stories would seem to offer clear support for that notion, in suggesting the emotional source of the comic attitude toward sex. It comes from "The Turkey," part of her master's thesis, and a work that was later revised to become "The Capture," when it was published in 1948. The story is about a boy, Ruller, who would seem to be the prototype of the later young prophets O'Connor returned to regularly—Hazel Motes, Tarwater—and the failed prophets as well—The Misfit, Rufus Johnson. For Ruller, like these others, considers himself a "very unusual child," and is likewise handled with comic irony by O'Connor. In the following passage, Ruller defines his essential difference from his brother Hane in terms which connect a sense of calling and "knowing" about things with sexual knowledge and—as the image of the snake suggests—Original Sin.

> He reckoned he was more unusual than Hane.
> He had to worry more than Hane because he knew more how things were.
> Sometimes when he was listening at night, he heard [his parents] arguing like they were going to kill each other; and the next day his father would go out early and his mother would have the blue veins out on her forehead and look like she was expecting a snake to jump from the ceiling any minute. He guessed he was one of the most unusual children ever.[90]

Though she chose to omit this version of the Fall—or rather the child's second-hand knowledge of it—from the later, published version of the story, it is, in a sense, behind the characterization of Ruller and behind the prophet Hazel Motes's obsession with sexual guilt and sin. To deal with sexuality, O'Connor developed (perhaps fell back on) a strategy of comedy and irony that is pervaded by a certain pessimism.

Perhaps the only story that treats a sexual encounter—or what one may read as such—without comic debasement is "Greenleaf." And there, as the reader will recall, Mrs. May's uncouth swain is a bull, whose charge signals a moment of discovery that is also the moment of death.

A Note on Style

The foregoing discussion has suggested some historical contexts within which Flannery O'Connor's qualities may be regarded, but the result of her peculiar synthesis, it must be admitted, is a tertium quid for which there is no exact precedent. The most obvious qualities of an O'Connor tale—qualities which account for its immediate appeal—are its striking plot and the lucid, alive prose that is its medium. And though her earliest stories are not in themselves comparable to those written after *Wise Blood*, the rudiments of the characteristic strategy and style are evident.

"Wildcat," for example, is an apprentice's tour de force in the use of point of view—although that may be a misnomer, since old

Gabriel (O'Connor's only Negro protagonist) is blind and his experience is rendered entirely through the senses of smell, hearing, and touch. It is a study of fear, of a man living in wait of an animal's violent attack, and it anticipates O'Connor's subsequent use of extreme situations to try human emotions; moreover, in old Gabriel's grave concern with how he will die, one can see the first dark adumbration of the many deaths that will serve as the dramatic climaxes for the later tales: after being alone all day, Gabriel is eating a late dinner with his family.

> Their forks were scraping back and forth over their tin plates like knife teeth against stone.
> "You wants sommo' side meat, Grandpaw?"
> Gabriel put his fork down on the quilt. "No, boy," he said, "no mo' side meat." The darkness was hollow around him and through its depth, animal cries wailed and mingled with the beats pounding in his throat.[91]

The conclusion is theatrical and obvious, but it resembles the effects that would distinguish O'Connor's best fiction. The character experiences a perpetual moment; the story does not close neatly but, rather, opens up to the reader's imagination.

What is lacking in "Wildcat" and in the other early stories, however, is dramatic conflict—what O'Connor would later define as the central moment in a fiction, when there occurs "some action, some gesture of a character that is unlike any other in the story, one which indicates where the real heart of the story lies. This would have to be an action or a gesture which was both totally right and totally unexpected; it would have to be one that was both in character and beyond character; it would have to suggest both the world and eternity."[92] Such violent refusals and violent acceptances of grace begin only with the discovery of her major theme.

Another early story, "The Crop," is least like anything O'Connor subsequently wrote in deriving its interest from an inherently "literary" problem: it is about a writer who is writing a romantic story into which she daydreams herself only to be awakened by the commonplace demands of real life. During the course of this trompe-l'oeil tale, the heroine advances several theories about writing, and though they are presented with deprecating irony by O'Connor, they do suggest essential characteristics of her prose.

> Miss Willerton was a great believer in what she called "phonetic art." She maintained that the ear was as much a reader as the eye. She liked to express it that way. "The eye forms a picture," she had told a group at the United Daughters of the Colonies, "that can be painted in the abstract, and the success of a literary venture (Miss Willerton liked the phrase, 'literary venture') depends on the abstract created in the mind and the tonal quality (Miss Willerton also liked 'tonal quality') registered in the ear."[93]

It would, admittedly, be difficult to find a good example of this double appeal to eye and ear in the early stories (it was easier at first to talk about than to do it), but many passages from the later fiction would illustrate the technique. For example, the description of the priest's reaction to the peacock in "The Displaced Person."

> "Where is that beautiful birrrrd of yours?" he asked and then said "Arrrrr, I see him!" and stood up and looked out over the lawn where the peacock and the two hens were stepping at a strained attention, their long necks ruffled, the cock's violent blue and the hens' silver-green, glinting in the late afternoon sun. . . .
> The priest let his eyes wander toward the birds. They had reached the middle of the lawn. The cock stopped suddenly and curving his neck backwards, he raised his tail and spread it with a shimmering timbrous noise. Tiers of small pregnant suns floated in a green-gold haze over his head. The priest stood transfixed, his jaw slack. Mrs. McIntyre wondered where she had ever seen such an idiotic old man. "Christ will come like that!" he said in a loud gay voice and wiped his hand over his mouth and stood there, gaping. (238–39)

It is deceptive prose, this; seemingly artless, it conceals a precise modulation of rhythms and periods, a concretely evocative vocabulary, a use of sound patterns to reinforce imagery, and a precise notation of speech. I find little to back up Allen Tate's assertion that "the flat style, the cranky grammar, the monotonous sentence-structure were necessary vehicles of her vision of man."[94] There are occasions when this is true, but these occasions are deliberate. In general, the range of her style, which has been little appreciated, is quite wide, and wholly adequate to the range of her vision.

Her prose is always alive with surprising images and innuendos, capable of spanning the ludicrously broken and the triumphantly exultant, as these two different perceptions of the same youth (Powell, in "A Circle in the Fire") illustrate.

> He had on a sweat shirt with a faded destroyer printed on it but his chest was so hollow that the destroyer was broken in the middle and seemed on the point of going under. His hair was stuck to his forehead with sweat.[95]

And later, at the climax of the story—

> She stood taut, listening, and could just catch in the distance a few wild high shrieks of joy as if the prophets were dancing in the fiery furnace, in the circle the angel had cleared for them. (154)

As the above examples suggest, stylistic extremes accord with the extremes of the profane and the sacred, nature and grace. And when that style is "flat," it is often in the middle ground where the extremes meet, in the act of violence.

> [The Misfit] shot her three times through the chest. Then he put his gun down on the ground and took off his glasses and began to clean them. ("A Good Man Is Hard to Find," p. 29)

> [Mrs. McIntyre] heard the little noise the Pole made as the tractor wheel broke his backbone. The two men ran forward to help and she fainted. ("The Displaced Person," p. 250)

> [Old Fortune] lifted her head and brought it down once hard against the rock that happened to be under it. ("A View of the Woods," p. 80)

No emphasis is needed; our attention is riveted.

And just how controlled this prose is—how deliberately flattened—can be glimpsed by comparing it with the prose of a nonfiction piece, "The King of the Birds." For one can see in this piece the same imagination at work as in the fiction, but without the pressures of a momentous dramatic context. Here is a description of the peacock's cry.

> Frequently the cock combines the lifting of his tail with the raising of his voice. He appears to receive through his feet some shock from the center of the earth, which travels upward through him and

is released: *Eee-ooo-ii! Eee-ooo-ii!* To the melancholy this sound is melancholy and to the hysterical it is hysterical. To me it has always sounded like a cheer for an invisible parade.[96]

The tone here is familiar, personal; the imagination is not constrained by the tensions that, in the fiction, issue in comedy and tragedy. And yet it is the same imagination, working on the same material, and even transforming it metamorphically, in the same way that violence, in the fiction, is used to metamorphose reality. For this passage, a simple description of a peacock's pride, also reveals a meeting ground in the imagination of the extremes of nature and mystery. Whether she was glorifying a peacock's pride or deriding the various forms of human pride, O'Connor wrote at her best with power and unsentimental clarity.

Thinking now of the description just quoted of the peacock's cry, yet another interpretation occurs to me. I fancy her birds emitted that sound after O'Connor read her own fiction to them—and who can be sure she didn't? The response seems right.

2

WISE BLOOD

IN the fiction of Flannery O'Connor as a whole, a division is possible between two recurrent dramatic situations—two dramatic images—that are central to her imagination. And that division also happens to be generic: in the two longer works, *Wise Blood* and *The Violent Bear It Away*, the protagonist is *actively* engaged with God. He may resist his vocation, defy it even, but the terms of his defiance are determined by the hero's consuming passion to define for himself his place in the universe and his relation to a God that just might exist. The turning point in his struggle will involve an *act* (murder, in each case) that defines him in relation to another character or characters. And that act is followed, in each work, by what we may call a moment of grace, of heightened consciousness, in which the meaning of the act compels from the hero a new recognition of his identity—a moment, then, which is at once a conversion to Christ and an inversion of his former selfhood. Such is the imaginative pattern underlying the novels.

In the shorter works, however, the dramatic image is the reverse: the protagonist is pointedly engaged not in an active relationship with God but, more typically, in a *passive* one. There are, to be sure, figures in the stories who are defined in terms of their belief in, or active disbelief in, God (Mrs. Greenleaf exemplifies the former, The Misfit the latter), but they are not the protagonists of the action. Instead, our primary interest is directed toward "normal" folk. And in every case—whether proud (Mr. Head, Mrs. Turpin) or self-deceiving (Julian, Hulga) or hardheaded (Mrs. McIntyre, old Fortune) or simply misguided (Grandmother Bailey)—these characters suffer a radical insight into their condition, a moment of perception that reveals for them the depth of their ignorance of the order of reality. Thus, while the defining dramatic image in the novels is an *act* performed *by* the hero, in the stories the defining image is an *intrusion* of some outside figure *upon* the protagonist.

It is perhaps only a coincidence, but a coincidence worth noting, that in two writers, whose significance to Flannery O'Connor has already been noted—Edgar Allan Poe and Teilhard de Chardin— something close to this same imaginative structure can be seen as a shaping force. For both of them, the significant patterns of experience were complementary images of activity and passivity. In the case of Poe, for example, it can be noted that while several of his heroes actively exert their will in an effort to achieve a union with some dead but magnetically attracting object (as in "Ligeia," "Berenice," "Annabel Lee"), others seem passively to undergo the experience of transcendence, usually while lying flat in the bottom of a boat. And these two attitudes before the transcendental ideal, the erect and the supine, are analogous to the images that define O'Connor's characters before the mystery of grace.

The analogy between O'Connor and Teilhard de Chardin can be noted even more explicitly when the philosopher outlines the structure of *The Divine Milieu.*

> Since in the field of experience each man's existence can properly be divided into two parts—what he does and what he undergoes—we shall consider each of these parts in turn: the active and the passive. In each we shall find at the outset that, in accordance with his promise, God truly waits for us in things, unless indeed he advances to meet us.[1]

But what Teilhard then goes on to say would seem to draw a line between the two writers. "We shall marvel how the manifestation of his sublime presence in no way disturbs the harmony of our human attitude, but, on the contrary, brings it its true form and perfection." For, in O'Connor, as we have already noted, it is almost always the case that the "manifestation of his sublime presence" does disturb "the harmony of our human attitude." (Thus one difference between the philosopher's vision and the fiction writer's: the former fixes his sight on the higher reality, the latter on the drama of the will.)

In any case, the active figure in the dichotomous structure of O'Connor's imagination will occupy our attention for this and the following chapter. The subject itself—of the spiritually engaged hero—is as old as Moses and Aaron, or Jacob wrestling with the angel, and recurs throughout Western literature with inevitable regu-larity—from the Passion plays to The Faerie Queen to Pilgrim's Progress, on through contemporary literature. More often than not, however, the modern writer has been interested in "the spiritual career" as a hoax. In America, for example, the fraudulent man of the cloth has been ironically defrocked, from Harold Frederic's Dam-nation of Theron Ware to Sinclair Lewis's damnation of Elmer Gantry (compare O'Connor's treatment of Hoover Shoats—alias Onnie Jay Holy—and his assistant Solace Layfield, in Wise Blood). And, conversely, Sherwood Anderson's God-intoxicated Jesse Bentley (a character in some ways resembling old Tarwater) is an example of self-deceiving spirituality: a man of presumably deformed emotions seeking, in a world of failed human relationships, the lost God.

Where the religious is sympathetically treated (one thinks, for example, of Bernanos's Diary of a Country Priest and, in particular, of J. F. Powers's humanizing and ennobling characterization of Father Urban), such characters are essentially "normal" people, lack-ing the madness and compulsion that characterize O'Connor's proph-ets. In one respect, the closest we can come to O'Connor's long works is Chaim Potok's briefly popular The Chosen, which supplies some-thing of the fanaticism of old Tarwater or of Hazel Motes's grand-father in the Hasidic background of the hero; with its intense focus on the vocational choice, The Chosen seems a Jewish version—or perhaps inversion: the rabbinic tradition is denied finally—of The Violent Bear It Away or of Wise Blood.

The Background of Wise Blood

For the unprepared reader, the peculiar voice of Hazel Motes produces a sensation like walking into a glass door.

> "I preach the Church Without Christ. I'm member and preacher to that church where the blind don't see and the lame don't walk and what's dead stays that way. Ask me about that church and I'll tell you it's the church that the blood of Jesus don't foul with redemption.
> "... I'm going to preach there was no Fall because there was nothing to fall from and no Redemption because there was no Fall and no Judgment because there wasn't the first two. Nothing matters but that Jesus was a liar." (105)

The rhetoric is transparent, but the substance is resistant, and catches us up.

Wise Blood is the story of a young man, who, released from the army, returns home to find he no longer has a home: the town of Eastrod is deserted. Hazel Motes then journeys by train to the city of Taulkinham, where, believing himself liberated from his childhood obsession with sin and Jesus, he enjoys a brief career as preacher of an anti-Gospel for his own Church Without Christ. In Taulkinham he attracts the misguided religious devotion of Enoch Emery and the frustrated sexual devotion of Sabbath Lily Hawks. When Enoch brings Hazel an ancient mummy to serve as his new Jesus, Sabbath, intimating an unholy nativity, assumes "motherhood"; Hazel, enraged, smashes the mummy. Enoch Emery then pursues his own salvation, and we leave him gazing dumbly from a Pisgah view of Taulkinham—dressed in a gorilla suit. Apart from Enoch and Sabbath Lily, who likewise disappears from Hazel's life, the prophet has no other "believers."

He does, however, have imitators, and one of them, Solace Layfield, is eventually run over by Hazel in his automobile for being untrue to his unfaith. Hazel's automobile is itself subsequently pushed over an embankment by an unfriendly policeman, whereupon Hazel returns by foot to his rooming house; there he blinds himself and drags out the rest of his days—not many—walking in rock-filled shoes, his chest sheathed in barbed wire. He refuses the advances of his landlady, Mrs. Flood, who wants to marry him. Ultimately,

Hazel dies in a rain-filled ditch, only to be brought back, a corpse, to the fascinated Mrs. Flood.

What's going on?

A plot summary of *Wise Blood* is even less gratifying than are most plot summaries: like a profile silhouette, the contour is there, but the meaning of the expression is lost.

Before dealing with *Wise Blood* itself, it may be useful to note the author's early groping toward the character and theme that would later emerge so strikingly and completely in the novel. Two of her early stories (neither was actually used in the novel) seem particularly relevant in this respect: "The Capture" (1948; an earlier—1947 —version was known as "The Turkey") and "A Stroke of Good Fortune" (1953; revised version of "Woman on the Stairs," 1949).

In "The Capture," the major theme of vocation is first—humorously—broached. Ruller, earlier discussed in another context, comes across a wild turkey in the woods (characteristically, it is a limping, wounded bird) and sees in this providential gift a token of his own homespun grace: he believes himself to be an "unusual child."[2] And from there it is not very far to his seeing in the wounded fowl a special annunciation: "Maybe finding the turkey was a sign. Maybe God wanted him to be a preacher. He thought of Bing Crosby and Spencer Tracy. He might found a place to stay for boys who were going bad." (199; *Complete Stories*, 49) He is overwhelmed with gratitude for God.

But the logic of Ruller's comprehension of God and his (very) special providence can—circumstances changing—only invite a corresponding despair: if God is wonderful by virtue of his gift, what then is he if that gift is taken away? And taken away it is, by some impoverished country boys. Stunned by his loss, Ruller at last turns toward home.

> He walked four blocks and then suddenly, noticing that it was dark, he began to run. He ran faster and faster, and as he turned up the road to his house, his heart was running as fast as his legs and he was certain that Something Awful was tearing behind him with its arms rigid and its fingers ready to clutch. (201; *Complete Stories*, 53)

As the first "appearance" of God in O'Connor's fiction, the moment is worthy of notice. It is terrible, and it is funny, and it comes with the suddenness of the stage direction, "exit, pursued by a bear," that sends Antigonus fleeing offstage in The Winter's Tale. O'Connor's, however, is a not quite inexplicable nemesis. For if we are asked to see in this ending what we shall be asked to see in Wise Blood and in so much of the later fiction—that there can be no just computation of God's ways to man, no equivalence between our personal knowledge and God's knowledge, our own acts and God's grace—nevertheless the conclusion is a demonstration that God, in his way, attends to man. For the emotional meaning of that ending is that not only does Ruller (like Job) feel a personal chastisement before the Lord's revealing himself as unknowable but that, paradoxically, God is no more present in the gift of a turkey than he is absent from the heaven's changing light—"suddenly, noticing that it was dark, he began to run."

What is also interesting in "The Capture" are several extraordinary pages of comic monologue, where Ruller discovers within himself the Word—rather, the curse word. For, in view of O'Connor's later significant characterization of Hazel Motes as a blasphemer (Tarwater will also be seized by a spasm of blasphemy), it is as if we are discovering, in the tentative stammerings of Ruller, the trying out of a major voice in her work. The boy has been chasing the turkey in the woods and has just run into a tree. He falls to the ground in despair, and this new mistrust of the divine purpose breeds in him the following discourse.

Oh hell, he thought.
"Oh hell," he said cautiously.
Then in a minute he said just, "Hell."
Then he said it like Hane [his brother] said it, pulling the e-ull out and trying to get the look in his eye that Hane got. . . .
"God," he said.
He looked studiedly at the ground, making circles in the dust with his finger. "God," he repeated.
"God dammit," he said softly. He could feel his face getting hot and his chest thumping all of a sudden inside. "God dammit to hell," he said almost inaudibly. He looked over his shoulder but no one was there.
"God dammit to hell, good Lord from Jerusalem," he said. . . .
"Good Father, good God, sweep the chickens out the yard," he said and began to giggle. . . . "Our Father Who art in heaven, shoot 'em six and roll 'em seven," he said giggling again. Boy, his mother'd

smack his head in if she could hear him. God dammit, she'd smack his goddam head in. . . . God dammit, she'd dress him off and wring his goddam neck like a goddam chicken. (195–96; *Complete Stories*, 46)

It is a child's voice, and its effect is comic, as will be the effect of later uses of the voice. For, from the believer's viewpoint, blasphemy must seem like a man wearing a blindfold whistling in the dark. But also, for the believer, the comedy in the scene is not without its serious overtone, which will be deepened in the later fiction.

Next, in "A Stroke of Good Fortune" and the original version, "The Woman on the Stairs," certain additional adumbrations of *Wise Blood* become visible. Thus, for example, in this story about a woman, Ruby Hill, who discovers she is pregnant, the person who unsubtly reveals the true condition to the benighted protagonist is, in "Stroke of Good Fortune," named Laverne Watts, but, in the earlier version, Leora Watts. Not only the original name of this character but also her Rabelaisian sexual appetite foreshadows her role as the priestess-prostitute of *Wise Blood* who initiates Hazel Motes into the mysteries of sex.

Laverne has her appetitive eye on her friend Ruby's younger brother, whose name in the later version is Rufus (compare the young satanic antagonist of "The Lame Shall Enter First," Rufus Johnson) but whose original appellation is Hazel. Moreover Hazel, in the original version, along with Ruby, is from Eastrod, the same provenance as the protagonist of *Wise Blood*. And like Hazel Motes, Rufus exhibits a similar obsessive attachment to his natal landscape. "If Pitman [changed from the original Eastrod] had still been there, Rufus would have been in Pitman. If one chicken had been left to walk across the road in Pitman, Rufus would have been there too to keep him company."[3]

This is all we have of the ur-Hazel, for throughout the story Rufus is offstage. Nevertheless, it is possible to see in "A Stroke of Good Fortune," which was originally written during the time *Wise Blood* was being episodically published, an additional context for Hazel Motes's existence that was later excised from the novel and relegated to this thematically separate story. (Some other stories published during the four years preceding *Wise Blood* were to be reworked into

chapters of the novel [see Appendix 1].) And what it seems to indicate about the creative process of Flannery O'Connor is that her
fiction would take its start from an imagined character whose force-
ful presence would be the core of a plot or action designed—or, the
word O'Connor would have used, discovered—by the writer to be
the expression of some truth about the meaning of the character's
life as well as a seeing into the nature of reality.

But one cannot mention the antecedents of *Wise Blood* without
mentioning too the influence of Nathanael West. This, her first
important work, is the one most like West, and one can easily see his
influence—in the names of characters (Asa Hawks from Asa Gold-
stein in *A Cool Million*), in certain devices (the Miss Lonelyhearts
letter sent by Sabbath Lily), in certain characters (Enoch descends
from Lem's friend Sam, a lousy "pimple-faced ape," in *A Cool Million*), in the crazy exuberance of the plot, in the grotesque distor-
tions of environment, and in the use of blasphemy (see Shrike in
Miss Lonelyhearts). Even the notion of a church aberrant may have
been nurtured by the passage in *Day of the Locust*, where Tod visits

> the "Church of Christ, Physical" where holiness was attained through
> the constant use of chestweights and spring grips; the "Church Invis-
> ible" where fortunes were told and the dead made to find lost
> objects; the "Tabernacle of the Third Coming" where a woman in
> male clothing preached the "Crusade Against Salt"; and the "Tem-
> ple Moderne" under whose glass and chromium roof "Brain-Breath-
> ing, the Secret of the Aztecs" was taught.[4]

Hazel Motes's Church Without Christ is not far behind. Of course it
must be remembered that West and O'Connor wrote out of opposing
religious commitments: West's implicit denial of a supernatural force
is the ground for his protagonist's search for faith, whereas Hazel
Motes flees Christ in a world where grace is operative.[5]

Hazel Motes

Hazel Motes is a character whose obsession with Jesus defines him
as rigidly as Ben Jonson's humor characters are defined or as an allegorical hero is defined. The disguises of pleasantry, the buffer zones
of polite conversation—indeed, the conventional and undistinguish-
ing clothing that surround the unoffending—do not surround him.
And, although, with the exception of his "sermons" and exhortations,

Hazel is a singularly taciturn character, whatever is on his tongue was just on his mind. His bones stick out. But, aside from the fact that he does not exist in a completely controlled allegorical environment, what distinguishes him from an allegorical hero is the greater inwardness of his spiritual exercises and the greater psychological motivation that O'Connor imputes to him.

The conflict within Hazel that gives shape to Wise Blood is over vocation. "Vocation" in the sense not of an active calling ("he knew by the time he was twelve years old that he was going to be a preacher" [22]) but, rather, of an internal, spiritual calling: will he, in other words, preach that Christ is the truth and the way—or, that " 'nothing matters but that Jesus was a liar' " (105)? It is not a question, therefore, of merely falling out of belief and into a secular indifference: the alternative to accepting Jesus is to preach that " 'nothing matters but that Jesus was a liar.' " In short, whichever of the poles of belief Hazel is finally drawn to, his life is predicated upon Jesus, and he must live within the theologically charged field of the redemption.

Through the use of dramatic flashbacks, the first few chapters make clear that the genesis of Hazel's spiritual career lies in the influence of his grandfather and his mother, both Tennessee backwoods believers, the variety of whose religious experience is intense and sinridden. Certain ineradicable memories are associated in Hazel's mind with these looming figures: the grandfather, for example, would preach to his limited but attentive audiences, using the nearest mean thing at hand—Hazel—as a tangible example of the democracy of redemption.

> Did they know that even for that boy there, for that mean sinful unthinking boy standing there with his dirty hands clenching and unclenching at his sides, Jesus would die ten million deaths before He would let him lose his soul? He would chase him over the waters of sin! . . . Jesus would have him in the end! (22)

With his mother, Hazel associates a beating he received at her hands following his viewing a naked woman at a carnival sideshow—an episode that confirms vividly his sense of sin.

> "What you seen," she said, using the same tone of voice all the time. She hit him across the legs with the stick, but he was like part of the tree. "Jesus died to redeem you," she said.

"I never ast him," he muttered.

She didn't hit him again but she stood looking at him, shut-mouthed, and he forgot the guilt of the tent for the nameless unplaced guilt that was in him. (63)

What is most interesting in this conviction of guilt is Hazel's response to the redemptive agency of Jesus: "I never ast him." For in placing upon Hazel the burden of sin and guilt, his mother and grandfather have unwittingly fused in his mind a restraining fear of Jesus, a fear of what, in *The Violent Bear It Away*, will be called the "TERRIBLE SPEED OF MERCY" (italics added). "There was already a deep black wordless conviction in him that the way to avoid Jesus was to avoid sin." (22)

What other novelists might take as the more likely subject for a modern (that is, post-nineteenth-century) Bildungsroman—the falling away from religion—hardly interests O'Connor at all. What she is interested in is how one falls back in. Accordingly, her account of Hazel's conversion to the world (which is how we find him) is quick and to the point: in the army, he is invited to go to a brothel by some other soldiers; but he refuses on the grounds that it might imperil his soul. "They told him he didn't have any soul and left for their brothel." (24) And that is the spur to Motes's anti-conversion. "He took a long time to believe them because he wanted to believe them. All he wanted was to believe them and get rid of it . . . without corruption, to be converted to nothing instead of to evil." (24) No more soul, no more evil, no more Jesus. (What might otherwise seem a flaw—were psychological verisimilitude aimed at—must here be taken as a necessary plot device.) Discharged from the army, Hazel thinks himself still uncorrupted, but, lest we are tempted to agree with him, the author inflicts upon Motes a festering wound that seems symbolically equivalent to the loss of his soul. Later, the suggestion of "war poisoning" is reiterated and broadened in implication when we are told that Hazel gets money from the government for "something the war had done to his insides." (214)

Such then are the early influences on Hazel's character: he has been so stamped by the forces of his Eastrod background and by the army that he can only stamp, machinelike, his own obsessive character on everything he touches. Like an allegorical hero, he carries his talismanic objects—not, however, as adornments from the hand of the author so much as signs that are pressed outward on things from within himself. The comic aspects of such a character (the sort Bergson described) are inevitable, and O'Connor's narrative tone ably exploits them: buying a new white hat to replace his "fierce black" one, Hazel is told by the salesman that white panamas are "really the thing and particularly if he was going to Florida." But he replies:

> "I ain't going to Florida. . . . This hat is opposite from the one I used to have is all."
> "You can use it anywheres," the man said; "it's new."
> "I know that," Haze said. He went outside and took the red and green and yellow band off it and thumped out the crease in the top and turned down the brim. When he put it on, it looked just as fierce as the other one had. (111)

What is at work so effectively in the prose is a comic irony born of the narrator's (and reader's) privileged perception that, against his will, Hazel is cooperating in a pattern of grace that, by just such indirections, is visible.[6]

It is evident, from a comparison of the first chapter of *Wise Blood* with its original version, "Train," that Flannery O'Connor discovered what would be the theme of *Wise Blood* and the essential character of Hazel Motes, and even her distinctive style, somewhere between the publication of the early fragments of the novel and the appearance of the completed work in 1952.

Thus, for example, O'Connor's original conception of Hazel's mother became, in the novel, more sharply defined: omitted from "Train" for being apparently out of character with the stern disciplinarian of *Wise Blood* is this comic sketch of the mother's habits while riding trains. "His mother had always started up a conversation with the other people on the train. She was like an old bird dog just unpenned that raced, sniffing up every rock and stick and sucking in the air around everything she stopped at."[7] Moreover, the main focus, in the early version, is on a Hazel who is obsessed quite simply with regaining his past. (It is the same longing for home felt by an exile that is the theme of O'Connor's first published story, "The Geranium.") What is most significantly added to the final version of chapter one is at the heart of the characterization of Hazel Motes:

an obsession with guilt and with Christ that will stay with him through the novel to his death.

This change in conception is most noticeable in the slight alteration of the conclusion of that chapter. Hazel, in his upper berth on the train, is dreaming of his mother's funeral back home in Eastrod, of the lid closing down on her coffin, and he transposes himself inside that coffin; here is the original ending.

> He opened his eyes and saw it closing down and he sprang up between the crack and wedged his body through it and hung there, moving, dizzy, with the dim light of the train slowly showing the rug below, moving, dizzy. He hung there wet and cold and saw the porter at the other end of the car, a white shape in the darkness, standing there, watching him and not moving. The tracks curved and he fell back sick into the rushing stillness of the train.[8]

In the final text, certain alterations are made in the rhythms of the passage, and the last sentence above is replaced by the following:

> "I'm sick!" he called. "I can't be closed up in this thing. Get me out!"
> The porter stood watching him and didn't move.
> "Jesus," Haze said, "Jesus."
> The porter didn't move. "Jesus been a long time gone," he said in a sour triumphant voice. (27)

In the first version, we have a conclusion that leaves our attention focused on Hazel—his sickness, his nightmare, and his fall back into the neatly phrased "rushing stillness of the train." The porter exists as a vaguely hostile, indifferently observing presence. In the later version, however, the porter's presence becomes more openly hostile, more actively malign. His implacable stance is emphasized. And, most significantly, when Hazel awakens from his nightmare and utters a half-frustrated, half-yearning cry of "Jesus," the porter replies with a literally accurate but theologically cynical, "'Jesus been a long time gone.'" Placed crucially at the end of the chapter, the porter's words reverberate and render him a dimension not merely of social indifference but of satanic malevolence.

Quite effectively the concluding exchange of the chapter directs our attention to the questions the book will deal with: Does Hazel need Jesus? Is Jesus dead?

The Uses of Perspective

The ambiguity of the conclusion of chapter one of *Wise Blood* defines a quality of Flannery O'Connor's prose that characterizes not only that book but her later work as well. It is a quality of felt tension, between the surface of the writing and its pregnant meaning, that invites a particular way of seeing. The ramifications of *seeing*, one might almost say, compose the aesthetic and moral key to the whole book (and much else that O'Connor wrote): for, on one level, how we, as readers, come to see Hazel Motes is the radical determinant of our experience with the novel; on another level, how the characters in the book see each other pointedly defines their relationships to one another; and, on a third level, the evolution of Hazel's spiritual career is an evolution in seeing into the nature of reality. On all three levels, there is the tension and discovery of the relationship between surface meaning and symbolic meaning.

Leaving aside for the moment the major question of how Hazel Motes sees the world, I would point to a passage (added to the final version of chapter one) that illustrates the other two modes of seeing involved in the novel.

> [Hazel's] suit was a glaring blue and the price tag was still stapled on the sleeve of it.
>   . . . [Mrs. Hitchcock] wanted to get close enough to see what the suit had cost him but she found herself squinting instead at his eyes, trying almost to look into them. . . .
>   She felt irked and wrenched her attention loose and squinted at the price tag. The suit had cost him $11.98. She felt that that placed him and looked at his face again as if she were fortified against it now. . . . his eyes were what held her attention longest. Their settings were so deep that they seemed, to her, almost like passages leading somewhere and she leaned halfway across the space that separated the two seats, trying to see into them. (10–11)

The passage is suggestive in several respects: the price tag on the suit portrays Hazel for the reader as a marvelously ridiculous figure; he is oblivious to external detail of appearance, his focus is inward. To Mrs. Hitchcock, however, the tag "places" him socially ($11.98 is not much to pay for a suit); but her own concern with the price of the suit as an index of Hazel's personal worth, in turn, places her. In addition, Mrs. Hitchcock's compulsion to look into Hazel's eyes suggests a significant aspect of the latter's personality: his charisma—a spiritual magnetism that his eyes reveal. We will find him attracting other characters too in this way. And, lastly, by admitting the reader to Mrs. Hitchcock's point of view, the passage forces him to look with her eyes and to see for himself into Hazel's, thereby creating a posture of fascination with the protagonist that is carried through to the end of the book.

Chapter one of *Wise Blood*, as the above discussion suggests, is structured mainly by the juxtaposition of various perspectives. And this continues to be a technique used throughout the novel. In addition, as certain words, phrases, and motifs recur in the texture of the work, O'Connor is able to enrich the structure of the reader's experience by creating ironic patterns of recognition that further contribute to our seeing into the meaning of the characters and situations.

An illustration of the increasing complexity of the book is chapter fourteen, the last chapter. It is entirely characteristic of O'Connor's work that the opening and concluding chapters of *Wise Blood* should form an envelope around the narrative, resonant with overtones from the whole texture of the book, but especially recalling, intensifying, and altering what was our initial impression of Hazel Motes. Hazel, it will be remembered, has blinded himself and is living alone in Mrs. Flood's rooming house. I shall return later to a consideration of the events leading up to the blinding, but let it suffice now to say that it signals Hazel's reversion to a belief in Christ and serves as a penance for his recognized sin and guilt. The purpose of the chapter, it will be seen, is to deepen our perception of the meaning of Hazel's career.

With the exception of the scene describing the retrieval of Hazel from a ditch by two policemen, the last chapter is narrated from Mrs. Flood's point of view. For after his self-blinding, Hazel's own eyes are closed to us as a narrative viewpoint, his utterances become fewer and fewer: a pall of silence enshrouds the figure. Nevertheless, he remains the focus of our attention, and, in fact, more intensely so, as the following passages clearly suggest.

> If [Mrs. Flood] didn't keep her mind going on something else when [Hazel] was near her, she would find herself leaning forward, staring into his face as if she expected to see something she hadn't seen before. (213)

> Watching his face had become a habit with her; she wanted to penetrate the darkness behind it and see for herself what was there. (225)

Mrs. Flood's obsessive curiosity must recall to us the initial scene in the train, when it was Mrs. Hitchcock who found herself, in front of Hazel's eyes, constantly "trying to see into them." And it neatly reinforces the reader's own curiosity.

Another detail adding to the circular structure of the narrative is O'Connor's use of a similar figurative language (Motes's "tunnel" vision) to describe both Mrs. Hitchcock's and Mrs. Flood's response to Hazel's magnetic power: thus Mrs. Hitchcock sees Hazel's eyes as "passages leading somewhere" (10), while Mrs. Flood imagines the inside of Hazel's head to be "like you were walking in a tunnel and all you could see was a pin point of light. She had to imagine the pin point of light; she couldn't think of it at all without that. She saw it as some kind of a star, like the star on Christmas cards. She saw him going backwards to Bethlehem and she had to laugh." (218–19) The metaphor culminates in the last lines of the book, taking Hazel from his initial ride on the literal train to a symbolic passage through a tunnel and concluding with his figurative apotheosis, when he is at last associated with the pinpoint of light at the end of the tunnel, the star of Bethlehem. The authority for this final vision is Mrs. Flood, who, though she has grown in her imaginative commitment to Hazel, remains unaided by grace, and hence "blocked at the entrance."

> She shut her eyes and saw the pin point of light but so far away that she could not hold it steady in her mind. She felt as if she were blocked at the entrance of something. She sat staring with her eyes shut, into his eyes, and felt as if she had finally got to the beginning of something she couldn't begin, and she saw him moving farther and farther away, farther and farther into the darkness until he was the pin point of light. (231–32)

Enclosing Spaces

Even more suggestive than the metaphor of the tunnel with its light at the end is the complex of associations built around the meaning of "home." Nothing is stronger in the last chapter than our sense that Hazel has indeed come home, and we cannot fail to note the richness of O'Connor's preparation.

In the first chapter, Mrs. Hitchcock anticipates Hazel's intentions from the mere look of him on the train. " 'I guess you're going home'" (10), she says. Hazel denies it of course (in his "sharp high nasal Tennessee voice" [13]), for he is going right now to the city of Taulkinham, but his thoughts are clearly back home. "Eastrod filled his head and then went out beyond and filled the space that stretched from the train across the empty darkening fields." (12) In fact, Hazel had already returned home immediately after his release from the army; he had gone there shorn of his belief in Jesus, he thought, but secure in the safety of a familiar environment. The place was deserted, however; the house bare except for his mother's chifforobe. Hazel had anchored the object securely to the floor and left a fiercely warning note in every drawer: "THIS SHIFFER-ROBE BELONGS TO HAZEL MOTES. DO NOT STEAL IT OR YOU WILL BE HUNTED DOWN AND KILLED." (26)

It is not hard to see in this chifforobe an image, in Hazel's mind, for his mother, and the conclusion of chapter one reinforces the nexus: for the space inside the chifforobe becomes transformed into the enclosing space of his mother's coffin, and it is into that space that Hazel dreams himself as he sleeps in the train's upper berth. "He had seen her face through the crack when they were shutting the top on her. . . . From inside he saw it closing, coming closer closer down and cutting off the light and the room." (26–27) It will be recalled that the dream ends with his awakening cry for mortal deliverance, "Jesus"—a cry which is answered only at his death at the end of Wise Blood.

Insofar as the book as a whole is thus a fulfillment of Hazel's original dream, it may be seen as a kind of dream romance, and, as such, Wise Blood has profound psychological validity. For what O'Connor has done is to lend a spiritual emphasis to a persistent rhythm of dreams and poetry. As Gaston Bachelard has written:

> . . . not only do we come back to [the nest or house], but we dream of coming back to it, the way a bird comes back to its nest, or a lamb to the fold. This sign of return marks an infinite number of day-dreams, for the reason that human returning takes place in the great rhythm of human life, a rhythm that reaches back across the years and, through the dream, combats all absence.[9]

While the chifforobe, then, seems associated oneirically with returning home to mother and, on the theological level, to Jesus, there is another sense in which enclosures hold for Hazel the feeling of unwanted confinement; opposed to Motes's drive to return "home" is an equally deep urge to leap out of confining spaces visible, indeed, from our initial view of him. "Hazel Motes sat at a forward angle on the green plush train seat, looking one minute at the window as if he might want to jump out of it, and the next down the aisle" (9); later, as Leora Watts holds him firmly by the arm, "he might have leaped out the window" (34); and, still later with Mrs. Watts, "his heart began to grip him like a little ape clutching the bars of its cage." (60) In each of these cases, it is interesting to note, Hazel desires escape from the company of some woman, and this pattern is repeated in a dream Motes later has, while sleeping in his car. He dreams that he is in a sort of exhibition case, and experiences terror when "a woman with two little boys on either side of her stopped and looked in, grinning. After a second, she pushed the boys out of view and indicated that she would climb in and keep him company for a while." (160)

That last passage suggests what might be behind this terror of enclosures. For the reader has earlier been introduced to the haunting source of Hazel's guilt—his early and accidental exposure to the side-show nude in a casket; he approaches some people "looking down into a lowered place where something white was lying, squirming a little, in a box lined with black cloth. For a second he thought it was a skinned animal and then he saw it was a woman." (62) In short, the enclosed space is not only identified with the security of home—and mother's chifforobe—but with the guilt and terror of his first discovery of the sin attached to women as sexual objects. It is his mother who chastises him on his return home, and, significantly, he later superimposes her long, straight-standing figure upon that of the fat woman who was in the actual casket. "He saw the lowered place and the casket again and a thin woman in the casket who was too long for it. . . . She had a cross-shaped face and hair pulled close to her head." (62–63)

In view of the guilt thus attached to sex, and the transposition of his mother to the feared sex object (and, significantly, both Leora Watts and Mrs. Flood "mother" Hazel), it is classically fitting that Hazel's defining act of penitence for the guilt of his generalized sin should be an Oedipal self-blinding.

Blindness and Vision

The inspiration for Hazel's self-blinding is not of course Oedipus, who is doubtless unknown to him, but rather Asa Hawks. For it is Hawks—more con man than prophet, more beggar than con man—who poses as a blind preacher.[10] What is behind Hawks's darkened glasses fascinates Hazel (as much as his own eyes fascinate Mrs. Hitchcock and Mrs. Flood), and he intently tries to peer through the glasses until, finally, he sees the truth—or, rather, the fraud. (162)[11] Thus Hazel's blinding of himself seems at least partially imagined by him as a refutation of the impostor prophet Hawks (whom he had looked upon earlier as a potential savior) and as an assertion of his own truer role of prophet.

While Hawks is the inspiration, the direct cause of the blinding is even more clearly designed to bring into relief Hazel's self-abuse as an act of self-definition. For the blinding occurs following the confrontation between Hazel Motes and another impostor-prophet, Solace Layfield. Layfield's introduction is very deliberately prepared for in the text: Hazel has been haranguing a crowd, in his characteristic but not quite inimitable manner, on the subject of conscience. " 'Your conscience is a trick,' he said, 'it don't exist though you may think it does, and if you think it does, you had best get it out in the open and hunt it down and kill it, because it's no more than your face in the mirror is or your shadow behind you.' " (166) Enter Solace Layfield, who is Hoover Shoats's partner in a two-man traveling evangelical show. Modeled on Hazel, whom Shoats had originally tried to interest in the business, Solace appears to Motes as his shadow, his mirror image—in short, his "conscience," for the absurdity and insincerity of Layfield's mechanical parody of Hazel's own anti-Christ gospel become uncomfortably and immediately apparent to the preacher. After watching Layfield's act, Motes declares ominously, " 'If you don't hunt it down and kill it, it'll hunt you down and kill you.' " (168)

But hunt him down Hazel does; after ramming Solace's car into a ditch, Hazel at last confronts his shadow. " 'You ain't true,' Haze said. 'What do you get up on top of a car and say you don't believe in what you do believe in for?' " (203) The prophet forces the impostor to take off his suit (a defrocking) and thereupon he ceremoniously runs him over with the guardian of his own faith, his Essex automobile. In the midst of the narration, however, we encounter a sudden ironic shift in viewpoint, from one in sympathy with Hazel to a strictly clinical, objective description of the indifferent body, stripped of its identifying guise and thus starkly human—and, as such, not a body that Hazel is willing to see.

> The man didn't look so much like Haze, lying on the ground on his face without his hat or suit on. A lot of blood was coming out of him and forming a puddle around his head. . . . Haze poked his toe in his side and he wheezed for a second and then was quiet. "Two things I can't stand," Haze said, "—a man that ain't true and one that mocks what is." (204)

For Hazel, then, if not for the reader, Layfield remains, even as he expires, a mockery of Motes rather than the distorted replica he in fact is: both, O'Connor implies, are frailly human; both are self-deceived. As for Layfield's "confession" of his sins to Hazel (which one critic has cited as "one of the few deeply moving scenes in the novel"),[12] in the context of O'Connor's unsentimental faith, this seems rather a parody of the "moving confession scene."

For O'Connor, Hazel is at the height of his blindness, and what is apparently required to save him is some act of grace. It comes to Hazel, ironically in the form of a patrolman with "a red pleasant face and eyes the color of clear fresh ice." (208) He stops Hazel for no apparent reason and folksily cajoles him into placing his car in the correct position for propulsion down the embankment. Appearing from nowhere as an allegorical agency of grace, this deus ex machina proceeds to push off the road Hazel's well-worn deus in machina, his Essex. (The car has been throughout the story the literal and figurative vehicle of Hazel's spiritual identity: " 'Nobody with a good car needs to be justified' " [113] etc.) Its sudden removal is, for Hazel, at once the melting of the calf—and the burning bush.

For the scene, described with a relishing comic detachment, leads directly to what is indeed, for Hazel, "the puttiest view" he has ever seen.

> The patrolman got behind the Essex and pushed it over the embankment and the cow stumbled up and galloped across the field and into the woods; the buzzard flapped off to a tree at the edge of the

clearing. The car landed on its top, with the three wheels that stayed
on, spinning. . . .

Haze stood for a few minutes, looking over at the scene. His face
seemed to reflect the entire distance across the clearing and on
beyond, the entire distance that extended from his eyes to the blank
gray sky that went on, depth after depth, into space. His knees bent
under him. . . . (209)

With the tonal quality of the prose modulating from its more usual
comic detachment to a gathering rhythm and rare lyric pitch, it is
the climax of the novel: in the flux of time, this is a still moment for
Hazel.[13] It describes a vision of space that seems, for the first time, to
allow him a cognizance of external reality: his eyes have been restored
to him. And it is an experience that gives the lie to his own earlier
preachment. " 'Nothing outside you can give you any place. . . . You
needn't to look at the sky because it's not going to open up and show
no place behind it.' " (165) The vision is an escape as well from the
confining, enclosing spaces that had been his nightmare prisons, a
resolution of the plaguing duality of the confining flesh and the
yearning spirit.

Mrs. Flood later sees the change in Hazel, and contrasts it with her
own "normal" being, in language that carries forward the metaphors
of space. "She could not make up her mind what would be inside his
head and what out. She thought of her own head as a switchbox
where she controlled from; but with him, she could only imagine the
outside in, the whole black world in his head and his head . . . big
enough to include the sky and planets and whatever was or had been
or would be." (218)

That Hazel's self-blinding implies a recognition of the error implicit in his blasphemy and pursuit (however masochistically) of sin
and sex is brought out clearly in the last chapter of the novel,
through the sparse interchanges between Hazel and Mrs. Flood.
Where Hazel had earlier affirmed to his companion the owl, in the
zoo, that " 'I AM clean' " (95), now he asserts to Mrs. Flood, " 'I'm
not clean.' " (224) And to his landlady's assertion that " 'I'm as good,
Mr. Motes . . . not believing in Jesus as a many a one that does,' "
Hazel replies: " 'You're better. . . . If you believed in Jesus, you
wouldn't be so good.' " (221) But while Mrs. Flood takes this latter
remark as a rare compliment from the man with rocks in his shoes,

what is really implied is that anyone who believes in Jesus cannot consider himself above the common sin and guilt of mortal man; as a nonbeliever, Mrs. Flood is entitled to her illusion of guiltlessness: Jesus's redemption, for O'Connor, implies our deserving—and needing—that redemption. And finally, when Mrs. Flood asks, "'What do you walk on rocks for?'" Hazel answers curtly, but with confidence, "'To pay.'" (222)

Throughout the tale, Motes is an absurd character; but we might note the significant change he undergoes, from being absurdly ridiculous to being more deeply absurd—that is, opposed to "manifest truth" (Webster's 2d) with a critical emphasis on "manifest." This change in the nature of Hazel's absurdity is paralleled by the shift in comic perspective, so that the reader's sympathy moves from the normal characters, who find Hazel so freakish, to a sympathy with Hazel himself. It is at last the normal, "sane" world of Mrs. Flood that we are led to regard as a comedy of error.

In certain ways Wise Blood resembles the form of classic tragedy: Hazel is a proud hero who scorns human limitations; he pursues sin, blasphemes God, and, in a moment of divine intervention and chastisement, suffers a recognition of his error that leads to a self-inflicted reversal of fortune. And, as Robert Fitzgerald has noted, O'Connor did indeed read Oedipus Rex while working on the novel.[14] And yet if we accept the premises of the story, then it is not as tragedy that we experience Wise Blood. O'Connor has superimposed a classic tragic shape upon a defiantly Christian world view; we may indeed feel a sense of awe and mystery at the end of the narrative, but Hazel is in fact the hero of a comic plot of salvation.

The Subplot of Enoch Emery

The design of Wise Blood includes several chapters on the adventures of Enoch Emery, chapters which some critics have seen as irrelevant to the main intention of the book and distracting from its central focus.[15] Yet it was O'Connor's habit to set up "doubles" at times in order to clarify her characterizations, and Enoch may be the first significant use of such a figure. More precisely, the story of Enoch Emery is designed as a parody of the story of Hazel Motes, and helps define, by contrast, the sense in which Hazel is a Christian hero.

Enoch, like Hazel, is a seeker; but, first and last, he is seeking friends. His dream is to be "THE young man of the future, like the ones in the insurance ads. He wanted, some day, to see a line of people waiting to shake his hand." (191) He is attracted to Hazel when the latter first comes to the city and, being himself a newcomer to Taulkinham, complains to him of the coldness of urban life; but Hazel, as he soon discovers, is an unfortunate choice for a friend. "'People ain't friendly here. You ain't from here but you ain't friendly neither.'" (58) While Hazel's attention is throughout directed toward "higher" things than man in his relations with men, Enoch's concerns are with man in his lowest relations—with animals. O'Connor dramatizes this obsession by portraying Enoch as a zoo-keeper, and one who, feeling greater kinship with his charges than with the visitors to the zoo, is, at best, precisely his brothers' keeper. Yet, like Cain and Abel, Enoch and the animals seem to entertain mutually hostile and rival attitudes.

The focusing symbol of Enoch's ethos, with its minimal claim to man's superiority over the animal kingdom, is a man whom other men have enabled to survive, materially, for a long time—a glass-encased mummy located in the temple known to Enoch mysteriously as MUVSEEVUM (thus Enoch pronounces MVSEVM). Taking Hazel as his divinely appointed spiritual mentor and hoping to please him, Enoch drags Motes to the mummy shrine. Although Hazel is manifestly uninterested in all this (he bolts out of the room), Enoch remains undaunted, and, obeying an impulse of his "wise blood" (Hazel and Enoch intermittently contest whose blood is "wiser"), he prepares his room for the mummy. Its tabernacle will be the washstand which had previously held a slop basin.

Chapter eight, which describes his preparations for the idol, is a masterful comic scenario; modulating deftly between ironic description and interior viewpoint, it exposes Enoch's world as an anarchic, metamorphosing environment, the appropriately distorting funhouse mirror of the man at its center: a portrait of a moose hangs on his wall with a menacing look of superiority; a rug disintegrates when he hangs it out the window; a chair bulges "around the legs so that it seemed to be in the act of squatting." (131) O'Connor's synecdochic picture of Enoch at last placing the idol in his washstand shrine speaks only too plainly: "From directly behind him, only the soles of his shoes and the seat of his trousers were visible." (175)

When Enoch finally brings the mummy to Hazel's house, the par-

ody of the Nativity reaches its climax. Sabbath Lily, Hazel's impos-
ing young mistress, eagerly accepts the figure and, raptly transfixed
by its universal and anonymous features, proclaims a new holy family,
positing herself and Hazel as its mother and father. But when Hazel
confronts madonna and child, he is adventitiously wearing his own
mother's silver-rimmed glasses, which he has kept with him since his
army days. Thus armed symbolically with her truth-seeing lenses and
having just suggestively seen his mother's face superimposed upon his
own in a mirror, Hazel acts decisively—as if with her power—against
this mockery of the Incarnation. But the detached language used to
describe the iconoclasm suggests the as yet impersonal nature of the
gesture, for Hazel has not yet, himself, gained his proper vision.

> The hand that had been arrested in the air moved forward and
> plucked at the squinting face but without touching it; it reached
> again, slowly, and plucked at nothing and then it lunged and
> snatched the shriveled body and threw it against the wall. The head
> popped and the trash inside sprayed out in a little cloud of dust.
> (187–88)

Nevertheless the idol smashing does foreshadow Hazel's eventual
recantation, for, although he doesn't yet realize it, the mummy, an
embodiment of man's merely physical and material, merely enduring,
"immortality," has been the exact apotheosis of his apocryphal faith.
" 'I'm member and preacher to that church where the blind don't see
and the lame don't walk and *what's dead stays that way.*'" (italics
added; 105) And Enoch had merely heeded what he imagined to be
his leader's call for a new Jesus, " 'one that's all man, without blood
to waste.'" (140)

The smashing means little to Enoch, however, for the adaptable
disciple has been gripped by a more durable image of success: Gonga
the Gorilla, film star, shaking the hands of admirers outside a movie
theatre. The ape had earlier proved unfriendly to Enoch, and so he
now plans to seize the costume and the role for himself. In eager
anticipation of that moment, Enoch experiences what will be the
utmost measure of grace alotted him; and it is a moment rendered
with brilliant parodic anticipation of Hazel's "still moment" on the
embankment: "Enoch left [the diner]. It was a pleasant damp evening. The puddles on the sidewalk shone and the store windows
were steamy and bright with junk." (194)

Once he has defrocked Gonga the Gorilla, and taken on the talismanic accouterments of his newfound role (compare Hazel's murder
and divesting of Solace Layfield), Enoch, with anxious anticipation,
extends his newly soft and hairy hand to the first human beings he
discovers (a pair of lovers gazing from a hilltop at the city), causing
them, alas, to flee their diverse ways. "He eased his arm from around
the woman and disappeared. . . . She . . . fled screaming down the
highway. The gorilla stood as though surprised and presently its arm
fell to its side. It sat down on the rock where they had been sitting
and stared over the valley at the uneven skyline of the city." (198)
That is the last image we are given of Enoch, and it remains in the
reader's mind to provide a parodic counterpoint to Hazel's view of
the landscape at his moment of enlightenment. It is a slightly pathetic image, this one of Enoch, but the visually comic rendering of
it does not permit us to indulge the feeling.

Enoch's quest for a rock of faith to rest his belief on has brought
him only as close as the rock earlier hurled at his head by Hazel and
the final cold stone on which he sits at the end of his career. Like
Hazel, Enoch ends in isolation; but his is a failed quest and, because
of the grotesque misdirection of it, an essentially ridiculous and
comic one. Accordingly, the narrative tone to which Enoch is subjected is throughout a detached and ironic one, while, as was noted,
Hazel, with his different sincerity, different evasions, and different
dispensation, sustains first a comic but then a more serious narrative
tone, indicating, thus decorously, the distinction in attitude toward
the ridiculous and the sublime.

The parody of Hazel's own career presented in the episodically
inserted subplot of Enoch Emery thus serves as a confirmation of the
meaning of the central story in *Wise Blood*. And the narrative control
implied by this ironic perspective is present not only in the larger
design of the book but in the narration of two little stories by Sabbath Lily Hawks as well. Sabbath Lily's stories alike portray the sorry
fate of goodness in a world of evil, and are perhaps imagined by
her (if not by the reader) as images of her own plight. One of her
stories goes:

"Listen, . . . this here man and woman killed this little baby. It was
her own child but it was ugly and she never give it any love. This
child had Jesus and this woman didn't have nothing but good looks

and a man she was living in sin with. She sent the child away and it come back and she sent it away again and it come back again and ever' time she sent it away, it come back to where her and this man was living in sin. They strangled it with a silk stocking and hung it up in the chimney. It didn't give her any peace after that, though. Everything she looked at was that child. Jesus made it beautiful to haunt her. She couldn't lie with that man without she saw it, staring through the chimney at her, shining through the brick in the middle of the night." (52)

The story bears a striking resemblance to the tale of Charles William Albright in *Huckleberry Finn*, not only in its emblematic function in the novel and in the substance of the story but in the style of narration as well. And, although Sabbath Lily could hardly mean it this way, it may also be seen as an ironic emblem of Hazel's own attempt to rid himself of Jesus, and of the hopelessness of that task.

The World of Wise Blood

O'Connor's use of irony as a device for narrative control is evident not only in the subplot of Enoch Emery and in Sabbath Lily's stories but in smaller ways as well. These are not always successful, however, and, preliminary to an evaluation of the novel, it would be well to assess its more obvious stylistic flaws. One device that is overworked, for example, is the counterpointed dialogue. Such a dialogue opens the book, and is the standard form of noncommunication between Hazel and the "normal" characters—truck drivers, policemen, soda jerks, mobs, and Sabbath Lily. One of many possible examples will suffice. " 'Will you get your goddam outhouse off the middle of the road?' " a truck driver demands of Hazel, who is staring at a sign advertising Christ. " 'I don't have to run from anything because I don't believe in anything' " (76), Hazel replies. Designed to provide a comic contrast (normal man versus the possessed man), to direct our seeing, the device ends by merely tiring our eyes.

Other stylistic flaws also seem present because of the author's too obvious desire to point her moral and adorn her tale. Thus, for example, the description of a diner's "poisonous Eastern voice" (16) in chapter one merely betrays, to at least one Easterner, O'Connor's regional eccentricity. Likewise the description of Mrs. Watts—"It was plain that she was so well-adjusted that she didn't have to think any more" (60)—seems bluntly uncute. The used-car salesman's remark about his sullen son's reiterated curses—" 'Something's wrong with him howcome he curses so much'" (72)—also strikes me as cudgeling. And too, Mrs. Flood's repeated obtuseness almost grows irritating—" 'There's only one kind of clean, Mr. Motes.'" (224)

O'Connor's occasional preference for the broadsword over the stiletto in making her points can be particularly irksome when it mars such otherwise fine ironies as the following, where the omission of the penultimate sentence might well have improved the effect.

> The black sky was underpinned with long silver streaks that looked like scaffolding and depth on depth behind it were thousands of stars that all seemed to be moving very slowly as if they were about some vast construction work that involved the whole order of the universe and would take all time to complete. No one was paying any attention to the sky. The stores in Taulkinham stayed open on Thursday nights so that people could have an extra opportunity to see what was for sale. (37)

But these criticisms are different from others that have been leveled at *Wise Blood*. Some readers are unwilling to accept as convincing the characters themselves, their situations, and the world they inhabit: Why should the characters be so "agitated"? How can Motes be anything but crazy, and how can one take a crazy man seriously? How can a character who seems to have no choice escape being grotesque?[16]

The implicit assumption of such questions is that it is legitimate to measure the characters and their world by the "real" world, or by the probable world we are accustomed to find in the realistic novel. Granting that assumption, one must concur: *Wise Blood* is unbelievable. But the limitations of such an assumption are obvious, excluding, as it would, "unbelievable" characters from Othello to Prince Myshkin. The issue does raise, however, certain related fundamental questions about just what kind of belief is demanded by a fiction.

The first point is that, obviously, there are several kinds of "fiction": *Pride and Prejudice* is not *Pilgrim's Progress*. *Great Expectations* is not *Gulliver's Travels*. *Madame Bovary* is not *Moby Dick*. And each kind states implicitly its own intentions, and` demands, accordingly, its own evaluation. True, no one lives in Taulkinham, and no one will ever meet Hazel Motes. It is even part of the strategy of the book to use such skepticism ironically: thus, as we have noted, Mrs. Flood and many other characters provide within the book the "normal" viewpoint espoused by such criticism: "What possible reason," Mrs. Flood asks, "could a sane person have for wanting to not enjoy himself any more?" (211) It is admitted, by virtue of these characters, that Motes is "unbelievable" from the viewpoint of the "probable" world.

Is the book, then, asking us to believe in the existence of some different reality, which would then make Motes believable and Mrs. Flood "unbelievable"? Is it asking us to reject the standard of the world and accept the Passion of Christ and the passions of his believers? In a sense, yes: *Wise Blood* is asking us (and some readers may respond affirmatively) to accept personally the validity of its vision; and certainly it was written from a committed viewpoint. It is not, however, as a work of fiction, demanding that assent.

What the book does legitimately demand is that it be read as one *image* of Christian reality. And images may represent a version of reality without demanding a belief in the image itself, just as fables do not demand a belief in their own probability. Like the world of the fable or, as suggested earlier, the romance, *Wise Blood*'s atmosphere is morally charged. Unlike the romances of Hawthorne and Melville, however, the characters inhabit, quite frankly, a satirically distorted world. But neither is it a satire as, for example, Swift wrote satires, for it contains explicitly an affirmative pattern of Christian mystery that more readily recalls Bunyan. But neither is it an allegory in the traditional sense, for it attempts to render an image of experience that is more complex than that of the traditional allegory and that cannot be so easily translated, at every point, into its theological or dogmatic equivalent; and it has more of the random surface texture of real life.

But the precise nature of that surface texture is crucial, for it provides the environment in which the characters exist; and their distorted figures would be aesthetically out of place within a novel that did not provide a reality correspondingly distorted to contain them: Hazel Motes would expire in Hemingway's universe.

Reading *Wise Blood* requires, as I have suggested, a special seeing; and while I have examined some ways in which the reader's perception of Hazel Motes is directed and illuminated, it remains to look briefly at the overall context, the environment in which the images of the characters exist. What we are judging is an image of Christian reality, and we must judge it not by its congruity to the outside world but by the congruity and consistency, the shape and texture of the image itself. Here we must make a sharp division in the novel between a nature that is redeemed and a nature that is despoiled. Each of these worlds is a distortion of "reality" or "life as we know it"—and purposely so. The two are contrasted sharply in the passage quoted above from the beginning of chapter three, where one can easily see this difference between sacred nature (the stars over Taulkinham) and the profane world that is chiefly visible in the city (the stores in Taulkinham). Most significantly, the image of redeemed nature occurs at Hazel's moment of insight into mystery, his moment of grace, also quoted earlier, in which his face "seemed to reflect the entire distance across the clearing and on beyond, the entire distance that extended from his eyes to the blank gray sky that went on, depth after depth, into space." (209) But that is a singular moment in the book, precisely as rare as a moment of grace.

For the rest—the great expanse of time—is unredeemed, emphatically so, and the tone used to present that unredeemed time, the major and distinguishing tone in Flannery O'Connor, is a comic one. The imagery of unredeemed time and nature creates a brilliantly ugly texture of stylized grotesquerie. "Reality," as we know it, is metamorphosed into a mechanized, anarchic environment as far from normality as are Hazel Motes and Enoch Emery.

Some examples will illustrate the features of the world the characters inhabit: mechanical movements are animated—

> It began to drizzle rain and he turned on the windshield wipers; they made a great clatter like two idiots clapping in church. (74)

Landscapes take on the aspect of clothing—

> There were patches of field buttoned together with 666 posts. (74)

Machines refuse to work—

> Haze started pounding his horn and he had hit it three times before he realized it didn't make any sound. (75)

Women appear rising from swimming pools like monsters—

> First her face appeared, long and cadaverous, with a bandage-like bathing cap coming down almost to her eyes, and sharp teeth protruding from her mouth. (84)

They are transformed into dogs—

> Then she rose on her hands until a large foot and leg came up from behind her and another on the other side and she was out, squatting there, panting. She stood up loosely and shook herself, and stamped in the water dripping off her. (84–85)

Human cows sell ice cream—

> On the wall facing the door there was a large advertisement for ice cream, showing a cow dressed up like a housewife. (88)

Women evoke mops—

> She was a tall bony woman, resembling the mop she carried upside-down. (106)

Mops become owls—

> He squinted close to the wire and saw that the piece of mop was an owl with one eye open. (95)

Nothing—and no one—can be just itself—

> A gentleman in a polo shirt stepped up and shook hands vigorously [with Gonga the Gorilla], like a sportsman. He was followed by a boy of about three who wore a tall Western hat that nearly covered his face; he had to be pushed ahead by the line. . . . The small boy was followed by a lady in shorts, she by an old man who tried to draw extra attention to himself by dancing up instead of walking in a dignified way. (195)

Surveying all the phantasmagoria is a heaven populated, on occasion, by blatantly theomorphic clouds—

> The sky was just a little lighter blue than [Hazel's] suit, clear and

even, with only one cloud in it, a large blinding white one with curls and a beard. (117)

It is in the context of such an imagined reality that Hazel and Enoch, Asa Hawks and Hoover Shoats, Solace Layfield and Sabbath Lily exist. These images of humankind are distorted—as is the world they inhabit—but O'Connor's archly comic (yet, in their cumulative effect, oddly saddening) descriptions create an aesthetic authority that gains our assent and compels our moral consideration. In the tradition of the romancer, O'Connor cuts the cable tying the fictional world to the real world (to borrow James's image) and in so doing allows us to suspend our disbelief. Whether we suspend our disbelief in the theological sense after reading the book is, as I have suggested, a matter of personal choice—though some of the general questions raised by fiction of a religious nature I have left for the last chapter. Here I will say that despite the occasionally too obvious intentions of *Wise Blood*, the cumulative effect of the narrative is to convince the reader of the authenticity and intensity of Hazel Motes's career. Given the absurdity of that career, O'Connor's first novel is no small accomplishment.

3

THE VIOLENT BEAR IT AWAY

W<small>HAT</small> was to be the first chapter of Flannery O'Connor's only other novel was published in 1955, but the completed work—*The Violent Bear It Away*—did not appear until 1960, eight years after *Wise Blood*. During the intervening years a number of short stories were published that dealt in a variety of ways with the sudden intrusion of mystery into the lives of the unsuspecting. But in her second novel, O'Connor returned her central focus to an extraordinary character, who, in his violent struggle against the possession of his soul by God, would bear a strong family resemblance to the hero of *Wise Blood*. "On n'a jamais fini de se battre contre Dieu," said Proudhon, and no better illustration of that remark could be found than in these works.

Narrative Structure

The vehicle for the novel is a plot whose shape is only slightly less angular and eccentric than the story of Hazel Motes and his Essex. Old Mason Tarwater, sole lord and prophet (and practically sole resident) of Powderhead, Tennessee, dies leaving his nephew, Francis

Marion Tarwater, two charges: to give him a decent Christian burial, and to baptize the boy's idiot city cousin, Bishop Rayber. The baptism will be the first official act of young Tarwater's own ascendancy as prophet. On the day of old Tarwater's death, however, and with the encouragement of a disembodied "stranger," Tarwater drinks himself into a stupor, sets fire to the house containing (he believes) his great-uncle's body, and goes to the city. There the youth takes up residence in the household of George Rayber, Bishop's father. Rayber, a fiercely rationalist schoolteacher-psychologist, exposes the youth to the culture he has missed; but Tarwater, though unwilling to baptize the child Bishop, is equally unwilling to have himself baptized in Rayber's secular, atheistic cult. The boy's inner conflict comes to a head when, just as Rayber thinks himself on the verge of winning Tarwater's soul, the latter drowns Bishop, thus doing away— he thinks—with a chief source of his vocational anxiety. Indeed, Tarwater believes himself to have achieved a double renunciation: of old Tarwater's mad prophetic mission, and of the ineffectual scientism of Rayber. But the murder was preceded by Tarwater's involuntary utterance of the baptismal pronouncement; and it remains to be seen whether the deed or the word will have determining power over Tarwater's soul. Thinking himself divested at last of the prophet's mantle, however, the boy retreats to Powderhead; but on the way home he is quite literally divested of his quite literal clothes, and sodomically raped by his old stranger "friend," whose true satanism is thus made manifest. Tarwater returns to Powderhead, setting fire along the way to the profaned woods, only to find that old Mason has already been buried by a Negro friend. Having burned his secular bridge behind him, the youth undergoes a transforming vision, and this time, with the determined conviction of the prophet, he sets out once more for the city, "where the children of God lay sleeping." (243)

Although a younger man than Hazel Motes, the hero of *The Violent Bear It Away* is equally possessed by his backwoods religious background and equally engaged in a life-and-death struggle with it. Hazel Motes's struggle, it will be recalled, takes the form of a public ministry of nihilism; conviction found, his belief is acted out in silence and exile, with his withdrawal culminating in a quietly triumphant death. In *The Violent Bear It Away*, O'Connor reverses the pattern and discovers in Tarwater a conflict between an acceptance of his sacred prophetic role and a disbelief in it. The resolution of that conflict issues in a demonstration of faith not through silence but through the mission of public prophecy. Accordingly, the novels deal with complementary aspects of the single major Christian theme of vocation. ("Calling," while it originally meant a movement of the spirit toward God, came to mean as well, after the Reformation, one's active enterprise in the world.[1]) The mirror image of Hazel Motes's Christian martyrdom is, in The Violent Bear It Away, the picture of a prophet's initiation.

Yet other differences between the novels should be remarked. One cannot say of The Violent Bear It Away what O'Connor herself said of Wise Blood when she prefaced the 1962 edition of that novel by asserting that "the book was written with zest and, if possible, it should be read that way." Not that her second novel is flat or lack-luster—certainly many passages of description and dialogue are as comically evocative as Wise Blood; but we find in The Violent Bear It Away passages of a tonal quality absent from the story of Hazel Motes. Mostly these describe experiences and visions from Tarwater's point of view, but they are written in a language and a voice more recognizably the author's. An example might be the section where Tarwater approaches the city for the first time.

> He was sitting forward on the seat, looking out the window at a hill covered with old used-car bodies. In the indistinct darkness, they seemed to be drowning into the ground, to be about half-submerged already. The city hung in front of them on the side of the mountain as if it were a larger part of the same pile, not yet buried so deep. The fire had gone out of it and it appeared settled into its unbreakable parts. (54–55)

One does not read such a passage with "zest." And if one compares it with, for example, the passage from Wise Blood (p. 37) contrasting the peaceful stars over Taulkinham with the stores that remain open late at night in the city, one can readily see the difference: where the earlier work makes a sharply ironic contrast between nature and the city in a tone of comic detachment, the later work metamorphoses the city into a grotesque image of a waste pile, and in a tone of far more somber irony.

Yet another difference between the two novels can be seen in their uses of narrative perspective. In Wise Blood, the normal viewpoint

(Hazel as seen by Mrs. Hitchcock, or Mrs. Flood) is used ironically to define an image of the Christian life and set it off from the unredeemed life; whereas in *The Violent Bear It Away* certain similar techniques (counterpointed dialogues between Tarwater and the salesman Meeks or between the prophet and the truck driver who later gives him a ride) are used mainly for their value as plot transitions and for filling in some antecedents of the plot.

Where *Wise Blood* portrays the outward appearance of a soul reaching a religious commitment, *The Violent Bear It Away* is concerned chiefly with representing the inward nature of that struggle. Accordingly, in her second novel, O'Connor uses juxtaposed narrative perspectives to illuminate the inner dimensions of certain actions or events. One illustration of this technique is the key episode in part two where, during an outing in the park, Rayber, Tarwater, and Bishop are sitting on a bench near a fountain. Of what ensues we are ultimately given three slightly—but significantly—different accounts. Chapter six, which is written from Rayber's point of view, furnishes the following narrative.

> Bishop let loose his hand and galloped away.
> . . . In a second he was over the side and in [the water]. "Too late, goddammit," Rayber muttered, "he's in." He glanced at Tarwater.
> The boy stood arrested in the middle of a step. His eyes were on the child in the pool but they burned as if he beheld some terrible compelling vision. The sun shone brightly on Bishop's white head and the little boy stood there with a look of attention. Tarwater began to move toward him.
> . . . In an instant of illumination he understood. Tarwater was moving toward Bishop to baptize him. . . . Rayber sprang and snatched the child out of the water. . . .
> . . . He felt that he had just saved the boy from committing some enormous indignity. He saw it all now. The old man *had* transferred his fixation to the boy, *had* left him with the notion that he must baptize Bishop or suffer some terrible consequence. (145–46)

Later, in chapter eight, Tarwater ruminates on his stay with Rayber and the opportunities he has had to baptize Bishop—if he'd really wanted to, that is. He remembers the episode at the fountain, but with certain details given an emphasis different from the one Rayber gave them. In particular, Tarwater senses a more spiritually intimate significance in the sunlight on Bishop's head and the felt presence of old Tarwater.

> The sun, which had been tacking from cloud to cloud, emerged above the fountain. A blinding brightness fell on the lion's tangled marble head and gilded the stream of water rushing from his mouth. Then the light, falling more gently, rested like a hand on the child's white head. His face might have been a mirror where the sun had stopped to watch its reflection.
> Tarwater started forward. He felt a distinct tension in the quiet. The old man might have been lurking near, holding his breath, waiting for the baptism. (164)

It is then, as we have seen, that Rayber intervenes, preventing the baptism.

Tarwater's stranger friend—who was silenced temporarily during this moment—then offers his own view, the third, of the episode at the fountain.

> Well, that's your sign, his friend said—the sun coming out from under a cloud and falling on the head of a dimwit. Something that could happen fifty times a day without no one being the wiser. . . . Listen, he said, you have to quit confusing a madness with a mission. . . . If you baptize once, you'll be doing it the rest of your life. If it's an idiot this time, the next time it's liable to be a nigger. Save yourself while the hour of salvation is at hand. (165–66)

Although—even at this point in the novel—the reader may not doubt that Tarwater's visionary account is the viewpoint of authority here, rather than the rationally psychological one of Rayber or the cynically irreverent one of the stranger, it does remain a question to Tarwater himself, until the very end of the book, precisely whether such "signs" as the sunlight on Bishop's head are just that—signs—or whether they are mere psychological aberrations and accidental illusions. The intention of the multiple viewpoint narration seems, then, not so much to elicit a condemnation of Rayber's or the stranger's perspectives as to intensify and expand the context of Tarwater's internal conflict.

This technique of suspending the narration of a key episode over several points of view is found in the treatment of the background history of the characters as well, and gives a special shape to the book's structure. Thus certain key events and situations in the lives of the characters—old Mason Tarwater's abduction of Rayber when the latter was a child, Rayber's return to old Tarwater at his parents' death, the marriage of Tarwater's parents, Tarwater's birth, Tarwater's baptism by Mason and Rayber's comical counter-baptism, old Mason's abduction of Tarwater, Rayber's attempted rescue of Tarwater and his being shot in the ear—the reader finds told and retold from different angles, and with different interpretations put upon them. The total effect is that of a statue being rotated on a pedestal: with each turn, the observer perceives some new plane, some new relationship between the planes, until at last the whole pattern takes shape in the clarity of its meaning.

Of course the use of multiple viewpoints is not, in itself, a new narrative technique; yet the particular use O'Connor makes of it is interesting, for it implies the process whereby meaning is wrested from history and, a corollary, whereby present action gains significance from its contextual historical pattern. More specifically, the structure of *The Violent Bear It Away* is based upon an alternation of past time and present time; the action in the present time centers on Tarwater's baptism of Bishop, while the historical context, which gives meaning to this action, and from which the proper meaning must itself be wrested, is supplied by the past events in the interrelated lives of Tarwater, old Tarwater, and Rayber. Certainly the meaning of Hazel Motes's career in *Wise Blood* could be ascertained only from the reader's knowledge of his background—the forces shaping him and against which he shaped himself. But in *The Violent Bear It Away*, that knowledge is not simply rendered through expository flashbacks or through the dreams of the hero but is woven into the structure of the work in a more organic way. The effect is similar to that achieved by Faulkner in, for example, *Absalom, Absalom!* or, better, in part two of *The Sound and the Fury*, where a present action (Quentin's last day, ending in his suicide) gains its meaning from a retelling of certain obsessive events in the history of his family, events which are rotated through the narrative consciousnesses of other characters in the other parts of the book.

In another respect, the structure of *The Violent Bear It Away* bears a close resemblance to *As I Lay Dying*, for both suspend over a week's length a narrative dealing with contorted family relations and the burial of a focal character. In O'Connor's novel, of course the suspension is within Tarwater's mind only, since, as the reader is told in the first sentence, old Tarwater was in fact buried on the day of his death.

> Francis Marion Tarwater's uncle had been dead for only half a day when the boy got too drunk to finish digging his grave and a Negro named Buford Munson, who had come to get a jug filled, had to finish it and drag the body from the breakfast table where it was still sitting and bury it in a decent and Christian way, with the sign of its Saviour at the head of the grave and enough dirt on top to keep the dogs from digging it up. (3)

With its several syntactical shifts of tense, this first sentence is a prototype of the stratified temporal pattern of the book as a whole.

Yet beyond this initial exposition, the "present action" in part one is slow to progress, though gaining some momentum in parts two and three. What we have, instead, in part one is the reader's discovery of Tarwater's background, conveyed through the ritualistic recitation of the family chronicle according to old Tarwater.

> "Well go on," Tarwater would say irritably, "get on with the rest of it." The story always had to be taken to completion. It was like a road that the boy had travelled on so often that half the time he didn't look where they were going, and when at certain points he would become aware where they were, he would be surprised to see that the old man had not got farther on with it. Sometimes his uncle would lag at one point as if he didn't want to face what was coming and then when he finally came to it, he would try to get past it in a rush. At such points, Tarwater plagued him for details. "Tell about when he came when he was fourteen years old and had already decided none of it was true and he give you all that sass." (65–66)

As an expository technique, it is as familiar as Prospero's first-act narration to Miranda of long-standing family feuds. But in The Violent Bear It Away, this retelling of family history takes on an added significance, as the paragraph just cited indicates. What Tarwater is learning from old Tarwater is as important to his own formation as it is to the reader's awareness of what's going on. For Tarwater's acts take their meaning from that history and carry it forward.

Moreover, family history, for Tarwater, exists not in isolation but in the context of world history, as old Tarwater would have it. "His

uncle had taught him Figures, Reading, Writing, and History beginning with Adam expelled from the Garden and going on down
through the presidents to Herbert Hoover and on in speculation
toward the Second Coming and the Day of Judgment." (4) And it
is precisely Tarwater's identity in the context of old Mason's sacred
history of the world that Rayber is determined to tear down, in part
two of the novel, in order to model the boy on his own plan.

Old Tarwater, Tarwater, and Rayber

Old Mason Tarwater's authority for raising young Francis Marion
Tarwater in the wilderness of Powderhead, for making of him, as
Meeks the salesman later puts it, " 'a captive audience' " (79) to his
prophecy, was the "rage of vision" the Lord had sent him, telling
him to "raise [the child] up to justify his Redemption." (4–5) But
O'Connor is willing to let the reader, at least initially, entertain some
doubt as to that authority ("The old man had been Tarwater's
great-uncle, or said he was" [3–4]; "the old man, who said he was a
prophet" [5]), and it is a successful strategy, forcing the reader to
hold in abeyance his judgment and letting the emerging conflict
within Tarwater between his great-uncle and Rayber gain in intensity
before the reader's own commitment is made.

At one point in the story, young Tarwater's stranger friend calls
old Tarwater "a one-notion man. Jesus. Jesus this and Jesus that."
(39) Though cynical, his remark is accurate, and recalls the single-
minded grotesques of Sherwood Anderson's *Winesburg, Ohio*. In fact,
the relationship between the great-uncle and his nephew is rather like
that between God-intoxicated Jesse Bentley and his grandson David
in Anderson's tale "Godliness." Shades of Huck Finn and his Pap also
linger around the Tarwaters' Powderhead existence far from civilization, and, indeed, Tarwater's choice, like Huck's before him, will
press itself as one between emulation of a spiritual sire and adoption
of the city's code and culture. (A third alternative, that of staking
out one's own territory, is, for Huck, the final resolution but, for
Tarwater, only a temporary and false one—sought, held in his mind
briefly at the end of the work, but at last not viable.)

Young Tarwater's resistance to Mason's indoctrination repeats the
pattern of Hazel Motes's resistance to his calling in *Wise Blood*.
Learning from old Tarwater that his baptism into freedom is through
the death of Jesus Christ, Tarwater, like Hazel, rebels in his heart,

feeling a "slow warm rising resentment . . . that Jesus had to be the Lord." (20–21) And while the boy is certain that he is not hungry for the "bread of life," which is Jesus, he is "secretly afraid" that "it might be passed down, might be hidden in the blood and might strike some day in him and then he would be torn by hunger like the old man, the bottom split out of his stomach so that nothing would heal or fill it but the bread of life." (21) It is a fear entirely justified.

A further resistance Tarwater feels to the idea of his taking over the family business of prophecy is, interestingly, that as a vocation it lacks glamour, romance, adventure. What could be more prosaic to a boy fed on the literary imagery and visions of Old Testament stories of Elijah and Elisha, Ezekiel, Jonah and Daniel, than the fulfillment of the old man's particular dream. "The boy would have a hideous vision of himself sitting forever with his great-uncle on a green bank, full and sick, staring at a broken fish and a multiplied loaf." (62) On the contrary, what Tarwater hungers to see are "wheels of fire in the eyes of unearthly beasts." (22) Yet when Tarwater himself prematurely anticipates his own vision and holds his breath, "as if he were about to hear a voice from on high," the sign is at best disappointing. "After a few moments he heard a hen scratching beneath him under the porch." (13) (Ironically, Tarwater is to get several of the "right kind" of signs, but it is the logic of divine calling that unless the prophet is, within himself, at the right stage of the journey, the signs don't signify.[2])

When Tarwater, fresh from his first incendiary activities and with more than just a chip on his shoulder, presents himself at the doorstep of his uncle Rayber, the latter's even limited knowledge of the boy could not have led him to think of the foundling as exactly a tabula rasa on which to write his own theories of education and human life. His quondam wife had given him fair warning: for when the psychologist and Bernice (who is a social worker) had sought to retrieve Tarwater from Powderhead and were answered with a gun fired by old Tarwater at Rayber's leg and then at his ear, Bernice had seen on the baby Tarwater's face an unforgettable expression.

> [It] had no more changed when the gun went off than the old man's had. . . .
> . . . Its face was like the face she had seen in some medieval paintings where the martyr's limbs are being sawed off and his expression

says he is being deprived of nothing essential. . . . [The face expressed] the depth of human perversity, the deadly sin of rejecting defiantly one's own obvious good. (180–81)

The passage is ironic, and in a way that makes it liable to misinterpretation: the "obvious" good, O'Connor implies, is not necessarily the ultimate good; and the language ("deadly sin") parodies the devoutly secular reasoning of the welfare woman. Rayber, however, hopes he can defeat Tarwater's perversity, and it takes the duration of the week to convince him finally of the accuracy of Bernice's view.

The choice that Rayber offers to Tarwater is essentially the humanist's or the existentialist's—though his rhetoric is unsubtle. " 'The great dignity of man,' his uncle said, 'is his ability to say: I am born once and no more. What I can see and do for myself and my fellowman in this life is all my portion and I'm content with it. It's enough to be a man.' " (172) But Rayber's humanism is espoused at great cost to himself, O'Connor makes clear. For although Rayber's role vis-à-vis Tarwater is as antagonist to old Tarwater, in fact the psychologist and his nephew share a great deal: the seed of the "affliction," as Rayber calls it, "lay hidden in the line of blood that touched them [both], flowing from some ancient source, some desert prophet or polesitter, until, its power unabated, it appeared in the old man and him and, he surmised, in the boy." (114) It is an affliction that strikes its victim as a rapturous, uncontrollable feeling of love, a mystic's vision of the stupefying beauty of the world, and for both Rayber and Tarwater it can be brought on, seemingly, by anything "looked at too long." (113) For Rayber, "it could be a stick or a stone, the line of a shadow, the absurd old man's walk of a starling crossing the sidewalk." (113) For Tarwater (and the passage is a clear parallel), it could be "a spade, a hoe, the mule's hind quarters before his plow, the red furrow under him." (22) Both do all they can to avoid this "threatened intimacy of creation." (22)

In fact, O'Connor implies, Rayber does too much: for he imposes a "rigid ascetic discipline" (114) on his feelings and sensations. "He was not deceived that this was a whole or a full life, he only knew that it was the way his life had to be lived if it were going to have any dignity at all." (114) The erect posture of the humanist, however, is discovered to be in reality the nervous and tentative angle of the funambulist. "He kept himself upright on a very narrow line between madness and emptiness, and when the time came for him to lose his balance, he intended to lurch toward emptiness and fall on the side of his choice." (115) (He does just that, we shall see, when Bishop is drowned.)

At odd moments, Rayber's facade of control is fissured and tension is released in facial expressions that reveal the grotesquely distorted personality that is being masked. Thus, for example, when the hotel clerk at the Cherokee Lodge glimpses the friction between Rayber and Tarwater, "Rayber looked at the woman helplessly and lifted his shoulders as if to say, 'I have more than one problem,' and shrug it off, but the gesture ended in a violent tremor. To his horror he felt the side of his mouth give a series of quick jerks." (154) Or, later, when he confesses to Tarwater that he had, himself, once tried to drown Bishop, "He leaned forward; his mouth opened and closed and then in a dry voice he said, 'Once I tried to drown him,' and grinned horribly at the boy." (169)

Rayber's disease, his disunity, results from the separation of the head from the heart.[3] Moreover, the space inside his head is grotesquely hypertrophied—a condition (or metaphor) consonant with his overdeveloped rationalism: thus old Tarwater, upon reading Rayber's article about him in which the prophet's drive is analytically dissected, feels that he has been "tied hand and foot inside the schoolteacher's head, a space as bare and neat as the cell in the asylum, and was shrinking, drying up to fit it." (76) Another time, Rayber suffers a dislocation of his ruling faculties when Tarwater asks him provocatively, while looking at the hearing aid battery the schoolteacher must wear, " 'Do you think in the box . . . or do you think in your head?' " (105) And earlier, when Tarwater tries to recall his impressions of Rayber, the conjured image repeatedly falls apart in his mind. (55)

By contrast, Tarwater's own personality, even if yet imperfect, is still so much of a piece that, like Hazel Motes's, it comically impresses its shape on the materials that clothe the body: Tarwater's hat, as Rayber perceives, has "the boy's own defiant quality, as if its shape had been formed over the years by his personality." (119–20) And after the week's effort at acculturation, Rayber still finds Tarwater looking exactly the same—"the filthy hat, the stinking overalls, worn defiantly like a national costume." (150) However eccentric his appearance, Tarwater projects an entire self.

Birth by Drowning

It does not take Tarwater long to realize that Rayber is "no more than a decoy the old man had set up to lure him to the city to do his unfinished business" (89), which is of course the baptism of Bishop; and it is to the working out of Rayber's and Tarwater's attitudes toward the child, whose name suggests the sacred role he is to play, that we now turn our attention.

Bishop is presented to the reader from a number of different viewpoints: O'Connor describes him, neutrally but punctiliously, as making peanut butter sandwiches by putting the bread inside and as feeding his spaghetti into sugar bowls. Another time, she shows him hanging out the window of a moving car, "letting the air dry his tongue." (180) At the Cherokee Lodge, before the drowning, he evokes two contrary reactions: the dancing teenagers are shocked into immobility and silence by his bellowing, as if he were a "fault in creation" (190), while the hotel clerk regards " 'that there kind' " as something "holy." (155) This latter response seems closer to the "correct" view of the child, which old Tarwater had at one point exclaimed to Rayber, " 'Precious in the sight of the Lord even an idiot!' " (33)

Moreover, it is a view reinforced ironically in the scene where Bishop and Rayber visit Powderhead: Rayber, seeing the wooded land he has inherited from old Tarwater, translates the natural resource into lumber, which, in turn, becomes the dollars and cents that will pay for young Tarwater's college education. Later, the schoolteacher picks a blackberry for Bishop and hands it to the idiot. "The little boy studied it and then, with his fallen smile, returned it to him as if they were performing a ceremony. Rayber flung it away and turned to find the trail through the woods." (184) The two attitudes toward nature stand in stark opposition: Rayber's is the acquisitive, destructive, possessive one; Bishop's is the respectful, admiring, Adamic one—the least berry being the occasion for a ceremony of innocence.

"The Lord," old Tarwater says, "had preserved the one child [Rayber] had got out of [his wife] from being corrupted by such parents. He had preserved him in the only way possible: the child was dim-witted." (9) O'Connor's Bishop thus joins that odd file of American literary idiots—including Benjy in *The Sound and the*

Fury, Lennie in *Of Mice and Men,* perhaps even translogical Jim in *Huckleberry Finn*—all of whom serve, in the context of decaying cultural, emotional, and spiritual values, as a repository of whatever good remains. Though scorned by the world, they preserve, in their ironically incorruptible form, that innocence superior to defeat.

Rayber's own attitude toward Bishop reflects the general tensions in his personality, and, in fact, brings them to a focus. On the one hand, Bishop is "an x signifying the general hideousness of fate" (113), fit victim for a more enlightened future's euthanasia. But, on the other hand, as Tarwater himself perceives at one point, father and son are "inseparably joined." (93) For Rayber had learned through his attempted drowning of Bishop that "his own stability depended on the little boy's presence. He could control his terrifying love as long as it had its focus in Bishop, but if anything happened to the child, he would have to face it in itself. Then the whole world would become his idiot child." (182)

But Bishop was, it would seem, born to be drowned; and if Rayber had failed in his attempt, Tarwater does not in his. Indeed, as the prophet walks slowly down the dock toward the boat that will carry Tarwater to his calling and the idiot to his death, Rayber, watching the scene, unknowingly glimpses the providential order of what is to follow. He sees in the two an apparent reversal of roles—"that it was Bishop who was doing the leading, that the child had made the capture." (197) He is right, but not in the sense he thinks. For Bishop does "capture" Tarwater not on Rayber's behalf but on old Tarwater's. The young prophet of course does not yet realize himself that the intended drowning will also be a baptism.

The drowning is the central action in the novel; everything leads up to it, and only in its aftermath is the meaning of the novel revealed. Even in the description of Tarwater's first contact with Bishop, it is foreshadowed: when the former calls Rayber, Bishop answers the phone and Tarwater hears over the line "a kind of bubbling noise, the kind of noise someone would make who was struggling to breathe in water." (83) Face to face with the child, the prophet realizes "with a certainty sunk in despair, that he was expected to baptize the child he saw and begin the life his great-uncle had prepared him for." (91) Not as the conqueror, then, but as the "forced servant of God" (93) does Tarwater look into Bishop's

eyes—eyes that in their resemblance to old Tarwater's make present
the old man's force of prophecy and grotesquely conjure an image of
Bishop as "the old man grown backwards to the lowest form of
innocence." (111)[4]

The moment of the drowning, like the moment of near baptism at
the fountain, is first perceived by the reader through Rayber's point
of view, and his attention is equally focused on the effect this witnessing will have on the would-be rationalist. Rayber's vantage point
is the window of his room overlooking the lake, from which he can
see the two figures sitting in the boat near the middle of the lake.
"All he would be was an observer" (200), he thinks introspectively;
before the dissatisfactions of life, "this indifference was the most that
human dignity could achieve, and . . . he felt he had achieved it. To
feel nothing was peace." (200) Continuing his ruminations, he comes
to see the time spent with Tarwater as "five days of madness" (201),
and he resolves to offer him an ultimatum: Tarwater must allow
himself to be tested and must throw away his talismanic hat; otherwise, he cannot stay with Rayber. But the psychologist's firm resolve
is subtly undermined, for, even as he goes back to his cot and dozes
off, he imagines himself and Bishop fleeing in the car, a "tornado just
behind them." (201) It is an ominous image, for it recalls an earlier
"wild dream" Rayber has had, "in which he chased Tarwater through
an interminable alley that twisted suddenly back on itself and
reversed the roles of pursuer and pursued. The boy had overtaken
him, given him a thunderous blow on the head [compare the "tornado" image above], and then disappeared." (139–40) O'Connor
uses these dreams of Rayber to foreshadow the fated reversal that
will follow.

The dramatic climax itself is ushered in with classical stage machinery: Rayber awakens with the moon staring in at him through his
window, "a pale messenger breathlessly arrived." (202) Thus alerted,
the psychologist stands at the window and sets his face against the
painful sound of Bishop's bellowing, and the sounds "seem to come
from inside him as if something in him were tearing itself free"
(202), for Bishop's death is also, for Rayber, the deracination of a
part of himself. Thus passively witnessing what he knows now is the
drowning of his son, Rayber becomes himself an accomplice in the
act—"as if . . . the two of them together had taken the child and

held him under until he ceased to struggle." (203) The scene recalls the similarly dramatized complicity of Miriam and Donatello in the death of the model in Hawthorne's *Marble Faun*; yet it is interesting to observe that where Hawthorne bases the subsequent growth of his characters upon their recognition of the gravity of their deed, O'Connor shows the pain of Rayber's response to issue not from his complicity in an act committed but in his recognition of something that is, for O'Connor, more terrible—his very failure to feel pain. "He stood waiting for the raging pain, the intolerable hurt that was his due, to begin, so that he could ignore it, but he continued to feel nothing. He stood light-headed at the window and it was not until he realized there would be no pain that he collapsed." (203) Rayber's anesthetization of his feelings, his separation of head from heart, has been successful, but at the cost of near total dehumanization. Not, however, quite total, for his collapse at the end must be taken as a feeling reaction to his failure to react, and, as such, may initiate some process of spiritual renewal, a process, however, which the reader is excluded from witnessing. For that is the last we see of Rayber.

Tarwater's renewal following the drowning of Bishop, on the other hand, is the subject of the final part of the book; but, here again, we might observe that the emphasis will be not on Tarwater's recognition of his guilt but, rather, on what accompanied—and gave meaning to—the murder: the baptismal blessing he pronounces over the drowning child (a similar understatement was accorded Hazel Motes's equally self-defining murder of Solace Layfield). Rayber, upon hearing Bishop's bellowing, was as certain that the child was being drowned as he was that Tarwater had baptized the child and "was headed for everything the old man had prepared him for, that he moved off now through the black forest toward a violent encounter with his fate." (203) And he is right of course, although Tarwater does not yet know it.

The Act and the Word

From Tarwater's point of view, the drowning of Bishop is one more instance of his ability to act where his uncle has failed; for he regards his own life as a conscious acting over again, a correction, so to speak, of Rayber's life. When the latter's parents died, for example, the schoolteacher burned all their possessions and went off to old Tarwater to tell him they were dead. It is of course as an imitation of that denial that we must read Tarwater's burning of the house at Powderhead when his great-uncle dies and his announcing the death to Rayber. In drowning Bishop, Tarwater not only symbolically renounces his great-uncle's command to baptize the idiot child; in the face of Rayber's own earlier failed attempt to drown Bishop, he is also asserting his equal renunciation of Rayber's ineffectuality. "'All you can do is think what you would have done if you had done it. Not me. I can do it. I can act.'" (196) Or, as he later puts it, "'You can't just say NO. . . . You got to do NO.'" (157)

But the decisive act—in which he drowns Bishop while pronouncing the baptismal words over him—itself undermines the boy. He *does* NO, but he *says* YES. Ravaged by the conflict of wills within him, Tarwater cannot, try as he will, will a unity of being; and, even in his telling of the drowning to the truck driver who later gives him a ride, the word has a force of its own, independent of his will.

> "I drowned a boy," Tarwater said.
> "Just one?" the driver asked.
> "Yes." He reached over and caught hold of the sleeve of the man's shirt. His lips worked a few seconds. They stopped and then started again as if the force of a thought were behind them but no words. He shut his mouth, then tried again but no sound came. Then all at once the sentence rushed out and was gone. "I baptized him."
> "Huh?" the man said.
> "It was an accident. I didn't mean to. . . . The words just come out of themselves but it don't mean nothing. You can't be born again." (209)

What emerges, then, from O'Connor's narration is a complex relationship, between word, deed, and some outside force, that is at the heart of the concept of significant action in the novel. The act of drowning is the occasion for the baptismal word, but its involuntary utterance seems to give it a force independent of Tarwater, and prior to his act.

In short, the *wholly* self-determined action that Tarwater wills is an illusion; in the world of the novel, there is a force surrounding the characters which they cannot help but respond to. Yet O'Connor validates the psychology of the moment by revealing this watching, waiting force through the dream Tarwater has, after the drowning, in which he relives the act. Thus, for example, he feels that Bishop's eyes are "fixed on him as if they were waiting serenely for a struggle already determined." (215) Other eyes too witness the event: "the sky was dotted with fixed tranquil eyes like the spread tail of some celestial night bird." (216) There is also a kind of historical force in the moment, felt when O'Connor alludes to an earlier reluctant prophet in describing Tarwater's struggles. "His pale face twitched and grimaced. He might have been Jonah clinging wildly to the whale's tongue." (216)

As night fades, Tarwater awakens from his dream crying out the words of the baptism, and, such is the power of words, the blessing causes the stranger-devil (who has advised the boy during the drowning) to depart in haste. But Tarwater chooses to ignore his dream. The chapter concludes with his walking back to Powderhead to "begin to live his life as he had elected it, and where, for the rest of his days, he would make good his refusal." (218)

If this were a different novel and Flannery O'Connor a different novelist, perhaps that sentence, with its final cadence, would close *The Violent Bear It Away*. But it doesn't. As just noted, there are other forces in O'Connor's world besides those that permit one to dispel a dream by closing an inner eye, and these must be attended to. Rayber, whom O'Connor uses not only as a rationalist antagonist to Tarwater but as an occasional mouthpiece of a plausible psychology, has earlier put it this way: "'Do you know . . . that there's a part of your mind that works all the time, that you're not aware of yourself. Things go on in it. All sorts of things you don't know about.'" (171) Tarwater of course dismisses his "underhead" (171), as he calls it, with scorn; but while Rayber's rhetoric is perhaps not congenial to O'Connor either, the existence of a deeply rooted ambivalence within Tarwater, of a conflicting will, is definitely implied.

What resolves that conflict—acting as an unholy catalyst—is the sexual violation of Tarwater by the stranger who gives him a ride on his way home. (Where classical gods liked to impersonate animals and men in order to work their sexual desires, in O'Connor—leaving aside the "Greenleaf" bull—it is the agency of darkness that evinces sexual energy.) The identity of the stranger is not of course a secret: his lavender eyes and panama hat echo the description of the Miltonically deceptive, subtle reasoner in chapter one. (35) There he had seemed to emerge from Tarwater's own divided consciousness, but his later malign physical incarnation would seem to suggest the persistence and potency of evil in O'Connor's world.[5] Tarwater had put Satan behind him, so to speak, only to find that that may be an even more dangerous place for his adversary.

The rape itself is stripped of much of its potentially shocking quality by the language used in framing it—as if the natural order has been tranquilized, if not made tranquil: "The woods were silent except for an occasional trill or caw. The air itself might have been drugged." (231) There is even a touch of comic absurdity when Tarwater awakens from his disturbed sleep: "Then he got into his clothes so quickly that when he finished he had half of them on backwards and did not notice." (232) This sort of before-and-after treatment allows the reader to accept what might otherwise be a disruptive scene. For O'Connor, evil is part of a larger necessity, and so this sodomic rape by a plundering devil (he steals Tarwater's corkscrew) is made decisive without annihilating the aesthetic tension in the book.

It is of great importance to notice the psychological propitiousness of the moment and its consequent purifying effect on Tarwater. Before the rape, the boy's self-confidence is high, his control of the world is certain. But just such self-delusion about man's true place in the world preconditions, in O'Connor, the inevitable Fall, the unavoidable assertion of reality. In timing and function, the scene is comparable to the sudden gratuitous destruction of Hazel Motes's car in *Wise Blood*—when Hazel was himself sure of his control of things and of his identity. And the effect of the rape is also similar to the effect on Hazel of his calamity. For afterward, like Isaiah, Tarwater has had his vision burned clean: his eyes "looked small and seedlike as if while he was asleep, they had been lifted out, scorched, and dropped back into his head. . . . They looked as if, touched with a coal like the lips of the prophet, they would never be used for ordinary sights again." (232-33) And Tarwater, in turn, enacts his own ritual purification—burning first the evil ground of his seduction. Then, the stranger reappearing for the last time to urge an alliance, the prophet lights "a rising wall of fire between him and the grinning presence. . . . [He] saw that his adversary [at last recognized as such] would soon be consumed in a roaring blaze." (238)

But a subtler sign of the change wrought in Tarwater after the violation is the silence that descends upon him. Before the rape, in a confrontation with the judgmental, angelic "large woman" at the store (224), Tarwater had sought to answer for his freedom, to "make bold his acts" (225), but "to his horror what rushed from his lips, like the shriek of a bat, was an obscenity he had overheard once at a fair." (225) Now, his will purified and almost perfected, Tarwater begins to enter a country that, though familiar to him from infancy, suddenly seems "strange and alien." (233) It is the country whose borders he has been on the verge of crossing, the country he has felt surrounding him throughout his journey. And it is the same silent country that appeared to be reflected "in the center of [Bishop's] eyes. It stretched out there, limitless and clear." (160) Previously hidden from his daily sight, it is now present to his inner eye.

Secular Time and Sacred Time

In the last chapter of the novel, Tarwater completes the circle of his journey and returns to Powderhead. From thence he will start out again for the city in fulfillment of his true calling. It is as perfectly written a last chapter as one could hope for, and almost every sentence is resonant with the accumulated themes and images of the book, the whole shaping a conclusion which, as Tarwater passes through the chapter and out of the book, is at once a new beginning. As with the conclusion of *Wise Blood*, it leaves one with a feeling of completion and, at the same time, a feeling of open-endedness. It will easily bear a close reading.

Throughout the novel, the landscape has been used symbolically. Never just a place where things happen, it is part and parcel of a larger spiritual process; now inimical, now hospitable, it wears the colors of the Holy Spirit. As Tarwater approaches the precinct of Powderhead, his senses seem stunned. He hears a woodthrush call from "somewhere deep in the wood . . . and as if the sound were a key turned in the boy's heart, his throat began to tighten." (236) It calls again. "With the same four formal notes it trilled its grief against the silence." (236) It is the same bird Tarwater heard days earlier at Powderhead when he went deep into the woods to fill the Negroes' jugs with whiskey: then it had seemed a mere naturalistic detail. But it gained a symbolic dimension when Bishop's ears were attuned to the call—and it stopped his breath—when he and Rayber had visited the area.[6] Now, as Tarwater himself comes to the forked tree that affords a Pisgah view of old Tarwater's lot, the bird image is internalized: "His gaze, like a bird that flies through fire, faltered and dropped. Where it fell, two chimneys stood like grieving figures guarding the blackened ground between them." (236) As he watches, moving closer to the sight, a deep-filled quiet pervades everything. The sun, which has been an angry witness of the week's events, retires. "The encroaching dusk seemed to come softly in deference to some mystery that resided here." (239)[7]

On the threshold of the definitive revelation Tarwater has looked for throughout the novel, the boy's eyes encounter Buford Munson, who, fulfilling a priestly role, has buried old Tarwater (thus allowing a later resurrection that cremation would have precluded), set a cross over his head, and plowed the old man's corn field. Before the grave, Tarwater stares at the sign of old Tarwater's Saviour, and the descriptive imagery suggests a redemptive agency at work. "His eyes . . . stared downward at the cross as if they followed below the surface of the earth to where its roots encircled all the dead." (240) ("'The world was made for the dead'" [16], old Tarwater had once declared.)

The atmosphere is charged to its utmost, and Buford himself—a priest of sorts, though not privy to a prophet's vision—must depart. Tarwater's subsequent revelation comes upon him with the irresistible force of grace, recalling, in its homely grandeur, Piers Plowman's vision of a fair field full of folk.

> The boy remained standing there, his still eyes reflecting the field the Negro had crossed. It seemed to him no longer empty but peopled with a multitude. Everywhere, he saw dim figures seated on the slope and as he gazed he saw that from a single basket the throng was being fed. His eyes searched the crowd for a long time as if he could not find the one he was looking for. Then he saw him. The old man was lowering himself to the ground. When he was down and his bulk had settled, he leaned forward, his face turned toward the basket, impatiently following its progress toward him. The boy too leaned forward, aware at last of the object of his hunger, aware that it was the same as the old man's and that nothing on earth would fill him. His hunger was so great that he could have eaten all the loaves and fishes after they were multiplied. (241)

With this new recognition and acceptance of the meaning of his hunger, the submerged pattern of his life—struggled against throughout the novel—stands out at last, for Tarwater and for the reader, in high relief. The baptismal word, uttered seemingly involuntarily over the drowning Bishop, emerges as the central defining action of Tarwater's life—a true expression of the self—and the action itself is assimilated into the larger pattern of the prophet's life as old Tarwater and those before him had lived it. The reader can see at last the present action of the novel in its fully asserted historical context.

> He felt his hunger no longer as a pain but as a tide. He felt it rising in himself through time and darkness, rising through the centuries, and he knew that it rose in a line of men whose lives were chosen to sustain it, who would wander in the world, strangers from that violent country where the silence is never broken except to shout the truth. He felt it building from the blood of Abel to his own, rising and engulfing him. (242)

And, in a last vision, the revelation Tarwater had hoped would be his, the particular sign he had waited for, breathlessly but in frustration—that too is vouchsafed him.

> He whirled toward the treeline. There, rising and spreading in the night, a red-gold tree of fire ascended as if it would consume the darkness in one tremendous burst of flame. The boy's breath went out to meet it. He knew that this was the fire that had encircled Daniel, that had raised Elijah from the earth, that had spoken to Moses and would in the instant speak to him. (242)

Throwing himself on the grave he had refused to dig, he hears the command, which seems to come from beneath the earth—"GO WARN THE CHILDREN OF GOD OF THE TERRIBLE SPEED OF MERCY. The words were as silent as seeds opening one at a time in his blood." (242) The image of the seed, dropped in the boy's blood by old Tarwater, has run throughout the book, and is rooted of course in the New Testament ("But he that received seed into the good ground is he that heareth the word, and understandeth it; which also beareth fruit, and bringeth forth, some an hundredfold, some sixty, some thirty." Matt. 13:23). But O'Connor raises the image from its merely illustrative level in a parable and endows it with a self-generating force of its own: the word-seeds, "silent, hidden in his blood stream, were moving secretly toward some goal of their own." (61) Thus independent of Tarwater's conscious will, old Mason's word has been germinating within the young prophet, has issued in the involuntary baptism of Bishop, and, at last, flourishes in this final fierce imperative to the boy to leave the sanctity of Powderhead and warn the city of "THE TERRIBLE SPEED OF MERCY."

The title of the book and the scriptural passage upon which it is based (Matt. 11:12) have been variously interpreted, but everything O'Connor wrote suggests her reverence for energy, and it must be in this sense that "the violent bear it away"—in defiance of such counsels of moderation as Rayber's ("'You want to avoid extremes. They are for violent people'" [145]), and in affirmation of the potency of the Tarwaters.

The conclusion of *The Violent Bear It Away* is charged with intensity: both space and time seem lifted above the familiar, set apart from the everyday, and imbued with a spiritual presence. In this sense, the locale of Powderhead (the name suggests its potential as a source of energy) comes at the end to be recognized by Tarwater for what it had been all along to old Tarwater: a first world, an Edenic wilderness far from the main-traveled roads of civilization. While Powderhead is "redeemed" as a place, so is the time redeemed in which Tarwater's vision occurs. For, as in *Wise Blood*, there are two cycles of time in the novel: regular, earthly time—the time of the city; and this redeemed time outside the diurnal round—the moment of prophetic insight. (And, for O'Connor, this is not merely a subjective difference: old Tarwater, in his youth, had vainly called for the sun to burst, only to witness the usual earthly cycle of rising and setting, and of seasonal change [see p. 5]. You can't will a miracle.) Thus, in adopting old Tarwater's threadbare mantle (and the robes of many a prophet before the two), the boy repeats a pattern of prophetic calling that lends a momentous context to the conclusion.

One source of the great power in Flannery O'Connor's writing lies in just this ability to render an almost mythic consciousness of human life. And what Thomas Mann says of the "mythically oriented artist" seems applicable to her as well. "What is gained is an insight into the higher truth depicted in the actual; a smiling knowledge of the eternal, the ever-being and authentic; a knowledge of the schema in which and according to which the supposed individual lives, unaware, in his naïve belief in himself as unique in space and time, of the extent to which his life is but formula and repetition and his path marked out for him by those who trod it before him."[8] But of course what happens in The Violent Bear It Away is precisely Tarwater's arrival at an awareness of his mythical role, so that the work itself is more properly of that kind in which the mythical point of view becomes, as Mann says, "subjective."[9]

In fact, one can locate the turning point of awareness in the change of narrative tone in the novel, a change parallel to that which occurs in Wise Blood. While the unknowing Tarwater is acting out his "naïve" part in the pattern, the gaze of the artist, as Mann says, is "ironic and superior . . . for the mythical knowledge resides in the gazer and not in that at which he gazes."[10] Accordingly, the style of the work until the conclusion reflects the author's ironically detached attitude. But with the conversion (in the last chapter), when the mythic knowledge turns in on Tarwater himself, irony disappears and is replaced by a tone of sympathetic awe and mystery.

One is struck, however, with this sharp difference between the portrayals of old Tarwater and young Tarwater: the former is given an air of farce (see, for example, virtually the whole first chapter: Mason's account of defending Powderhead against the rationalist invaders [6–9], his instructions regarding his burial [13–16], his efforts to baptize Bishop [31–35]); while the latter, when he accedes to his divine mission, is clothed in an atmosphere which is, though rude and rustic, almost epical. One reason for this difference in decorum and attitude may be that old Tarwater's commissioned vocation is already a part of his character (this would illustrate, by the way, Mann's observation that an air of farce, of theatrical performance, is appropriate to a character who is subjectively conscious of his role in an epic), whereas with young Tarwater, that vocation is merely at hand; and so to emphasize the awe and seriousness of this moment of celebration, of feast (compare Tarwater's vision of the throng feeding on the bread and fish), O'Connor abandons the comic tone of the festival farce and brings out instead, with great effect, the solemnity of the festival epic.[11]

The Problem of Narrative Control

Some early readers of The Violent Bear It Away, mistaking O'Connor's irony, thought it anti-Catholic; others were affronted by what they saw as an affirmation of a God of wrath. Still others, of a more literal bent perhaps, saw it as cranky, provincial, lacking in universality. More recently, critics have tended to accept the characters on face value, exploring, instead, the themes and imagery of the work. Yet it seems to me that at the heart of the book there remains a problem that might be phrased tentatively as how convincing it all is or, rather, how it goes about being convincing. O'Connor touched on the problem in a response she made once to a friend's objection that old Mason Tarwater was theologically eccentric. She argued that old Tarwater was "a prophet, not a church-member. As a prophet he has to be a natural Catholic. Hawthorne said he didn't write novels, he wrote romances; I am one of his descendants." And her premise, in invoking the romance tradition, was that there are different kinds of "realism." "The lack of realism would be crucial if this were a realistic novel or if the novel demanded the kind of realism you demand. I don't believe it does."[12] But here is the crux of the matter: What "kind of realism" does the novel demand?

The question, for *The Violent Bear It Away*, is somewhat different from what it is for *Wise Blood*. The universe of O'Connor's second novel is a less distorted, more plausible world; hence it becomes relevant to judge the plausibility of Tarwater's motivation. The choice for the hero is approximately the same as in *Wise Blood*—to believe or not to believe—but it seems to have been precisely O'Connor's intention to illuminate and dramatize the making of Tarwater's choice in a way not attempted for Hazel Motes. What is required therefore in *The Violent Bear It Away* is a psychological realism: one must ask how convincingly Tarwater's choice is imagined and how convincingly the resolution of his conflict is worked out.

O'Connor's conception of Tarwater's choice apparently required that his chief antagonists tread a fine line between a narrowly allegorical and a more broadly representative quality—as can be seen from her reply once to an interviewer's question about the "message" of the book.

As for its being too allegorical and all the rest, I can't agree. I wanted to get across the fact that the great Uncle (Old Tarwater) is the Christian—a sort of crypto-Catholic—and that the schoolteacher (Rayber) is the typical modern man. The boy (young Tarwater) has to choose which one, which way, he wants to follow. It's a matter of vocation.[13]

If her response seems equivocating, it is indicative of the difficulties
O'Connor risks in her ironic characterizations: old Tarwater must
not be *too* *obviously* a "crypto-Catholic"; Rayber must not be *too*
obviously a "typical modern man" (with the full opprobrium that
phrase carries for O'Connor); rather, their negative and attractive
qualities must be somehow balanced—and yet ultimately discernible
—so that the choice for Tarwater will be not only a dramatically
convincing one but, finally, one whose validity can be judged accu-
rately by the reader.

I do not think, myself, that the dramatization of old Tarwater is
at all a problem; though literally dead from the first sentence in the
book, the aged prophet is more convincingly alive than any other
character. His presence is felt throughout the narrative—in the
scenes of his earlier days, and in the dialogues between Rayber and
Tarwater; it is felt in the young boy's mind at the fountain where
Bishop is almost baptized, and whenever Tarwater looks into Bishop's
eyes; and of course it is felt in the commanding voice that seems to
issue from the grave on the last page.

Of the alternative pull in Tarwater's consciousness, however, one
must say that the dramatization is less than successful: Rayber is, I
think, a victim of O'Connor's too palpable intentions. The problem
with his characterization would seem to be O'Connor's unwillingness
merely to *show* the reader Rayber's inadequacies: she insists on *tell-*
ing us them as well. And the effect of this is to weight heavily, at
times, the irony of the narrative. For if the reader is asked to regard
the conflict within Tarwater as a real one, then it must be dramatized as such. The presentation of Tarwater's own attitude toward
Rayber is successful enough: from the boy's subjective viewpoint, it
is consistent that he should find the schoolteacher at times ridiculous.
But O'Connor goes further, and makes Rayber's absurdity too patent
a premise of her authorial viewpoint; and this becomes evident in
the uncertainties of tone that slip into passages dealing with the character, in the too obvious sarcasm Rayber is subjected to.

Thus, for example, when Rayber initially appears at the door to
greet Tarwater, he is without his hearing aid and so cannot hear the
boy; in capital letters, we imagine the message: Rayber is deaf to
Tarwater. Similarly, Rayber's scientific-rationalist viewpoint is too
deliberately undermined by the repeated descriptions of his machinelike qualities (the hotel clerk thinks that "his eyes had a peculiar

look—like something human trapped in a switchbox" [154]). Too pointedly the author's mockery says of him, a ridiculous fool. "[The clerk] observed as his feet passed the level of her head that he had on one brown sock and one grey" (154); chasing Tarwater through the streets of the city, barefoot, "he walked over something sticky on the sidewalk and shifted hurriedly to the other side, cursing under his breath." (120) Small boys shout at him in his disarray, "'Hi yo Silverwear, Tonto's lost his underwear!'" (121) He pauses before a bakery window where Tarwater had all too clearly eyed a loaf of bread (read: bread of life); and the psychologist thinks, with extravagant obtuseness, "If he had eaten his dinner, he wouldn't be hungry." (122) When Rayber lectures Tarwater on the meaninglessness of baptism, we are told, unnecessarily, "His words had a disconnected sound." (195) The cumulative effect of this simplistically satirical characterization is that our very last view of the man (when his feelings are supposedly in tragic conflict) seems oddly jarring—prepared for but not quite convincing.

Curiously enough, O'Connor seems to have been as obsessed with the sham intellectual as she was by the prophet. One of her earliest stories, "The Barber" (1947), for example, is concerned with a similar figure, also called Rayber (the name seems destined for derision by O'Connor), who is merely the first in a series of such characters (Asbury in "The Enduring Chill," Thomas in "The Comforts of Home," Julian in "Everything That Rises Must Converge," and others). What distinguishes the Rayber type is a desperate liberal zeal, a predictably thwarted sexual or married life, and an impulse toward self-martyrdom. The nemesis of supernatural values also suffers from an inability to act effectively, in whatever role. Yet O'Connor seems to have felt a peculiar ambivalence toward the character—evidenced by her recurrent desire to make him at once the object of ironic satire and the subject of a tragic experience. Particularly with the Rayber who is Tarwater's antagonist, the satire tends to obscure the tragedy.

Old Mason Tarwater, the other pole in Tarwater's consciousness, is also treated satirically, but with a difference. The prophet may be a fool of God, but he is no fool. For example, in the following exchange, the old man's religious preparedness (every moment his last) is lightly mocked, along with the scantiness of his wardrobe, but it is a mockery that laughs along with, rather than at, its object; Old Tarwater and the boy discuss the former's sojourn with Rayber.

> "I told him, I said, 'I may live two months or two days.' And I had on my clothes that I bought to be buried in—all new."
> "Ain't it that same suit you got on now?" the boy asked indignantly, pointing to the threadbare knee. "Ain't it that one you got on yourself right now?"
> "I may live two months or two days, I said to him," his uncle said.
> Or ten years or twenty, Tarwater thought. (71)

In contrast, the kind of insight communicated by the following passage is pointedly at Rayber's expense, and reveals him as an unknowing parody of the old man.

> "God boy," he said, "you need help. You need to be saved right here now from the old man and everything he stands for. And I'm the one who can save you." With his hat turned down all around he looked like a fanatical country preacher. (174)

What the passage further points to, however, is the narrowness of Tarwater's alternatives as conceived by O'Connor: the boy's choice is less one between two men, or two possible ways of life, than one between two preachers—a "false" and a "true."

From Rayber's point of view, Tarwater's choice is between God and man; " 'The great dignity of man,' " he says, in a passage quoted earlier, " 'is his ability to say: I am born once and no more. . . . It's enough to be a man.' " (172) Thus Rayber implicitly subverts the entire dualistic theology of Tarwater's old world (God or the devil) only to substitute another equally uncompromising dualism. But O'Connor is careful to undercut this alternative by having the stranger-devil, earlier in the book, suggest an almost identical choice.

> You can do one thing or you can do the opposite [the stranger said].
> Jesus or the devil, the boy said.
> No no no, the stranger said, there ain't no such thing as a devil. I can tell you that from my own self-experience. I know that for a fact. It ain't Jesus or the devil. It's Jesus or you. (39)

With obvious irony, the passage implies that such a choice is, in fact, a choice between Jesus and the devil. The net effect of this "guilt

by association" is that Rayber's point of view—which is an amalgam
of scientism, existentialism, and humanism—becomes tantamount to
the devil's point of view, and Rayber seems at times almost a devil
in disguise.

Thus frequently the reader, if not Tarwater, is cajoled by the
unsubtle irony into being made (all unwillingly) a party to the conflict. What should be the implicit conclusion of the drama is built
into the narrative viewpoint, tending therefore to cut short, at certain points, the reader's full experience of Tarwater's inner strife. But
if the reader cannot take Rayber very seriously, Tarwater at least
can, and the latter's ambivalence toward him is closer to what ours
ought to be. The novel may be flawed in this regard, but not fatally
so, and the sympathetic reader can still perhaps regard Tarwater's
engagement with Rayber as a serious one.

A second judgment we must make is harder: Is the resolution of
Tarwater's conflict plausible? It may seem at first that this question
is related to the question of whether Tarwater (to raise a philosophical ghost) has free will—that the plausible resolution would perforce
assume free will. I do not think this is the case, however. O'Connor's
own comment on the point seems to beg the question, but in fact
implies the answer. "Tarwater is certainly free and meant to be; if
he appears to have a compulsion to be a prophet, I can only insist
that in this compulsion there is the mystery of God's will for him,
and that it is not a compulsion in the clinical sense."[14] As far as I
can see, "the mystery of God's will for him" implies that his will is
not completely his own. Of course no fictional character truly has
free will, but Tarwater, in addition, does not seem to have free will:
the world of the novel is fraught with forces of good and evil, forces
Tarwater is sensitive to.

Does it really matter, though? What does matter, I think, is that
the forces do not seem to be imposed from without. Rather, they
seem real, subjectively, to Tarwater, and hence the psychology of
his conversion remains plausible. Of course the nature of the world
Tarwater inhabits (both physically and psychically) is determined
by O'Connor's own beliefs about the world, but, given those beliefs,
her image of that world is a convincing one. We do not, for example,
have to believe in the devil in order to "believe" in the devil who
violates Tarwater. Whoever it was that did it, it was a devilish thing

to do. Moreover, we know that morally there is a logic to the rape—not, certainly, because Tarwater deserves it but because it is axiomatic that, one way or another, innocence is destroyed. And we can understand how it might prepare the boy for the confirming vision that comes to him soon after.

If Tarwater seems, at the end, to yield to his "fate" like an inverted Huck Finn—"All right, I'll go to Heaven"—what finally matters is that those passages describing the force of the heavenly pull—in his dreams, perceptions, visions—are among the strongest, most "plausible" in the book. They derive their unquestionable authority from a prose that is modulated to the precise emotional key of the experience—a prose that communicates emotion through the vivid details of physical sensation. Here, for example, is Tarwater's arrival at the Powderhead clearing for the last time.

> Instantly at the thought of food, he stopped and his muscles contracted with nausea. He blanched with the shock of a terrible premonition. He stood there and felt a crater opening inside him, and stretching out before him, surrounding him, he saw the clear grey spaces of that country where he had vowed never to set foot. (239)

Another example might be the devil's jeering denial of the spiritual root of Tarwater's hunger, which ends by evoking that hunger even more tangibly for the reader. "And as for that strangeness in your gut, that comes from you, not the Lord. When you were a child you had worms. As likely as not you have them again." (161) Or, another example, the girl-prophet Lucette's singing message of Christ's love and redemption, his meanness and exaltation, which is heard by an entranced Tarwater and an anguished Rayber, and which captures for the reader the full intensity of the belief that is at the core of the book.

> "The world said, 'How long, Lord, do we have to wait for this?' And the Lord said, 'My Word is coming, my Word is coming from the house of David, the king.'" . . .
> She began again in a dirge-like tone. "Jesus came on cold straw, Jesus was warmed by the breath of an ox. 'Who is this?' the world said, 'who is this blue-cold child and this woman, plain as the winter? Is this the Word of God, this blue-cold child? Is this His will, this plain winter-woman?'
> "Listen you people!" she cried, "the world knew in its heart, the

same as you know in your hearts and I know in my heart. The world
said, 'Love cuts like the cold wind and the will of God is plain as the
winter. Where is the summer will of God? Where are the green sea-
sons of God's will? Where is the spring and summer of God's
will?' . . .

"If you don't know Him now, you won't know Him then. Listen to me, world, listen to this warning. The Holy Word is in my
mouth!" (131–33)

One can see something of the range of O'Connor's rhetoric in these
examples, a rhetoric that functions not only in its specific dramatic
context—as an integral part of the plot—but that sustains throughout the book an engrossing tension.

The aesthetic principle which *The Violent Bear It Away* fulfills
is Thomas Aquinas's, and O'Connor was fond, herself, of citing it:
art is reason in making (*recta recto factibilium*). The novel was
indeed long in the making and, if it is not entirely successful, it may
be because there was in fact too much reason in making it. It has a
fine, farcical beginning and an awesome ending; the middle passage,
where Rayber figures, may be the hard one.

4

THE SHORT STORIES

In turning from the novels to the shorter fiction, we might note a comparison O'Connor herself made between the two forms.

> The novel is a more diffused form and more suited to those who like to linger along the way; it also requires a more massive energy. For those of us who want to get the agony over in a hurry, the novel is a burden and a pain. But no matter which fictional form you are using, you are writing a story, and in a story something has to happen.[1]

It is interesting that the distinction she draws between the forms seems to be one of pacing and quantity, rather than of quality and design. This may account in part for the thinness in texture that we find in her novels, when compared with those of many other writers. While in general the best short-story writers strive for a single effect and tell a single tale, one might say that the best novelists seem to tell many stories, or a story with many parts. It is not so much, for them, a question of lingering along the way as of reaching the destination by a multiplicity of ways.

I do not mean to underestimate the considerable achievement of *Wise Blood* and *The Violent Bear It Away* when I say that they seem like long short stories. The essential principle of composition in them is the same as in the shorter works: in fiction, O'Connor observed, "Detail has to be controlled by some overall purpose, and every detail has to be put to work for you. Art is selective. What is there is essential and creates movement."[2] The results of such an aesthetic, then, are novels that are thin in nonessential details—background, setting, minor characters, subplots—and richly dense in meaningful detail. But this same aesthetic, when applied to the writing of stories, produces an effect wholly consonant with the natural requirements of the form: brevity demands an economy of characters; singleness of effect demands a simplicity of plot and action; and intensity of meaning demands highly charged detail. So that one must say that for O'Connor, as for Hawthorne, the shorter forms were the more congenial.

While the texture of Flannery O'Connor's fiction is fairly consistent, in none of her shorter works is the major subject of the two novels treated. For a study of vocation, by its very nature, requires a fuller exposition of motivation, inner conflict, and resolution than can be managed in a short work. So that, following the distinction made above in Chapter 2, our focus shifts now from the prophet freak who is actively engaged in a struggle to define himself spiritually to the more normal character—passive and complacent before the universe—upon whom a "definition" of self in relation to the mysterious nature of reality is suddenly intruded.

And yet the intruding agents in these tales themselves often resemble the heroes of the longer fiction—except that they are failed prophets, as I have called them earlier. These include The Misfit ("A Good Man Is Hard to Find"), Tom Shiftlet ("The Life You Save May Be Your Own"), Rufus Johnson ("The Lame Shall Enter First"); and we might stretch the term to encompass as well the Powell boy ("A Circle in the Fire"), the Wellesley College girl ("Revelation"), even perhaps Sarah Ham ("The Comforts of Home"). Allowing for admitted differences between them, each is significantly different from the figure he intrudes upon by virtue of a slightly mad, slightly diabolic element in his character. Each is more or less thoughtful and troubled, but capable of some outrageous, evil action which upsets the usual balance of the world.

Not all of the intruding figures fit this description, however. In fact, not all of the intruding figures are even "human." For this same function is served by images as diverse as the descending bird Asbury imagines in a water stain on his ceiling ("The Enduring Chill"), the bull in "Greenleaf," the plaster statue in "The Artificial Nigger," and the image of Christ tattooed on Parker's back.

Another distinction to be drawn between the novels and the short fiction is that where the former attain their depth of vision within an explicitly theological framework, the stories shape their ends in ways that are theological only in the broadest sense: God may, to be sure, reveal himself in diverse shapes at times, but more often he is known by his absence, or by implication only—or as some force one senses behind the scenery and drama of human life. And even in stories where an overtly theological language is used, the effect is of an intru-sion of mystery into the lives of these passive, unsuspecting charac-ters—a mystery that cannot be narrowly or dogmatically defined but that comes to a character, often at the moment of his death or suf-fering, as an insight into the pain and misery of life, and into an order of reality that has been hidden from him. And where the novels expand upon the moment of grace that befalls their heroes, in some measure detailing the effects of conversion and the life of vocation, the tales stop short at the moment of perception itself. Effects are achieved with greater suddenness and economy, and with a charac-teristically stunning conclusion; accordingly, irony is more consis-tently used to heighten the meaning of an action, an irony that has often been prepared for throughout the story.

Some moment there is, then, in each of the stories, that illumi-nates a relationship, resolves a conflict, or induces a self-recognition in so momentous and startling a manner that the reader feels that, if not God himself, at least some revelation is at hand. From a Chris-tian viewpoint, the tales mirror a "balanced" picture of the world, where "grace, in the theological sense," as O'Connor wrote, "is not lacking."[3] Yet one hardly needs to point out that in the context of modern literature this "balanced" picture, as she called it, is some-thing of an anomaly. For what we get if we imagine a world devoid of grace—where redemption is not at hand, where no salvation is possible, where a set of characters endure misery without passion, and where there is no meaningful intrusion upon their lives—is Gogo and Didi, waiting for Godot. Beckett's world is, one might say, precisely antithetical to O'Connor's; and if one were to speak of works representative of "our age," one would surely have to choose the metaphysics of Beckett over the theology of O'Connor. O'Connor of course recognized as much, and may even have had Beckett in mind, when she said:

> There is another type of modern man who recognizes a divine being not himself, but who does not believe that this being can be known anagogically or defined dogmatically or received sacramentally. . . . Man wanders about, caught in a maze of guilt he can't identify, trying to reach a God he can't approach, a God powerless to approach him.[4]

In fact, the simplest way to define Flannery O'Connor might be to say she is the "opposite" of Samuel Beckett. And one might adduce the following passage from the end of "The Artificial Nigger"

> Mr. Head stood very still and felt the action of mercy touch him again but this time he knew that there were no words in the world that could name it. . . . He realized that he was forgiven for sins from the beginning of time, when he had conceived in his own heart the sin of Adam, until the present, when he had denied poor Nelson. He saw that no sin was too monstrous for him to claim as his own, and since God loved in proportion as He forgave, he felt ready at that instant to enter Paradise.

and then place it alongside the slave Lucky's oration in *Waiting for Godot*

> [Lucky says] that man in Essy that man in short that man in brief in spite of the strides of alimentation and defecation wastes and pines wastes and pines and concurrently simultaneously what is more for reasons unknown in spite of the strides of physical culture the practice of sports such as tennis football running cycling swimming flying floating riding gliding conating camogie skating tennis of all kinds dying flying sports of all sorts autumn summer winter winter tennis of all kinds hockey of all sorts . . . in a word for reasons unknown in Feckham Peckham Fulham Clapham namely concurrently simultaneously what is more for reasons unknown but time will tell fades away.[5]

In short, says Lucky, "man . . . fades away." In spite of the "labors lost of Steinweg and Peterman"—in spite of the way of the Rock-Church and of the man called Peter.

The dramatic image, then, that is at the core of O'Connor's short fiction insists that it is possible for Godot to come—that he does, indeed, come, and often in a violent, unexpected form. In this chapter I shall discuss some of the variations within that basic image; certain character types may recur, but the dramatic situation in no two stories is exactly alike, and the effects range from ironic tragedy to ironic comedy. "There may never be anything new to say," O'Connor wrote, "but there is always a new way to say it, and since, in art, the way of saying a thing becomes a part of what is said, every work of art is unique and requires fresh attention."[6] Here I have not had room to give "fresh attention," however, to every work, and so will restrict myself to the half dozen I feel are her most interesting.

A Good Man Is Hard to Find

The epigraph to the collection A Good Man Is Hard to Find reads: "The Dragon is by the side of the road, watching those who pass. Beware lest he devour you. We go to the father of souls, but it is necessary to pass by the dragon" (St. Cyril of Jerusalem).[7] It is especially fitting for the title story itself, which begins by seeming, innocently enough, like a happy journey from Atlanta to Florida; before it is over, however, a dragon has not only materialized but has quite devoured the entire traveling Bailey family. Yet Grandmother Bailey, at least, seems to have gone on to "the father of souls." Her deliverer is an escaped convict who calls himself The Misfit.[8]

The various members of the Bailey family are nicely individualized, as to both physical and moral attributes: Bailey, the pater familias, is an irritable, harassed, and stubborn man, who doesn't "like to arrive at a motel with a cat."[9] His wife's face is "as broad and innocent as a cabbage" (9), and she ties around her head a green kerchief with "two points on the top like rabbit's ears." (9) The couple's obnoxious children read comic books, fight among themselves, and are noticeably rude to strangers. But the story is focused on the grandmother, who—foolish, xenophobic, racially condescending, and self-righteously banal—is set off from the others in still more telling ways. Chiefly, she is the only one of the family who, in some way, expresses care: her personality moves outward toward others, toward the landscape, even toward her cat (significantly named Pitty Sing), whom she will not leave at home for fear he might accidentally turn on the gas and asphyxiate himself. And it is precisely this outward expression of care that will trigger The Misfit's cold rage.

One of the oblique signs of her grace, if we may prematurely call it such, is her graciousness, which O'Connor describes with her characteristically macabre humor: "Her collars and cuffs where white organdy trimmed with lace and at her neckline she had pinned a purple spray of cloth violets containing a sachet. In case of an accident, anyone seeing her dead on the highway would know at once that she was a lady." (11) And she is somewhat prescient in this regard, for if she is not precisely dressed to kill, this remnant of Southern gentility is, as it turns out, dressed to be killed.

The plot device which sets in motion the confrontation with the intruding Misfit, is the travelers' diversion from the main road in search of a nice old mansion that the grandmother, remembering from the days of her youth, thinks is nearby. And there is a rightness about this search for the house that is not at first apparent. Significantly, the grandmother has been dozing off, and it is upon awakening, as if the splendid house had taken shape in her dreams, that she recalls it. An old plantation house, an idyllic memory of antebellum Southern life in all its imagined innocence and order, the image stands in sharp contrast to the depicted shabbiness of present-day life. And the old lady, in a successful effort to arouse the interest of the party, craftily embellishes her description by adding a secret panel, where the family silver was said to be hidden before Sherman's march.

What is barely concealed beneath the literal description of the mansion is its symbolic equivalence to a heavenly mansion; and the addition of the secret panel suggests its mysterious containment of the treasures of the past. It is home in the broadest sense—the place one starts out from, the place to which one returns. This favorite image of O'Connor's has already been noted in the homelier versions of Hazel Motes's Eastrod shack and the Powderhead cabin of the Tarwaters; and we have noted too the association of returning home with the image of the coffin (see "Judgement Day"); hence it is probably more than a merely accidental detail that Grandmother Bailey awakens from her nap at "Toombsboro" (the name of a real and desolate little town near Milledgeville, Georgia, by the way) to remember the mansion. What is suggested in these associations is a return, through death, to an earlier state of innocence and purity, to a place far off the main road, away from the sterility of the city, where one was a child, and to which one can return again only as a child. It may seem a small detail in a brutal image, but the woman's dying posture suggests her saving innocence: the killers look down "at the grandmother who half sat and half lay in a puddle of blood with her legs crossed under her like a child's and her face smiling up at the cloudless sky." (29)

The agent of her death is of course The Misfit. No vulgar criminal, The Misfit, as his daddy said of him, is " 'a different breed of dog' " (24) from his brothers and sisters; " ' "it's some that can live their whole life out without asking about it and it's others has to know why it is, and this boy is one of the latters." ' " (24) Along with his metaphysical obsession (though the phrase sounds incongruous when applied to so homespun a character), The Misfit evinces a distinguishing gentility of manner, which the old lady, with her desperate equation of manners and morals, mistakes for goodness.

As The Misfit's co-disaffiliates (they, however, are just "common") proceed to murder the Bailey family, the lingering grandmother engages the escaped convict in a revealing dialogue. And in The Misfit's accented account of his past, O'Connor mixes just the right elements of classic American drifter and morbid sophisticate to lend credibility and authority to an essentially enigmatic figure. " 'I was a gospel singer for a while. . . . Been in the arm service . . . been twict married, been an undertaker, been with the railroads, plowed Mother Earth, been in a tornado, seen a man burnt alive oncet. . . . I even seen a woman flogged.' " (25) At the root of The Misfit's meanness, however, are not these experiences but a cosmic sense of injustice—of a universe out of kilter: " 'I call myself The Misfit . . . because I can't make what all I done wrong fit what all I gone through in punishment [he has escaped from a penitentiary].' " (28) And the paragon of all who are wronged is, for The Misfit, Jesus. And yet, what complicates his problem vastly is precisely the grander aspects of Jesus: " '[Jesus] thown everything off balance. If He did what He said [raise the dead], then it's nothing for you to do but thow away everything and follow Him, and if He didn't, then it's nothing for you to do but enjoy the few minutes you got left the best way you can—by killing somebody or burning down his house or doing some other meanness to him. No pleasure but meanness,' he said and his voice had become almost a snarl." (28)

It is a violent logic, and it draws so sharp a line between the total commitment of faith and the total commitment of disbelief that there is no middle course. Moreover, it is the same logic that applied to Hazel Motes in his career and that we have seen exemplified in what would be the later conflict between the principles of old Tarwater and those of the devil. The middle way—the way of humanism (for example, Rayber)—is, for O'Connor, the way of self-deception and self-destruction. Unless we understand the argument, we are likely to misread The Misfit as an equally perverse logician and theologian. Such is not the case, however, for if he is diabolically misguided in his inexorable commitment to his logic, the logic of his commitment is, for O'Connor, itself inexorable.

Put another way, what The Misfit lacks (and what Hazel and Tarwater, for example, are given) is a vision of grace: and, nostalgically, he yearns for just that; but the language in which he phrases his desire points to his implicit denial of the ongoing action of mercy, and, instead, fixes the redemptive act (Jesus' raising of the dead) in a single historical moment of time. " 'It ain't right I wasn't there because if I had of been there I would of known. Listen lady,' he said in a high voice, 'if I had of been there I would of known and I wouldn't be like I am now.' " (29) It is at this point, the moment of his confessed privation from grace, that the grandmother is given her moment of grace. "She saw the man's face twisted close to her own as if he were going to cry and she murmured, 'Why you're one of my babies. You're one of my own children!' " (29)

Though he has taken her dead son Bailey's shirt, The Misfit is unwilling to acquiesce in the proffered adoption. In her last gesture of gracious care toward the world, the old lady reaches out to touch him on the shoulder. "The Misfit sprang back as if a snake had bitten him and shot her three times through the chest." (29) For the old lady's gesture, like Christ's, throws everything off balance, and it is perceived by The Misfit, ironically, as the Snake's temptation. His own act, then, of shooting the woman, is conceived by him, one imagines, as a reestablishment of the particular order of his own world. That, perhaps, is the meaning of his deadpan reply to his henchman Bobby Lee's question following the shooting, and it must strike the reader as at once logically inescapable and yet, with the extravagance of the iterative image, grimly humorous.

> "She was a talker, wasn't she?" Bobby Lee said, sliding down the ditch with a yodel.
> "She would of been a good woman," The Misfit said, "if it had been somebody there to shoot her every minute of her life."
> "Some fun!" Bobby Lee said.
> "Shut up, Bobby Lee," The Misfit said. "It's no real pleasure in life." (29)

But there is perhaps the seed of a new dissatisfaction in those last words of his, which deny what he had earlier affirmed ("No pleasure but meanness" [28]). O'Connor's own comment on the conclusion carries forward the suggestion. "I don't want to equate the Misfit with the devil. I prefer to think that, however unlikely this may seem, the old lady's gesture, like the mustard-seed, will grow to be a great crow-filled tree in the Misfit's heart, and will be enough of a pain to him there to turn him into the prophet he was meant to become. But that's another story."[10]

It is difficult to define the effect of a story like "A Good Man Is Hard to Find." We have been moved by an invisible narrative hand, from a gently satirical fiction with interesting shades of local color to a brutal confrontation that, while it ends with a massacre of innocents, yet does not permit us to sentimentalize their deaths (indeed the grandmother's death strangely elevates her)—but rather draws our attention to the figure of the killer, who is himself no vicious creation, but a comic character. And one cannot separate the effect of such a story from its style, so that, as Elizabeth Hardwick aptly put it, "You'll have to call *A Good Man Is Hard to Find* a 'funny' story even though six people are killed in it."[11] For the brutality and cruelty of The Misfit are carefully kept under control by the detachment of the narrative and the abstract logic of the drama. And yet, there is no denying "the puddle of blood" the old lady is left lying in.[12]

We might compare the effect of "A Good Man Is Hard to Find" with that of another tale written in 1953, "The Life You Save May Be Your Own." For the latter story reveals clearly how O'Connor could shift narrative gears while following basically the same road.

Both stories show a family subjected to the intrusion of a similarly polite but odd young man who works some harm upon them. Unlike The Misfit, however, Tom T. Shiftlet is no murderer. And where the grandmother in "A Good Man Is Hard to Find" is, presumably, delivered by violence unto her salvation, in "The Life You Save May Be Your Own," the passive victim is an idiot girl who is immune, by her innocence, to any real harm. What chiefly distinguishes the two stories, however, is the difference in focus and the difference in tone. For the intruder in the latter story is on the scene from the beginning—coming up the road in the first sentence. And throughout, O'Connor directs a sharply comic, sharply ironic eye on Shiftlet, so that he never assumes the dimension of The Misfit with his cosmic dilemma. He does, to be sure, resemble that character, but as Tom Sawyer resembles Huck Finn or as Laertes resembles Hamlet: where The Misfit agonizes over Jesus, Shiftlet extends his arms (one a stump) before the sun to form "a crooked cross"[13]; where The Misfit was, among other things, an undertaker, Shiftlet was an "assistant in an undertaking parlor" (57); and so forth.

Moreover, there is no sudden change in the atmosphere of "The Life You Save May Be Your Own," as there is in "A Good Man Is Hard to Find": no suspenseful preparation for the intrusion, and little feeling of mystery at the story's end—when Shiftlet, who has arrived by foot, leaves the idiot girl (whom he has reluctantly married) in a diner and departs by car. What we have, instead, is a conclusion that points with comic precision and satiric ridicule at the scapegrace protagonist, who, having left that poor "'angel of Gawd'" (66) dumbly behind, is overcome by disgust at "the rottenness of the world"! "'Oh Lord!' he prayed. 'Break forth and wash the slime from this earth!'" (67) The Lord's jeeringly reproachful answer, by way of O'Connor, is in the form of "a cloud . . . shaped like a turnip" (67) which descends over the sun, and another cloud which crouches behind his speeding car. "The turnip continued slowly to descend. After a few minutes there was a guffawing peal of thunder from behind and fantastic raindrops, like tin-can tops, crashed over the rear of Mr. Shiftlet's car." (68) (O'Connor was fond of sardonically noting, by the way, that when this story was adapted for television, the ending was slightly altered: Shiftlet has a change of heart and goes back for his idiot bride. Needless to say, the author had not been consulted.)

The imagination that could behold a Shiftlet with comic equanimity, and without wavering into either a sentimental conclusion or a bitterly ironic one, is the same that could more fully and more complexly engage our sensibilities in "A Good Man Is Hard to Find" without merely shocking us or merely drawing tears.

Good Country People

In "Good Country People," a pattern similar to the one behind the two stories just considered is discernible, though serving now what one might call an ironic moral fable. In all three tales, a stranger, deceptively polite and unexpectedly malignant, intrudes upon the domestic tranquility of a family. And where the murderous Misfit comes away with Bailey's shirt, and Tom T. Shiftlet with a resurrected automobile, Manley Pointer, the Bible salesman of "Good Country People," leaves the story with Hulga Hopewell's wooden leg. In the two earlier stories, ironic judgment is directed chiefly against the intruding figures; but in this later one, the passive victim of the intrusion is more emphatically exposed by the author's irony —as are, in fact, all the characters in the story: Hulga's blindness and limitation may be the focus of our attention, but we are also given to see the deceptive Bible salesman through the eyes of the girl's mother, Mrs. Hopewell, and through those of her aide-de-camp, Mrs. Freeman; with a fine narrative control, O'Connor discovers in each a purblind viewpoint.

The setting of the story is a rural Southern farm, not unlike the farm where O'Connor herself lived and wrote, and it will recur in over half of her stories as a disarmingly routine environment, yet one strangely capable of serving as an arena for disarmingly unroutine revelations. Once again O'Connor carefully lays the groundwork for the final dramatic scene—and with a meticulousness one hardly realizes until a second reading. The present action of the plot takes place on a single morning, the date of Hulga's tryst with Manley Pointer, but that climax (or anticlimax, as it turns out) is withheld until the characters involved have been fleshed out. And O'Connor uses to this end a combination of brief backward glances, witty authorial description, and, most impressively, dialogue.

> When Mrs. Hopewell said to [Mrs. Freeman] . . . "You know, you're the wheel behind the wheel," and winked, Mrs. Freeman had

said, "I know it. I've always been quick. It's some that are quicker
than others."
   "Everybody is different," Mrs. Hopewell said.
   "Yes, most people is," Mrs. Freeman said.
   "It takes all kinds to make the world."
   "I always said it did myself." (171–72)

While there is something as yet indefinably sinister about Mrs.
Freeman in the early pages of the story, and something innocuously
well intentioned about Mrs. Hopewell, both women mouth apo-
thegms with a self-styled sagacity. They are the unacknowledged
legislators of the world, these women, with a force of utterance stag-
gering in its banality. " 'Why!' " Mrs. Hopewell cries, " 'good country people are the salt of the earth! Besides, we all have different
ways of doing, it takes all kinds to make the world go 'round. That's
life!' " To which the Bible salesman replies, " 'You said a mouth-
ful.' " (179) Bounded by the prefabricated walls of the cliché, neither
Mrs. Freeman's nor Mrs. Hopewell's perception of the world pene-
trates beyond outward appearance.
   From Hulga's point of view, neither does her mother turn her gaze
inward: " 'Woman! Do you every look inside? Do you ever look
inside and see what you are *not*? God!' " (176) Yet O'Connor keeps
an equally ironic distance from Hulga too (her "God" is an expletive,
not a deity), whose knowledge of reality stops at the scientifically
knowable, and who is stridently unconcerned with the nothing that
is anything else. Mrs. Hopewell finds the following passage under-
lined in her daughter's book.

> "Science, on the other hand, has to assert its soberness and serious-
> ness afresh and declare that it is concerned solely with what-is. Noth-
> ing—how can it be for science anything but a horror and a phantasm?
> If science is right, then one thing stands firm: science wishes to know
> nothing of nothing." (176)

The effect of the passage is to underline for the reader Hulga's own
determination not only to know nothing of the Nothing that isn't
there but to know nothing of the Nothing that is. And one ramifi-
cation of this involution is that, for Hulga, nothing comes of nothing:
"she didn't like dogs or cats or birds or flowers or nature or nice
young men." (176)

Enter nice young man. For against Mrs. Freeman's and Mrs. Hope-well's knowledge of "everything" and Hulga's philosophical knowl-edge of "everything knowable," O'Connor places the Bible salesman, with his disarming affirmations of his simple "Chrustian" (178) piety. The older women remain safely outside Manley Pointer's pur-view, mere unseeing witnesses of the comings and goings of the sales-man. It is for Hulga that O'Connor designs the special intrusion of Pointer; she it is who suffers passively the recognition of her true, broken condition and the recognition as well of the Nothing that is all around her.

The scenes that follow, in which first Hulga dreams of seducing the "innocent" young salesman and is then seduced, in a fashion, by him, are among O'Connor's raciest—if that is the word to describe the thwarted sexual encounter of a thirty-year-old wooden-legged Ph.D. in philosophy and a fetishistic confidence man. Actually the scene in the hayloft—a fake Bible stuffed with whiskey and contra-ceptives, the climactic surrender of a prosthetic device—has the mak-ings of a crude, perverse joke; and, to be sure, it is that—and much more. For with her usual cool detachment, O'Connor effects a dou-ble exposure of Hulga, a self-exposure of the salesman, and a final unmasking of the sturdily omniscient farm women.

When Hulga first sorties out to meet Manley (armed with the scent of Vapex), the reader gets his first glimpse at the pious sales-man's true nature: he is nowhere to be seen at first, but then the phallic Manley Pointer stands up, "very tall, from behind a bush on the opposite embankment" (187)—smiling his villainous smile. As they walk across the meadow, conversing, the Bible salesman expresses astonishment at Hulga's daring disbelief in God, pausing every now and then to kiss her heavily. And O'Connor is careful to note the girl's controlled reaction. "Even before he released her, her mind, clear and detached and ironic anyway, was regarding him from a great distance, with amusement but with pity." (188)

But the salesman presses his suit and although the girl becomes confused (how easy this all is; who's seducing whom?), she cautiously affirms her love. In all honesty, however, Hulga feels compelled to add (with that wonderfully indefinite plural), " 'I have a number of degrees.' " (191) Having gotten one foot in the door, the salesman presses on with the single-minded determination that only a fetishist can muster, demanding next that Hulga prove her love by showing

him where her wooden leg is attached. At this, Hulga is touched to
the quick, so to speak; she begins to lose her footing—presently her
very foot. With swift and shrewd instinct, Pointer declares: "'it's
what makes you different. You ain't like anybody else.'" (192) And
she yields.

That is O'Connor's first exposure of Hulga, and it hinges on two
ideas: first, that Hulga has let her wooden leg deform her whole character; and, second, that she believes that in surrendering the leg to
Manley she will achieve the happiness that she only now admits
has not been hers.

> No one ever touched [the leg] but her. She took care of it as someone
> else would his soul, in private and almost with her own eyes turned
> away. . . .
>   When after a minute, she said in a hoarse high voice, "All right,"
> it was like surrendering to him completely. It was like losing her own
> life and finding it again, miraculously, in his. (192)

In surrendering the leg to Manley, Hulga surrenders what is at once
her strength and her weakness: she is the Philoctetes of Georgia, and
both her wound and her bow are taken from her. She has let her
stump separate her from biped humanity; her soul—by a grotesque
metonymy—has become her leg. And in rendering that leg to Manley, she renders herself helpless. One cannot miss, either, in the passage quoted above, the romantic parody of the Christian renunciation that O'Connor works into Hulga's surrender, which echoes as
well Pointer's own solecistic adaptation of the Gospel—"He who
losest his life shall find it.'" (181)

Because she is so caught up, so mastered by the brutish Mr.
Pointer, all knowledge deserts Hulga; gone is her former ironic detachment, replaced by a helpless dependence on the salesman. At this
juncture, Pointer exposes himself: out of his salesman's valise comes
the hollow Bible, and there is no judging this book by its cover. The
obscene deck of cards and the other paraphernalia of seduction that
are contained within unmask the pious fraud: "'Aren't you . . . just
good country people?'" Hulga asks in bewilderment; and Uriah Heep
replies, "'Yeah . . . but it ain't held me back none. I'm as good as
you any day in the week.'" Hulga then falls back on her sure knowledge of hypocrisy, and "hisses": "'You're a fine Christian! You're
just like them all—say one thing and do another.'" But she is wrong:

Manley may be a hypocrite and as bromidic as the farmwomen, but he is no Christian. " 'I hope you don't think,' he said in a lofty indignant tone, 'that I believe in that crap! I may sell Bibles but I know which end is up and I wasn't born yesterday and I know where I'm going!' " (194–95) And with that he disappears down the hayloft ladder, with the leg to add to his collection of " 'interesting things.' " (195)

Here then is the second exposure of Hulga: as Manley climbs down the ladder and scurries across a field, we know that Hulga has been tricked of course; but, in O'Connor's view, she has also tricked herself—by her proud certainty of what is and what can be. At the center of her tightly constructed, thoroughly known, scientifically accounted for universe, a chasm opens up. Before an incomprehensible evil—before "Nothing"—she is powerless and helpless. And that is the reader's last image of Hulga—"sitting on the straw in the dusty sunlight." (195)

But we are given a final image of the villainous salesman in a scene that offers the reader a final exposure of self-assuredness in "Good Country People."

> "Why, that looks like that nice dull young man that tried to sell me a Bible yesterday," Mrs. Hopewell said, squinting. "He must have been selling them to the Negroes back in there. He was so simple," she said, "but I guess the world would be better off if we were all that simple."
> Mrs. Freeman's gaze drove forward and just touched him before he disappeared under the hill. Then she returned her attention to the evil-smelling onion shoot she was lifting from the ground. "Some can't be that simple," she said. "I know I never could." (195–96)

Well, some can't smell the evil under their nose, as Mrs. Freeman might say. The metaphor for mechanical perception that O'Connor uses in this last paragraph echoes the opening lines of the story, thus shaping an ironic frame around the narrative; but it suggests as well the underlying concern of the fable: vision. It is not simply that one must drive carefully; in order to drive at all, one must see, and see truly.

Like many of O'Connor's titles, "Good Country People" takes on a sardonic shade by the end of the story. Manley of course has been thus honorifically titled by Mrs. Hopewell, and we know just how good *he* is. But what is interesting in this regard is that Mrs. Freeman is drawn by O'Connor as just such a good country person, though one does not at first recognize the parallel between her and Pointer. But the similarities of viewpoint are there: both have pierced through the girl to the "Hulga" identity she has forged for herself, and both take a perverse relish in using that name rather than the name her mother calls her by, Joy. And, what is more, Mrs. Freeman shares with Manley not only steel-pointed eyes (174, 193) but a fascination with the wooden leg. And like Pointer, with his collection of assorted prosthetic devices, Mrs. Freeman is fascinated by the medical anomaly, especially "secret infections, hidden deformities, assaults upon children. Of diseases, she preferred the lingering or incurable." (174) While one effect of this resemblance between the decidedly sinister Mrs. Freeman and the Bible salesman is thus to universalize the presence of evil in the world, still another effect is to accentuate the blindness of Hulga. For the girl's asserted uneasiness in the face of Mrs. Freeman's perversity fails to sensitize her perception of Pointer—until it is too late.

With dispassionate irony and a detached, finely controlled comic sense, O'Connor reveals in "Good Country People" the world as it is—without vision, without grace, without knowledge. And, what is relatively rare in her fiction, she stops short of describing in Hulga any final recognition of her self or the world. So that we are left to ourselves to construe the meaning of the experience by looking back and again looking back at the various implications of the action. It is a ribald moral fable—harsh, cold, and funny.

The Displaced Person

The shape of the plot in "The Displaced Person" is approximately the same as that which informed "Good Country People," and recalls as well the other stories we have considered so far: an alien intrudes upon the settled life of a farm and deeply unsettles it. But the intruder in this story—a Polish refugee named Mr. Guizac—differs significantly from his counterparts in being not a figure of genial malignity but the reverse—a well-meaning, if innocently naïve, man who is so much a doer of good on the farm that he is thought by Mrs. McIntyre, the owner, to be the salvation of the place. Yet strangely, he seems to bring out the worst in people, and by the story's end he has been himself destroyed and has served as a catalyst for the disruption of the whole farm.

"The Displaced Person" is rather longer than O'Connor's other tales: the version that was collected in *A Good Man Is Hard to Find* is actually double the length of the original version published in the *Sewanee Review* in 1954, which stopped at the end of section one. In fact, the story as it now stands has two separate movements, two separate climaxes—thus resembling in its structure (though far shorter) the two novels, each with its double climax (Enoch Emery and Hazel Motes in *Wise Blood*; Rayber and Tarwater in *The Violent Bear It Away*). Two characters, in succession, serve as the focus of our interest in the story, and serve too as the successive points of view for the telling of it. Thus the first part concerns Mrs. Shortley (Mrs. McIntyre's lieutenant on the farm) and her quietly enraged response to the Polish refugee; and the second and third sections, which were added later, shift to Mrs. McIntyre and her growing frustration with herself and with Guizac. To each of these women, in different ways, comes the experience of death, failure, and evil—dimensions of reality that had been safely hidden beneath the surface of their cloistered lives until the intrusion of the saintly Pole. The effect of the addition of the tragic confrontation between Mrs. McIntyre and Guizac is to give to the story as a whole a unity and complexity greater than the sum of its parts, a unity that centers on Guizac.

The meaning of Mrs. Shortley's encounter with Guizac is somewhat elusive, and to read it aright we must be attuned to the irony implicit in O'Connor's use of the woman as a center of consciousness for the first section. Thus, for example, the story opens with an image of Mrs. Shortley surveying the countryside in expectation of the arrival of the foreign intruder and his family. She is described as a mountainous woman, and her icy blue gaze pierces forward "surveying everything." (197) Or rather, not quite everything: for she ignores the afternoon sun, which is described as an intruder. Leaving aside the association of the intruding Guizac with this image of the sun, we might remark the larger question implied by the opening— of just what Mrs. Shortley is able to see—a question obliquely called to the reader's attention through O'Connor's use of the attendant peacock, which, by the way, was added to the original version, apparently for emphasis: for the peacock is not only himself an image of unearthly majesty, but has fixed his *sight* on something in the distance that "no one else could see" (197)—particularly Mrs. Shortley.

The bird is used again a little later to define more precisely Mrs. Shortley's spiritual qualities. Thus after Mr. Guizac has arrived (himself a stormy petrel) and after the woman has felt the gravity of his threat, Mrs. Shortley prophesies to the Negro workers on the farm that they might themselves be "displaced" by the hard-working displaced person. O'Connor judges her authority for such pronouncements severely: standing directly in front of the peacock's tail, Mrs. Shortley remains oblivious to the wondrous thing. "She was having an inner vision instead." (205) She imagines billions of European refugees pushing their way onto America while she—"a giant angel" (205)—tells the Negroes to move elsewhere. The vision (especially her own role in it) pleases her immensely.

In short, the woman's visionary apparatus (a vestigial organ of Southern fundamentalism) is an inner light that shines solely for Mrs. Shortley, its purpose self-magnification. Hers is a disembodied vision—one that takes no interest in the created world, the "map of the universe" before its eyes but, instead, charts its own eccentric way. The reader's authority for taking the peacock as a spiritual touchstone is established by O'Connor in her descriptions of other reactions to the bird, particularly that of the Catholic priest, Father Flynn, who has engineered the arrival of the Polish family in the first place. "'What a beauti-ful birdrrrd!'" the priest murmurs. "'So beauti-ful. . . . A tail full of suns.'" (202) And O'Connor adds, in her own voice, "The peacock stood still as if he had just come down from some sun-drenched height to be a vision for them all." (202)

But he is not, in actuality, a vision "for them all"—not for Mrs. Shortley, not for Mrs. McIntyre. And the blindness of the former extends to her perception of the Polish Mr. Guizac, whom she sees, xenophobically, as an agent of the devil. But while Mrs. Shortley gives the Guizacs a mere three weeks before the combination of their European stupidity, belligerence, and superstition proves them inferior workers to the Negroes ("'You can always tell a nigger what to do and stand by until he does it'" [216], she says), Mrs. McIntyre soon discovers that Guizac is a useful factotum on the farm.

So valuable does Mr. Guizac prove himself to be that Mrs.

McIntyre, in order to pay him more money, contemplates firing some of her other help. And in a bit of dialogue that implies more than a little about the custodial habits of whites in the South, it is not the Negroes but the Shortleys who fall from favor.

> "Five times in the last month I've found Mr. Shortley smoking in the barn," Mrs. McIntyre said. "Five times."
> "And arrre the Negroes any better?" [the priest asks].
> "They lie and steal and have to be watched all the time," she said.
> "Tsk, tsk," he said. "Which will you discharge?"
> "I've decided to give Mr. Shortley his month's notice tomorrow," Mrs. McIntyre said. (220)

Mrs. Shortley, overhearing this, is enraged, and, before Mrs. McIntyre can deliver her verdict, the Shortleys are crowded into their car which, like an unseaworthy ark, moves slowly away from the place of judgment.

The conclusion of section one, from the packing of the car to the moment of Mrs. Shortley's death in the front seat from an apparent heart attack (it had been intimated that her heart was incommensurate with her heavy mass), is narrated objectively, from a viewpoint outside Mrs. Shortley. The climax of this section has been masterfully prepared for, and is the key to O'Connor's final judgment of the woman.

What has haunted Mrs. Shortley in her thinking about the Europeans are grim imaginings of the ghastly dismemberment of human bodies: she recalls, for example, a newsreel image of a room heaped with dead, naked bodies—"their arms and legs tangled together, a head thrust in here, a head there, a foot, a knee, a part that should have been covered up sticking out, a hand raised clutching nothing." (200) And the image recurs to her periodically, associated in her mind with depths of evil unknown in America. She is convinced that, as time goes on, even more Poles will be imported to the farm until a battle will be joined between the dirty Polish words and the clean American words. The passage describing her vision of this linguistic Armageddon is an extraordinary one, fusing in Mrs. Shortley's primitive imagination the haunting newsreel image, the fervid Puritanism, and the unrestrained violence that make up, in equal parts, her obsession.

> She saw the Polish words, dirty and all-knowing and unreformed, flinging mud on the clean English words until everything was equally dirty. She saw them all piled up in a room, all the dead dirty words, theirs and hers too, piled up like the naked bodies in the newsreel. God save me! she cried silently, from the stinking power of Satan! And she started from that day to read her Bible with a new attention. (217)

Mrs. Shortley's "new attention," not unexpectedly, issues in an understanding of her own special part ("because she was strong" [217]) in the planned destiny of the world. And when, stimulated by her reading of the Apocalypse and the Prophets, she comes to experience a personal prophetic vision, she herself delivers the Word in a "loud voice" that carries forward her obsession: " 'The children of wicked nations will be butchered. . . . Legs where arms should be, foot to face, ear in the palm of hand. Who will remain whole? Who will remain whole? Who?' " (218–19)

Not, as it turns out, Mrs. Shortley. For when her death finally does come, she, if not the reader, is wholly unprepared for the ironic reversal implied in her last vision.

> She suddenly grabbed Mr. Shortley's elbow and Sarah Mae's foot at the same time and began to tug and pull on them as if she were trying to fit the two extra limbs onto herself. . . . She thrashed forward and backward, clutching at everything she could get her hands on and hugging it to herself. . . . (222–23)

Mrs. Shortley has all along imagined herself as the adamantine rock of the true faith, while the rest of the world—Negroes, the poor, Europeans—are the victims of divine retribution. We are not given, in this passage, Mrs. Shortley's vision itself at the moment of her death; but it is not hard to infer from the dramatic description of her frenzied, grasping response to it, and the "look of astonishment" that crosses her face, that it is not what she expected. She herself has become the dismembered European, she the child of wicked nations, she the displaced person. And the final sentence of the section ends with a metaphor which "places" her beyond the *national* boundaries

of grace she had contemplated, and suggests, instead, a more universal status—fallen, broken, displaced: for the first time, Mrs. Shortley
sees the "tremendous frontiers of her true country." (223)

In section two of "The Displaced Person," O'Connor shifts our
attention to Mrs. McIntyre, who, in section one, had rejoiced in the
economic advantages of Mr. Guizac's labor. As for the Shortleys'
hasty departure—"We've seen them come and seen them go" (223),
she says with satisfaction. There is, quite naturally, a lull in the
story as this new section begins; in a sense, one story is already completed—and was, as mentioned, published originally as a separate
entity. But O'Connor is not done with Mr. Guizac or with the self-
satisfied Mrs. McIntyre, and there soon develops, in this second part,
the grounds of the conflict that will rise to a climax in section three.

The old Negro Astor quietly drops the seed when he meticulously
discloses that Mr. Guizac is trying to bring his orphaned sixteen-year-
old cousin to America from a prison camp in Europe in the only way
he can—by giving her in marriage to the young Negro farmhand
Sulk, in exchange for the latter's payment of part of the transportation cost. Mrs. Shortley had known of the plan herself, and had
mischievously concealed it from Mrs. McIntyre, who learns of it
gradually, and with consternation.

When Mrs. McIntyre finally confronts Mr. Guizac with his
un-Christian intentions, the Pole replies: " 'She no care black. . . .
She in camp three year.' " (235) And in what amounts to her first
significant action, Mrs. McIntyre responds from the violent depths
of her own complacent, ordered universe that she is not responsible
for the misery of the world. "It is not," as Robert Fitzgerald has
written, "merely that [Mr. Guizac] has stumbled against the color
bar. It is the classic situation of tragedy in which each party to the
conflict is both right and wrong and almost incomprehensible to the
other."[14]

While the conflict between Mrs. McIntyre and Mr. Guizac defines
itself, O'Connor supplies, in the middle section, some details of the
former's character. If Mrs. Shortley regarded herself as recipient of a
personal, divinely favored dispensation, Mrs. McIntyre's identity is
founded on her own reiterated sense of power, of dispensation, of
material ownership. Her pride is in her hardheaded practicality and
shrewdness. Accordingly, it is interesting that O'Connor reveals in

this section Mrs. McIntyre's quite strong attachment to her first husband, the Judge. She had married the Judge when he was an old man, we are told, and because of his money but also (although she wouldn't admit it to herself) because she had liked him.

The old man had a certain style, it seems, a Southern gentility, and a fondness for making philosophical quips. But, above all, he had the appearance of being wealthy. Appearance indeed: when he died, he left a bankrupt estate. Still, Mrs. McIntyre managed to hold her own in the world, and the image of her past life with the Judge became enshrined in her memory. But the picture of the Judge we get in this section seems, ironically, to go beyond Mrs. McIntyre's understanding of him. Thus, for example, when Mrs. McIntyre remembers the Judge's fondness for saying, " 'Money is the root of all evil' " (224), the old Negro Astor (who has a richer memory of him) remembers: " 'Judge say he long for the day when he be too poor to pay a nigger to work. . . . Say when that day come, the world be back on its feet.' " (224–25) And Mrs. McIntyre responds, with an impoverishing literal emphasis: " 'Well that day has almost come around here and I'm telling each and every one of you: you better look sharp.' " (225) And later, when she goes to the old Judge's closetlike office space, where his safe is "set like a tabernacle in the center" (232) of his roll top desk, Mrs. McIntyre again seems to be worshiping the old man for the wrong reasons: the Judge's dramatic sense of his material limitations becomes, for his widow, a literal poverty. "It had been his first principle to talk as if he were the poorest man in the world and she followed it, not only because he had but because it was true." (233) (O'Connor would later call "the experience of limitation or, if you will, of poverty" the basis "of all human experience.")[15] Similarly, she keeps the Judge's last remaining peacock only because she fears offending him in his grave, oblivious to the finer feelings the Judge himself had had for them—"He had liked to see them walking around the place for he said they made him feel rich." (228)[16]

And when Mrs. McIntyre thinks of the granite angel the Judge had placed over his grave (partly for aesthetic reasons and partly because it reminded him of his wife), and which she herself had thought hideous, she nevertheless weeps quietly—remembering particularly that a former employee, on departing, had stolen the angel (or most of it, the thief's ax striking just above the toes). But her maudlin reaction is wholly out of countenance with O'Connor's description of the gravesite that closes this middle section—a description that provides a macabre perspective on the story, serving to bring the reader out of his involvement with the Pole and Mrs. McIntyre for a moment and to prepare him for the murder that concludes the story: for as the Displaced Person cuts the corn in the field, he gradually circles inward toward the center and toward a little island of grass—the Judge's graveyard, where he "lay grinning under his desecrated monument." (237) It is an odd image, this; and not until the end of the story does one realize that submerged in the picture of the Pole mowing the field like the grim reaper is, instead, an image of the Pole riding what will be the instrument of his own death. As he circles in toward the center, the Judge's grinning death's-head seems to disdain all this transitory world.

In the last part of "The Displaced Person," Mrs. McIntyre attempts to justify, both to herself and to the priest, her desire to fire Mr. Guizac. And the first of several conversations between Father Flynn and the lady of the farm, in which the latter tries to explain her reasons for dismissing the superb worker, is a beautifully designed counterpoint, concluding with a juxtaposition that states, as clearly as one could wish, the dramatic and symbolic function of Mr. Guizac in the story. For while Mrs. McIntyre is arguing the superfluity of the Pole, the priest's attention is fixed on the superfluous beauty of the passing peacock, which, raising its glorious tail, causes Father Flynn to exclaim gaily, "'Christ will come like that!'" (239) But Mrs. McIntyre charges on to summarize her position on Mr. Guizac. "'He didn't have to come in the first place,' she repeated, emphasizing each word." To which the old man, smiling absently, still with his eyes on the bird, replies, with unambiguous ambiguity, "'He came to redeem us.'" (239) The point is driven home in a subsequent conversation when, as the priest is speaking of Christ the redeemer, the obstinate Mrs. McIntyre interrupts fiercely, "'As far as I'm concerned . . . Christ was just another D.P.'" (243) Christ, Mr. Guizac, the peacock—they are all one and all of no use.

A few weeks after his departure, Mr. Shortley returns—alone—to the farm and, rehired by Mrs. McIntyre, he incites the demos to get rid of Mr. Guizac. His arguments (which impress the townsfolk) are marvelous parodies of logic—amusing and frightening in their mimetic accuracy.

> Mr. Shortley said he never had cared for foreigners since he had been in the first world's war and seen what they were like. . . . He said he recalled the face of one man who had thrown a hand-grenade at him and that the man had had little round eye-glasses exactly like Mr. Guizac's.
> "But Mr. Guizac is a Pole, he's not a German," Mrs. McIntyre said.
> "It ain't a great deal of difference in them two kinds," Mr. Shortley had explained. (240–41)

The cumulative effect of his suasion, on public opinion and on Mrs. McIntyre, finally leads the latter out to the machine shed to give the Pole notice. And the narrative tone of the ensuing scene, told from Mrs. McIntyre's viewpoint, takes on a tense and somber quality of expectation. The landscape itself seems to cooperate in forming an arena of silence for the action. As Mrs. McIntyre waits for Mr. Guizac to come out from under the tractor (only he knows how to fix it), Sulk and Mr. Shortley are present, also waiting.

Mr. Shortley gets on another tractor in front of the one the Pole is working on, and backs it out of the shed.

> He had headed it toward the small tractor but he braked it on a slight incline and jumped off and turned back toward the shed. Mrs. McIntyre was looking fixedly at Mr. Guizac's legs lying flat on the ground now. She heard the brake on the large tractor slip and, looking up, she saw it move forward, calculating its own path. Later she remembered that she had seen the Negro jump silently out of the way as if a spring in the earth had released him and that she had seen Mr. Shortley turn his head with incredible slowness and stare silently over his shoulder and that she had started to shout to the Displaced Person but that she had not. She had felt her eyes and Mr. Shortley's eyes and the Negro's eyes come together in one look that froze them in collusion forever, and she had heard the little noise the Pole made as the tractor wheel broke his backbone. The two men ran forward to help and she fainted. (249–50)

The verb tense of the narrative, shifting to the pluperfect as the murderous tractor moves forward, suggests that, even as it happens, the moment of aggregate guilt has been fixed forever in time. This scene too (like the drowning of Bishop in *The Violent Bear It Away*) seems to echo Hawthorne's *The Marble Faun*, when Miriam and Donatello hurl the model into the abyss, only to discover that they themselves, in that moment of evil, have fallen into a kind of abyss.

At the center of the story is the intruding figure—the patently Christlike figure—of the man the two ladies called, in fun, "Gobble-hook." But why Mr. Guizac? How is he the Christ of the tale?

He is not especially Christlike: he is hard-working, but not forgiving; he is mechanically skilled, but not a teacher of men; he is impatient and short-tempered in the face of others' blunderings. In one respect, however, he shares something of Christ's nature and experience, and in a way that is beyond the comprehension of Mrs. Shortley and Mrs. McIntyre: he has suffered. His coming to the farm demands from them some recognition, some empathy, something beyond their usual habits. And, in fact, Mrs. McIntyre seems on the threshold of such an awareness when she dreams that the priest calls on her and drones: " 'Dear lady, I know your tender heart won't suffer you to turn the porrrrr man out. Think of the thousands of them, think of the ovens and the boxcars and the camps and the sick children and Christ Our Lord.' " (245) But she is unable to act on this half-awareness, unable to move outside the sphere of her interests and conventions.

When Mrs. McIntyre returns to the scene of the accident (after having fainted again in the house), she comes as a stranger to her surroundings, as, herself, a displaced person, alien to the countryside and to the people gathered round the corpse. And where the reader first sees Mr. Guizac bent over, foolishly kissing Mrs. McIntyre's hand in greeting, he last sees him under the bent figure of the priest, receiving in his mouth the communion wafer. It is a ceremony from which Mrs. McIntyre is excluded.

Where Mrs. Shortley dies at the moment of her final vision, Mrs. McIntyre's revelation is followed by a prolonged aftermath. And, what is unusual in O'Connor's fiction, the last paragraph pulls together the loose threads of the various characters' lives, and, in the manner of many a concluding paragraph of many a nineteenth-century novel, sends them on their separate ways: Mr. Shortley quits the farm; Sulk sets off for points south; Astor retires; and Mrs. McIntyre herself comes down with a "nervous affliction" and, after a stay at a hospital, returns to a farm bereft of farmhands and animals. Bedridden, she is left with a single black woman to care for her. Her eyes—that saw truly once, and then to see her essential displacement —steadily fail her; and her voice (which had halted when she had started to shout to the Displaced Person) she loses altogether. (One thinks of Benito Cereno's wasting away following his own initiation into the dark sphere of human life.) Only the priest remembers to visit her. "He came regularly once a week with a bag of breadcrumbs and, after he had fed these to the peacock, he would come in and sit by the side of her bed and explain the doctrines of the Church." (251)

I am not sure whether this last paragraph of the story is needed. If it is read as the novelistic equivalent of a final wrathful judgment on all concerned, it would seem superfluous, perhaps opportunistic—a little too much to the point. But perhaps the best way to read the conclusion is not as a meting out of rewards and punishments but rather as a rapid denouement: and there is a fitness to the characters' fates being dismissed in a phrase—a fitness that derives from the essential incompleteness, open-endedness, of their lives after the day of Guizac's death. We are not, in fact, told what happens to them— but merely that they scatter from the scene of the crime, sufficient evidence in itself that something has "happened" to them. And, as for Mrs. McIntyre and the priest, that has a decorum all its own: not in the sense that what Mrs. McIntyre needs is Church doctrine but in the sense that that *is*, after all, what the priest would do: feed breadcrumbs to the birds and talk Christ to Mrs. McIntyre.

In her "Introduction to *A Memoir of Mary Ann*," O'Connor would put in abstract and unequivocal form a statement of some relevance to "The Displaced Person."

> In . . . popular pity, we mark our gain in sensibility and our loss in vision. If other ages felt less, they saw more, even though they saw with the blind, prophetical, unsentimental eye of acceptance, which is to say, of faith. In the absence of this faith now, we govern by tenderness. It is a tenderness which, long since cut off from the person of Christ, is wrapped in theory. When tenderness is detached from the source of tenderness, its logical outcome is terror. It ends in forced-labor camps and in the fumes of the gas chamber.[17]

One may disagree with these assertions, and one would certainly not want to reduce the story to such a formulation; but the view affirmed there is part of its meaning, and probably what is behind it. And she goes on to say, "Hawthorne could have put [these reflections] in a fable and shown us what to fear."[18] O'Connor already had, and it is surely one of her best tales.

The Artificial Nigger

In the stories we have considered so far—"A Good Man Is Hard to Find," "Good Country People," and "The Displaced Person"—the central dramatic image has been the intrusion of some alien figure, grotesquely evil or grotesquely good, upon the settled life of a character, with the result that a wholly new order of experience and (for those who survive) new identity has been forced upon the character. In the following three stories to be examined—"The Artificial Nigger," "The Comforts of Home," and "Parker's Back"—this same basic pattern can be observed, except that where the dramatic situation in the first group involved essentially the confrontation of the intruding figure and a single passive figure, this second group involves the intrusion of some grotesque upon the lives of two characters, with the result dramatized in terms of their relationship—whether it be that of Mr. Head and Nelson before the plaster statue, or Thomas and his mother before Sarah Ham, or Parker and Sarah Ruth before the tattooed image of Christ on Parker's back.[19]

"The Artificial Nigger" was named by Flannery O'Connor as her favorite story, and it has been the favorite of many others as well.[20] It is interesting to note, therefore, that it differs in several respects from the other stories in the canon. For one, its protagonists are a pair of Georgia backwoods characters who, in spite of—or perhaps because of—their failings, endear themselves to the reader. Many of O'Connor's characters are fascinating, or amusing, or shocking, but old Mr. Head and his grandson Nelson become almost lovable. The story is unusual in certain other respects as well: for the sense of failure and misery that comes to so many of her characters as a final experience comes to Head and Nelson as well—but not as a final experience. Instead, they are given a moment of grace at the end that reunites them after their sundering. And that moment is stated explicitly, in theological terms—the only such direct statement in the stories; and, concomitantly, the characters are not, in the end, the objects of an ironic viewpoint.

The shape of the plot is simple and traditional: Mr. Head and Nelson leave their shack in the country and journey to the city so that Nelson can see what life there is like. But the two soon get lost and peevishly mock one another's ignorance and naïveté, until the elder Head has the occasion to deny Nelson his support when the latter desperately needs it; feelings of betrayal and shame divide the two following that episode, at which low point the "artificial nigger" intrudes upon their lives and mysteriously unites them again. They return home together chastened and wiser. Though on a smaller scale, the story's basic structure—a journey from home ending in a transformation and return to home—is thus the same as that underlying both of the novels.

Although a deeply felt love and mutual dependence anchor the relationship between Mr. Head and Nelson, it is masked by much cantankerous caviling (old Tarwater and his grandnephew will echo this odd symbiosis). The chief matter of their rivalry is over who knows more about the world, and the trip to the city is conceived by Mr. Head in explicitly moral terms as a demonstration of his own superior knowledge, particularly with respect to the city itself. Yet the question of knowing the city soon comes down to the question of knowing the Negro. And visible in this equation (though in an admittedly comic, grotesque shape) is the shadow of the tangled complexity of white-Negro relations in the South—the association of the Negro with the city, with a dangerous knowledge, with knowing who one is, oneself.

There are three specific encounters with "the Negro," and each presents a different experience and a new knowledge to the two travelers. The first takes place on the train ride to the city: as a "huge coffee-colored man" slowly proceeds down the aisle wearing expensive and ornate clothing, Mr. Head, who has been gripping Nelson's arm, asks him, " 'What was that?' " And the boy replies " 'A man.' " (110) So the instruction continues:

> "What kind of a man?" Mr. Head persisted, his voice expressionless.
> "A fat man," Nelson said. He was beginning to feel that he had better be cautious.
> "You don't know what kind?" Mr. Head said in a final tone.

"An old man," the boy said and had a sudden foreboding that he was not going to enjoy the day.

"That was a nigger," Mr. Head said and sat back. (110)

The depths of Nelson's ignorance are uncovered. He must be taught the nature of the world by Mr. Head. And as the boy looks down the aisle after the "man," he feels he has been deliberately fooled and (here O'Connor's psychology seems flawless) he hates the Negro fiercely and, what is more, understands why his grandfather hates them.

The second confrontation with "Negro" soon follows, when Nelson is urged to ask directions from a "large colored woman leaning in a doorway" (118)—for the two have arrived in the city at last only to become promptly lost in the Negro section. The woman is drawn by O'Connor as a kindly and playfully sensual figure (when she speaks, Nelson feels "as if a cool spray had been turned on him" [118]), the most naturally sensual figure, in fact, in all of her fiction. (Taken together with Mark Twain's similarly singular portrait of the Negro woman Roxana in Pudd'nhead Wilson—even if she is only "one-sixteenth" black—this may say something about the persistence, in the Southern white imagination, of attitudes toward sexuality that will permit the release of certain emotions only when dealing with the Negro.) Face to face with the woman, Nelson experiences what amounts to a vicarious initiation into "dark" sexuality: his eyes rove over her buxom, sweating figure.

He suddenly wanted her to reach down and pick him up and draw him against her and then he wanted to feel her breath on his face. . . . He had never had such a feeling before. He felt as if he were reeling down through a pitchblack tunnel.

"You can go a block down yonder and catch you a car take you to the railroad station, Sugarpie," she said. (119)

It is an interesting passage, not only because it shows Nelson reacting again in his instinctively ignorant human way to "Negro" but because of the association O'Connor implies between his feelings and an earlier lesson he has learned. For the phrase "pitchblack tunnel," above, has occurred three pages earlier, in Mr. Head's explanation of the sewer system. Head had warned Nelson that the pipes contained sewage and rats, and that a man could be "sucked along down endless pitchblack tunnels. . . . He connected the sewer passages with the entrance to hell." (115–16) I am assuming that the repetition is deliberate, and that what is suggested is Nelson's profound ambivalence here—his great attraction to the earthy figure of the woman and, at the same time, his feelings of repulsion, of a loss of control tantamount to being sucked into the nether regions of the earth, into hell itself. At any rate, this is the feeling Mr. Head communicates to the boy when he pulls him away roughly from the woman. As they hurry away, the innocent's face burns with shame, and, in his recoil from the woman, he takes hold of Mr. Head's hand with a childish dependency.

Nelson's reactions to the Negro have so far passed from nonrecognition to irrational hatred, and from irrational love to revulsion. In his final encounter, with the "artificial nigger," he will share with Mr. Head a total bewilderment. But before considering that scene, we must first consider what directly precedes it.

For the confrontation with the last genus of "Negro" occurs when Mr. Head and Nelson have reached the all-time nadir in their relationship. That wily guide, the elder Head, has decided he must teach his charge still another lesson in humility; and so he removes himself from the fatigued and dozing child, thinking that, upon his awakening, Nelson will realize what a "sorry time" he would have if his grandfather weren't there. His plan doesn't work; or, rather, it proves his point only too well: for, upon awakening, Nelson is so panic-stricken that he dashes off down the street after Mr. Head, who, watching from an alleyway, dashes off after his fleeing grandson. When the old man does catch up with him, he finds him sitting on the ground with an elderly woman, the two surrounded by groceries of every description and a crowd of outraged women who are plucking at the shoulder of the dazed and terrified boy while the woman with whom he has collided shouts, " 'You've broken my ankle and your daddy'll pay for it!' " (122)

These words, along with the imminent arrival of the police, strike an equal terror into the heart of Head, and, in a moment of monumental weakness, he denies knowing his grandson, who all this time has been clinging to him. The women are so amazed by this (the two look as alike as the heads on two coins) that they fall back, leaving Mr. Head a space to walk through. "Ahead of him he saw nothing but a hollow tunnel that had once been the street." (123) And so

Mr. Head too enters the "pitchblack tunnel" leading to hell: in a moment, whatever superiority to Nelson he might have claimed is destroyed; his life is overturned; and as they walk away from the scene—Nelson assiduously staying twenty feet behind his grand-father—the latter begins to feel the depth of his denial and the heaviness of guilt. Nelson, dignified, and determined in his refusal to forgive the old man, ignores all of Mr. Head's efforts at reconcilia-tion. For both the old man and the boy, the dissolution of their relationship into guilt and hostility amounts to the dissolution of their entire world: order, meaning, coherence—all are gone. In a quiet, almost nondescript way, anarchy is loosed. It is precisely at this point that the two espy the plaster figure of a Negro "about Nelson's size" and sitting on a wall, but "pitched forward at an unsteady angle" and holding "a piece of brown watermelon." (127)

It is the third "Negro" they have confronted that day, but for the first time neither Nelson nor Mr. Head understands it. As they gaze dumbfounded at this monumental paradox, they cannot tell "if the artificial Negro were meant to be young or old; he looked too miser-able to be either. He was meant to look happy because his mouth was stretched up at the corners but the chipped eye and the angle he was cocked at gave him a wild look of misery instead." (127) And, significantly, the careful description of their postures before the statue—each a paradox of youth and age—shows them united, one to the other, and both to the "artificial nigger." "The two of them stood there with their necks forward at almost the same angle and their shoulders curved in almost exactly the same way and their hands trembling identically in their pockets. Mr. Head looked like an ancient child and Nelson like a miniature old man." (127) Both are of course ignorant of the statue's merely ornamental significance; instead, they see in it the symbolic meaning that, through a gro-tesque metamorphosis, it has taken on.

Ironically, it is only a decrepit statue that can make them both see, for the first time, the irreducibly human quality of "Negro." For if Nelson, in his innocence, had before identified the "coffee-colored" Negro in the train as "a man," it is in a different sense—gained from their common experience of misery, defeat, and betrayal—that they now both feel united to the "man" before them. (It is a character-istic pattern in O'Connor's fiction to abolish racial or social or even property distinctions in the face of the democracy of misery; see, for

example, the end of "Revelation" and the concluding insight given
the child in "A Circle in the Fire" that the face of the new misery
"looked old and it looked as if it might have belonged to anybody,
a Negro or a European." [154]) As the two Heads stand gazing at
the statue, they feel "as if they were faced with some great mystery,
some monument to another's victory that brought them together
in their common defeat. They could both feel it dissolving their
differences like an action of mercy." (128) The "victory" represented
by the monument is, in one sense, the victory of the white "home-
owner" thus symbolized in the model of the defeated Negro abjectly
gracing the front of his house; but in a larger sense, it is the victory
of evil that is inevitable in the fallen world.

Thus when Mr. Head, feeling the need to assure Nelson of his
abiding wisdom, declares: "'They ain't got enough real ones here.
They got to have an artificial one'" (128), it is at once what a Mr.
Head would have said, and the truth as well. His words are not the
"lofty statement" he wanted to utter at this moment, but they state
obliquely the defeat and misery that are truly implied in the statue:
apparently they do not have enough real ones. They do need an
artificial one. In addition, one cannot fail to note the analogy of the
crucifix and the statue that O'Connor implies: Christ's death too,
for O'Connor, was a victory of evil. And yet—the paradox of Christianity—it is also the victory of good, of the redemption: for through
that sacrificial death, salvation was brought into the world. And that
is precisely the effect of the statue of the Negro on Mr. Head and
Nelson.

Reunited, they go back home—"'before we get ourselves lost
again'" (128), as Nelson says. Their return is unambiguously a return
from a fallen world to a world of grace; and O'Connor does not
spare the imagery of an enclosing garden (compare the etymology of
"paradise") and a luminous world.

> . . . the moon, restored to its full splendor, sprang from a cloud and
> flooded the clearing with light. As they stepped off, the sage grass was
> shivering gently in shades of silver and the clinkers under their feet
> glittered with a fresh black light. The treetops, fencing the junction
> like the protecting walls of a garden, were darker than the sky which
> was hung with gigantic white clouds illuminated like lanterns. (128)

The train which had carried them to the moral crucible of the city glides past them and disappears, "like a frightened serpent into the woods." (129) Paradise regained, the Fall—if once is enough—can be called a fortunate one. "'I'm glad I've went once,'" Nelson says in the story's last line, "'but I'll never go back again!'" (129)

The movement of the story, from beginning to middle to end, is thus a completed circle—from home to city to home—and, through the merciful intrusion of the artificial Negro, that circle shapes a comic plot. In another sense, the story moves from an Old Testament atmosphere to a New. The first pages of the story are charged with an imagery of Old Testament stories of rulers and their servants, of guarding angels. Mr. Head himself has the self-convinced air of an Old Testament prophet, wise and wizened. (All of this is done, I might add, with a light touch.) In a sense, then, the action of the story—the humbling of Mr. Head followed by his restitution through grace—is a demonstration of the fallibility of merely human wisdom and the necessity of saving grace—in short, a movement toward the values of the New Testament. And that change is paralleled by the shift in the tone of the story as well, from the opening, lightly ironic description of the moonlight gilding the lowly cabin with mock splendor to the relatively more solemn image of the moon, at the end of the story, "restored to its full splendor" (128) and flooding the clearing with light.

On still another level, the story is a miniature Pilgrim's Progress. Not in the sense of its having a strictly allegorical basis but, rather, in the analogous progressive stages of the soul's ascent to God that are implied in the dramatic narrative: from pride to confusion to denial to despair to grace and, finally, to redemption.

The theological meaning of "The Artificial Nigger" is not only implicit in the structure and imagery of the story but is explicitly stated in the penultimate paragraph, which is almost the only occasion on which Flannery O'Connor adopted a fictional strategy so direct:

> Mr. Head stood very still and felt the action of mercy touch him again but this time he knew that there were no words in the world that could name it. He understood that it grew out of agony, which

is not denied to any man and which is given in strange ways to children. . . . He realized that he was forgiven for sins from the beginning
of time, when he had conceived in his own heart the sin of Adam,
until the present, when he had denied poor Nelson. He saw that no
sin was too monstrous for him to claim as his own, and since God
loved in proportion as He forgave, he felt ready at that instant to
enter Paradise. (128–29)

And yet one feels that the paragraph does not add anything essential
to the story, not to mention its being out of character for Mr. Head
to think such thoughts. In addition, it has the effect of somewhat
limiting the far richer meaning of the dramatic image itself—the
confrontation with the inexplicable statue, the identity of postures
before the figure, the return home. And O'Connor herself has written
that a "piece of fiction must be very much a self-contained dramatic
unit." Which means, she went on,

> that it must carry its meaning inside it. . . . any abstractly expressed
> compassion or piety or morality in a piece of fiction is only a state-
> ment added to it. It means that you can't make an inadequate dra-
> matic action complete by putting a statement of meaning on the end
> of it or in the middle of it or at the beginning of it.[21]

But if, in fact, the work is dramatically complete—and surely
"The Artificial Nigger" is—then why add that paragraph? Possibly
O'Connor felt that while the experience of tragedy is so much a part
of the world that any clarification would be superfluous, the experience of grace is so uncommon as to warrant some emphasis. Or, possibly, she felt that without the authorial interpolation, not only the
specifically Christian meaning of the story but any meaning would
be impaired; perhaps she suspected that "The Artificial Nigger" relies
so heavily on materials that have been freighted with sociological and
political overtones that it would be mistaken for something that it
assuredly is not. For whatever political meaning is implicit in the
story is there by indirection only. Whether or not the Heads undergo
a change in their attitude toward Negroes is rather doubtful; what is
clear, however, is that two individuals have been reunited with each
other and with God through the chance intrusion of a plaster statue.
And it is precisely as unlikely, as grotesque, as "impossible" an intrusion as, for O'Connor, is Christ's intrusion into the fallen world.

A story that perfectly complements "The Artificial Nigger" is the later "Everything That Rises Must Converge" (1961). For there we see a pair of characters, Julian and his mother, brought together not in any overt sense (Julian runs for help as his mother dies, failing even to recognize her son) but—if at all—in an ironic one: Julian recognizes the depth of his misery and loneliness and—what he has been unable to admit—his dependence upon his mother. And the violent intruder in this story is a Negro woman; but in neither tale is the focus of attention ultimately on the issue of race. In this regard, one might contrast O'Connor's fiction with Faulkner's. For "The Artificial Nigger" is not the first time a white writer has imagined the Negro as an agent of salvation: Nancy is such an agent in *Requiem for a Nun*. But where an essential meaning of Faulkner's drama lies in Nancy's being Negro, in O'Connor the "Negro-ness" of the image is, in a fundamental sense, accidental. Certainly one does not want to deny the crucial dramatic significance of "Negro" in O'Connor's story—it is as important to the tale as leaves and branches are to a tree—but the root meaning of the "artificial nigger" to Nelson and Mr. Head lies in its being not an image of Negro suffering but an image of common human misery.

The Comforts of Home

One is tempted to posit, without solemnity, the existence of something like a "charity group" of tales within the O'Connor canon. These might include "A Circle in the Fire," "The Comforts of Home," "Everything That Rises Must Converge," "The Lame Shall Enter First," and even *The Violent Bear It Away*. All of these works deal in some way with a character whose sense of virtue is expressed through acts of charity—often involving a guest brought into the house: What do we do with the guest? Do we reform him? Let him be? Throw him out? Educate him? Give him gifts? These are the questions the stories seem to ask, and beneath them is the larger question—What is charity? And yet, if we attempt to generalize on the basis of this approach, we soon run into a tangle of contradictions, clearly visible when, for example, "The Lame Shall Enter First" is compared with "The Comforts of Home." In both stories, a delinquent youth is brought into the home by a parent who energetically tries to rehabilitate the incorrigible intruder. But the effect of the intrusion is to upset the domestic tranquility of the household, threatening the security of the only child whose sole domain it was. Beyond these similarities, however, the stories radically differ. In "The Comforts of Home," O'Connor weights her sympathy toward the charitable mother, while her son Thomas bears the brunt of the author's ironic judgement. In "The Lame Shall Enter First," however, the agent of active virtue (Sheppard) is handled ironically, while sympathy is accorded both the intruder and the neglected child who becomes his disciple.

Apart from the generally implied virtues of humility and self-knowledge, a definite moral norm in these stories is hard to find. What they do portray, finally, is not the effect of misguided charity upon the world but how moral failure and limitation are related to modes of being and perception.

"The Comforts of Home" opens with the moment of crisis near at hand: son Thomas watches from a window as the intruding "little slut," as he calls her, and his mother return home after another day in which the latter has tried to locate a job for the girl and a place for her to live.[22] Only this was to be Sarah Ham's last day in the house, for Thomas had delivered an ultimatum to his mother, declaring that he would leave if the girl were brought back. As his mother and the girl enter the house together, Thomas alters his plans: not only does he not know how to begin to leave home but, deciding that his mother was counting on just such a weakness, he steels his will against her and determines that she must be shown.

That moment in the plot is then suspended until the end of the story, and in the intervening pages we are given the background of the conflict between Thomas and his mother. And it is noteworthy that their relationship is narrated from Thomas's point of view, right up until the very end, when the viewpoint is significantly altered, as we shall see. Moreover, throughout the story, Thomas's mother is known by no other name than simply "his mother," as if to emphasize not only the point of view from which the tale is narrated but the single most defining element in the woman's identity—adding some poignance to the climax of the conflict, in which the old lady is accidentally killed by her son.

On the surface, the conflict between the two concerns the degree to which virtuous feelings should be translated into charitable actions. From Thomas's viewpoint, his mother has a definite tendency, despite her good intentions, "to make a mockery of virtue, to pursue it with such a mindless intensity that everyone involved was made a fool of and virtue itself became ridiculous." (117) The son, for his part, believes in a golden mean of virtue—"that a moderation of good produces likewise a moderation in evil." (118–19) The reader of *The Violent Bear It Away*, published the same year as "The Comforts of Home," would of course be suspicious of such immoderate moderation, but, in case we have missed the implicit irony, it is restated with further elaboration in a description of the virtues the boy has inherited from his mother and father (the latter deceased). "Thomas had inherited his father's reason without his ruthlessness and his mother's love of good without her tendency to pursue it. His plan for all practical action was to wait and see what developed." (121) The elements in him are so mixed that, in short, he usually does nothing.

But the conflict between mother and son goes even deeper than this, and raises the question that O'Connor never tires of raising: What is the nature of reality? For Thomas's mother is possessed by a sense of the real presence of evil and misery in the world that is balanced only by her intense feeling of compassion. Both extremes of perception and feeling are alien to Thomas, so that whereas he finds the girl who has been removed from jail and placed in his home by his mother unendurable, and therefore not to be endured, his mother seems "bowed down by some painful mystery that nothing would make endurable but a redoubling of effort." (121–22) And it is his mother's abstract knowledge of the mysterious presence of evil in the world that gives her face "a disconcerting omniscient look," as if she were a "sibyl"—though wearing only her "bathrobe and a grey turban around her head." (127)

The image is, to be sure, a funny one, and the old lady is, perhaps, a "fool of virtue." But O'Connor's point is that it is a foolishness that conceals a deeper wisdom. For behind her modest and not very effective gestures of decency is a force of love that recalls in its intensity Rayber's and Tarwater's in *The Violent Bear It Away*. "There were times when it became nothing but pure idiot mystery and [Thomas] sensed about him forces, invisible currents entirely out of his control." (118) When that love is translated into charity, it becomes an almost impersonal force—a counterbalance to her abstract sense of the world's misery—and this impersonal quality destroys Thomas's pleasure in her attentions to him. Thus, for example, when his mother learns from a lawyer the full extent of Sarah Ham's malady, her compassion for the girl is redoubled and (a wonderful touch) "to [Thomas's] annoyance, she appeared to look on *him* with compassion, as if her hazy charity no longer made distinctions." (122) And the further growth of her sorrowful compassion, following Sarah's half-hearted suicide attempt, annoys even Sarah Ham, "for it appeared to be a general sorrow that would have found another object no matter what good fortune came to either of them. The experience of Sarah Ham had plunged the old lady into mourning for the world." (133) The mother's compassion is thus something like tumultuous, and we might note the difference between it and the merely "hazy compassion" elsewhere condemned by O'Connor for excusing "human weakness because human weakness is human."23

In the face of the old lady's sorrow, the extremes of Thomas's "good" and Sarah's "evil" meet, joined in a common bond of human fallibility. (Actually it is by no means a foregone conclusion that Thomas is morally superior to Sarah. Taking the family dog as a litmus test, one would have to say that Sarah elicits the more favorable response: the dog bounds toward her, "overjoyed, shaking with pleasure" [115] when she appears. Compare that greeting with the apathy Thomas's arrival, later on, inspires: "The dog was asleep on the back doormat. At the approach of his master's step, he opened one yellow eye, took him in, and closed it again." [138] Also a perfect emblem of the young man's moral posture: let sleeping dogs lie.) But if Thomas and Sarah seem to share a moral affinity when opposed to the deeper feeling of the mother, it is certainly not an affinity that Thomas would admit; and the conclusion of the story clearly illustrates this. Caught by his mother in the act of framing the girl by planting his pistol in her pocketbook (the sheriff has been summoned to "find" the evidence of her theft), "Thomas damned not only the girl but the entire order of the universe that made her possible." (140) And as the moment is forced to its crisis through accusation and denial, Thomas longs to restore the "peace of perfect order" (141), to deny the moral imperfection of the fallen world. He fires the gun at Sarah Ham. "The blast was like a sound meant to bring an end to evil in the world." (141)

At this moment, the narrative point of view shifts, the tableau is revealed through the eyes of Sheriff Farebrother, and "The Comforts of Home" seems to become transformed into a different story—or does it? What the sheriff sees is the old lady, lying dead "on the floor between the girl and Thomas." (141) Farebrother quickly assesses the facts: "The fellow had intended all along to kill his mother and pin it on the girl." (141) But then further insights are flashed to him: "Over her body, the killer and the slut were about to collapse into each other's arms. The sheriff knew a nasty bit when he saw it. He was accustomed to enter upon scenes that were not as bad as he had hoped to find them, but this one met his expectations." (142)

The reader's first impression of this ending must be puzzlement: why put an odd joke at the end of a tragedy? Thomas, we had thought, was a victim of his insistence of an impossible worldly perfection; he would murder evil instead of suffering it as inevitable; and his mother, we had thought, fell victim to this unearthly idealism. In that case, the ending might seem a minor effect of the kind Melville achieves in *Billy Budd*, where the truth of the narrative proper is distorted at the end by the various versions it spawns—ballad, official report, news account. And yet, it seems unlikely O'Connor would end a story in just this way unless she wanted to suggest some final view of things.

In fact, the final viewpoint suggests yet another skein in the tangled conflict within Thomas, and I must pause here to trace it before returning, with different emphasis, to that last scene. We must complement our view of the young historian's moral innocence by noting, in addition, his arrested emotional development. Thus Thomas's defense of his mother from Sarah Ham's helplessness, so to speak, is also a hysterical defense of his own home ground; he knows that his "saner virtues" (119) derive from his mother's well-ordered household, which is, for him, unequivocally womblike—"as personal as the shell of a turtle and as necessary." (130)

But it also seems evident that his hostility to Sarah (her preferred name, Star Drake, suggests her sexually aggressive nature—an echo of Temple Drake in Faulkner's *Sanctuary?*) is not the whole story: beneath his defenses there is a profound turmoil—"out of the reach of his power of analysis" (128)—and it is implied that his unmanageable aversion to her "small tragic spearmint-flavored sighs" (130) and other allurements actually conceals deeper feelings of attraction to her (not unmixed with accompanying self-loathing).

"The Comforts of Home" may be O'Connor's most involved family romance, and we cannot leave out of an account of Thomas's psyche his feelings of rivalry with his father. Throughout, Thomas feels that he is taking his father's place unworthily by allowing his mother's charitable foolishness to continue. "Numbskull," he imagines the old man saying to him, "put your foot down now." (126) Also in the back of Thomas's mind is his knowledge that the old man had harbored desires for revenge against the woman—and in fact died "with an angry glance at his wife as if she alone were responsible." (121)

The problem for Thomas, then, is how to reconcile his conflicting urges—to act with the forthrightness of his father, to keep the love of his mother, to punish his mother, to get rid of Sarah Ham, and to satisfy his repressed desire for the latter. If indeed this is what is going on in his mind, then one must say that O'Connor resolves the conflict with startling brilliance—in what would seem the sole way possible: prompted by his father, while his mother sleeps, with the ostensible motive of framing the girl, Thomas plants his pistol in Sarah's pocketbook; and the act is described in unmistakably sexual language. "He grabbed the red pocketbook. It had a skin-like feel to his touch and as it opened, he caught an unmistakable odor of the girl. Wincing, he thrust in the gun and then drew back. His face burned an ugly dull red." (140)

But he is caught in the act (we will not pause to ask whether he might have wanted to be caught), and Sarah's discovering words and the quality of her voice carry on the sexual undercurrent. " 'What is Tomsee putting in my purse?' she called and her pleased laugh bounced down the staircase. . . . 'Tomsee is being naughty,' she said in a throaty voice." (140) When Thomas's mother, awakening from her nap, enters the scene, the exchange between her and Sarah Ham reinforces the sexual symbolism, lending the lines a touch of unexpected, bawdy humor as well.

> "Tomsee put his pistol in my bag!" the girl shrieked.
> "Ridiculous," his mother said, yawning. "What would Thomas want to put his pistol in your bag for?" . . .
> "Thomas wouldn't put a gun in your bag," his mother said. "Thomas is a gentleman." (140–41)[24]

In frenzy and fury, damning the universe, his arm as if guided by his antifeminist father, Thomas fires the gun. Indeed, one can almost surmise in the expression on Thomas's face (before the shift to Sheriff Farebrother's viewpoint) the suggestion of a design that has been at last completed. "His expression for some few seconds was that of a man unwilling to admit surprise. His eyes were clear as glass, reflecting the scene." (141)

Any summary of the bare action in "The Comforts of Home" would inevitably sound tragic. Yet the death of Thomas's mother is hardly handled as a tragic spectacle; and Thomas himself is treated without pity. Instead, the tale is an uncommonly complicated moral satire with, in addition to the more obvious critique of parochial idealism, a criticism of the kind of self-deception that sees sexuality as the enemy of Christian love. Sarah Ham is of course no model of any sort (though neither does she seem a very bad sort); but Thomas's innocence, far from being a strength, is, rather, a weakness of his character. "Greenleaf" seems, in a way, to corroborate this point not only in affirming obliquely the analogy of sexual and Christian love in the major symbol of the bull but also in such casual satirical asides as, "[Mrs. May] thought the word, Jesus, should be kept inside the church building like other words inside the bedroom." (31)

With its various metaphysical, moral, and psychological levels intersecting, "The Comforts of Home" is a fascinating story. And we might well recall O'Connor's words on one occasion which, while spoken in an admittedly different context, easily carry a more general weight: "I am not, of course, as innocent as I look."[25]

Parker's Back

Like the two stories just considered—"The Artificial Nigger" and "The Comforts of Home"—"Parker's Back" describes the intrusion of an alien figure upon the relationship of two characters. And that intrusion serves not only to define and illuminate the relationship but (as with the other tales) to render to one character in particular an experience of the mystery of his human condition. Only, in "Parker's Back" the intruding figure is the image of Christ that is tattooed on the back of the hero, Parker. And what further distinguishes this tale from the others is precisely the implication that Parker has, in a sense, himself become the Christlike intruder.

Parker is an odd blend of earlier characters in O'Connor's fiction: he has something of The Misfit's and Shiftlet's background as a footloose drifter and something of Hazel Motes's and Tarwater's backwoods bearing; and yet he specifically lacks any conscious pre-occupation—much less obsession—with Jesus and the redemption; and he is not at all bothered by the carnal face of sin. His wife, Sarah Ruth Cates, has no real precedent, however, being a fanatically puri-tan fundamentalist, born and bred in a briar patch. She bears a slight resemblance to Mrs. Greenleaf (though younger), but is pointedly without the latter's intimate knowledge and experience of Jesus. I might add that Parker and Sarah Ruth are among the very few char-acters in O'Connor's fiction to be married during the life of the story.

The reader's initial impression of their relationship is that a theo-logically "approved" character (Sarah Ruth) has been pitted against an atheist (Parker). But as the story moves to its climax, the conflict grows into a parody of the reverse situation: Christ-changed Parker is given a mock lashing by the pretender to the Christian mystery, Sarah Ruth. Never before in O'Connor has a "prophet" been so dis-honored in his own country: Sarah is no mere "intellectual" adver-sary and no mere church socializer—she is a rigidly fanatic Bible reader whose hatred of sin is equal to her hatred of the Church and Catholic idolatry. When she denies, in the end, the tattooed Christ on Parker's back, she is denying as well the doctrine of the Incarna-tion, of the corporeality of God. In that sense, it is a more or less technical theological conflict that polarizes these characters and yet (O'Connor seems to be saying) one that is more than skin deep.

The history of Parker's conversion, if we may call it that, is extrava-gant, whimsical, and ludicrous. What first awakens the spiritual pas-sion that will lead him, all unknowingly, to Christ is the sight of a tattooed man at a fair. "The man's skin was patterned in what seemed from Parker's distance . . . a single intricate design of brilliant color." As the tattooed man flexes his muscles, "the arabesque of men and beasts and flowers on his skin appeared to have a subtle motion of its own. Parker was filled with emotion, lifted up as some people are when the flag passes."[26] Although that last sentence suggests a cool amusement at Parker's emotion, it would be a mistake to under-estimate the importance of this initial sense of wonder. It is akin to the earlier association of the aesthetic and the spiritual in "The Dis-placed Person" when the priest exclaims rapturously over the beauty of Mrs. McIntyre's passing peacock. In both cases, a grotesque blend of the familiar and the exotic seems to be at the root of "wonder," and, in Parker's case, it leads him to marvel at the strangeness of life itself. "Until he saw the man at the fair, it did not enter his head that there was anything out of the ordinary about the fact that he existed." (223) O'Connor's first principle is thus rooted in the perception of the world and not in some disembodied cogito: rather, video ergo sum.

Thus begins Parker's spiritual career: in emulation of the tattooed man at the fair, he offers the tabula rasa of his body to a series of artists for their lines and colors, figures and words. And, what is more, the operations hurt him "just enough to make it appear to Parker to be worth doing. This was peculiar too for before he had thought that only what did not hurt was worth doing." (223) Parker thus receives O'Connor's characteristic initiation into suffering, and we know that, spiritually, he is henceforward a marked man.

Yet the mass of creation on his skin is, in a manner, without a Creator, and, with a subliminal urgency, Parker seeks some means of ordering his world. Thus he marries Sarah Ruth—for no apparent reason—and stays with her too—also for no apparent reason (she was "both ugly and pregnant and no cook" [231])—although the reader may well perceive in his attachment to the Bible zealot an as yet unrealized attraction to the Word. Still, Sarah Ruth is not enough, and, with his vague dissatisfaction growing, Parker takes himself to a tattoo parlor, where at last he fixes upon an image that will contain his malaise. Or, rather, the image chooses him, for staring out from the artist's catalog of possible pictures is "the haloed head of a flat stern Byzantine Christ with all-demanding eyes." (235)

What is so impressive in this story of course is how convincingly O'Connor manages to render the almost magical powers of this image of Christ; in a way that is more like Hawthorne than anything else she wrote (compare "The Birthmark" and "Egotism; or the Bosom Serpent"), O'Connor enforces a peculiar amalgam of literal physical detail and symbolic meaning. Thus, as the tattoo sinks into Parker's skin, the transformation—or second birth—begins: his heart beats slowly, "as if it were being brought to life by a subtle power." (235) When the image is fully complete, Parker is shocked into silence by the powerful eyes of the Christ—"eyes to be obeyed." (241) He drives back home to Sarah Ruth and, on the way, he experiences that alienation from self and surroundings that one recognizes, in O'Connor, as the sign of an impending revelation. Outside his own house at last, the image of the sun denotes a transformation in nature that is the mirror of Parker's own metamorphosis. "Then as he stood there, a tree of light burst over the skyline. Parker fell back against the door as if he had been pinned there by a lance." (242) The foreshadowing crucifixion imagery is unmistakable, and not without a humorous self-consciousness.

But the metamorphosis is not yet complete. Sarah won't let him into the house until he utters his full name ("'I don't know no O.E.'" that literalist says [242]); but when he does utter the name—Obadiah (lit.: worshiper of Jehovah) Elihue (lit.: whose God is He)—he at last fully creates for himself his new identity: and a gracious light pours through him, turning the unimportant "spider web of facts and lies" (241) that had earlier been his soul "into a perfect arabesque of colors, a garden of trees and birds and beasts." (243) The deliberate echo of Parker's initial perception of the carnival tattooed man (see 223) implies the fulfillment at last of Parker's "notion of wonder."

The fulfillment of his suffering soon follows. For although Parker had sought, in having tattooed on his back "just God" (234) (that is, only God), an image that would finally satisfy his wife's obsession with the Bible, Parker painfully discovers that Sarah Ruth does not recognize "God" when he is pictured right before her eyes. The word, for his wife, is disembodied. It is not "with God."

"Another picture," Sarah Ruth growled. "I might have known you was off after putting some more trash on yourself." . . .

"Don't you know who it is?" he cried in anguish.

"No, who is it?" Sarah Ruth said. "It ain't anybody I know."

"It's him," Parker said.

"Him who?"

"God!" Parker cried.

"God? God don't look like that!"

"What do you know how he looks?" Parker moaned. "You ain't seen him."

"He don't *look*," Sarah Ruth said. "He's a spirit. No man shall see his face."

"Aw listen," Parker groaned, "this is just a picture of him."

"Idolatry!" Sarah Ruth screamed. "Idolatry!" (243–44)

And the woman whose broomstick is mightier than her word proceeds to beat still another tattoo on the poor man's flesh.

> Parker was too stunned to resist. He sat there and let her beat him
> until she had nearly knocked him senseless and large welts had
> formed on the face of the tattooed Christ. Then he staggered up and
> made for the door.
> She stamped the broom two or three times on the floor and went
> to the window and shook it out to get the taint of him off it. Still
> gripping it, she looked toward the pecan tree and her eyes hardened
> still more. There he was—who called himself Obadiah Elihue—lean
> ing against the tree, crying like a baby. (244)

The ritual scourge Parker endures in this, the last scene of the
story, is the perfection of his "suffering" and exaltation. In some
respects, its effect might be compared with the scaffold scene in
Hawthorne's *Scarlet Letter* and too with the conclusion of Kafka's
"Hunger Artist," in both of which, as Edwin Honig has written perceptively, the ironic reenactment of Christ's ordeal "becomes terrifying and credible because it is revealed as an actuality of daily life
which repeats the original archetypal situation of Christ's lonely
death on the Cross. Passing into fiction in this way, the scriptural
event is given a new and different, one might say more starkly religious, value from the one now rigidified in the dogma."[27]
    And yet it would be false to the overall effect of "Parker's Back" to
push the analogy with Hawthorne and Kafka too far. For Christ's
"terrifying" and "lonely death on the Cross," in Honig's words, seems
after all to be somewhat distant from the tone of O'Connor's story.
The narration of the tale is quite clearly designed to place Parker's
"crucifixion" in a comic context, so that we may well associate
Parker, at the end, with blind, ascetic, suffering Hazel Motes who is
also the hero of a Christian comic plot (the Resurrection is implied
paradoxically in the Crucifixion). In addition, the structure of the
tale seems analogous to the traditional motif of the henpecked husband who can do nothing to please his shrewish wife. Our recollection
of Parker's first meeting with Sarah Ruth (she smacks his face for
cursing) casts a comic light on the repeat performance that closes
the tale.
    Moreover, the narrative style of "Parker's Back" suggests that

O'Connor took her usual rare delight in adopting the ironic, humorous voice of the storyteller.

> Sarah Ruth's father was a Straight Gospel preacher but he was away, spreading it in Florida. (229)

> When he could, [Parker] broke in with tales of the hefty girl he worked for. " 'Mr. Parker,' " he said she said, " 'I hired you for your brains.' " (She had added, "So why don't you use them?")
> "And you should have seen her face the first time she saw me without my shirt," he said. " 'Mr. Parker,' she said, 'you're a walking panner-rammer!' " This had, in fact, been her remark but it had been delivered out of one side of her mouth. (231)

And it is simply the final irony of the story that our last picture of Parker, after we have carefully observed his second birth into grace, should be—through his wife's eyes—as a pathetic crying baby. So outrageous, indeed, is the story, so humorous the telling of it, so overt the symbolism, that one hesitates to decide whether it is not as much a parody of the Christ figure in fiction as a seriously ironic achievement of that figure; or whether, through parody, O'Connor has not ironically reinvigorated the source.

While it is lacking in the deadly violence that characterizes many of her best tales, early and late, "Parker's Back" evinces a confidence in handling that is indicative of the writer who is sure of himself and his materials. In this respect, it bears comparison with earlier tales like "The River" (also an overtly "theological" tale) and "A Temple of the Holy Ghost" (where the symbol of the grotesque body also carries a theological meaning)—in both of which that maturity seems lacking. And if we take O'Connor's attitude toward Parker as at once playfully comic and seriously ironic, one cannot but marvel at the rightness of her symbolism. For the tattooed body of O. E. Parker becomes at once a splendid and beautiful microcosm of the world, an embodiment of his "spider web soul," and a literal emblem of his Christlike suffering—besides being the perfect naturalistic medium for Parker's aesthetic emotions.

And too, as Theodore Gaster has written, the tattoo has a long history in religious faiths as a sign confirming a belief in, and covenant with, God.

> The custom of tattooing passed even into Christianity. In early centuries, baptism was known as "sealing," and this was also the ancient

name for the rite of Confirmation, which originally followed immediately. Nor did the custom survive only in a figurative sense. To this day the Catholics of Central Bosnia tattoo themselves with religious symbols; while in the neighborhood of Loreto (Italy) it is common to do likewise in honor of the celebrated local Madonna. . . . and it is recorded of the German mystic, Heinrich Seuse, that he impressed the name of Jesus over his heart.[28]

Caroline Gordon has written, in an article on O'Connor, of a visit she paid to the writer in May, 1964, when the latter was hospitalized in Atlanta. This was of course a few months before O'Connor's death, and she was working at the time on "Parker's Back," hoping that she would be able to finish it for her forthcoming volume of stories, *Everything That Rises Must Converge*. Miss Gordon writes: "After the nurse had left the room Flannery pulled a notebook out from under her pillow. 'The doctor says I mustn't do any work. But he says it's all right for me to write a little fiction.'"[29]

5

JUDGEMENT DAY

THE fact that it is possible to talk about O'Connor as I
have been talking about her—in terms of recurrent dramatic images
or situations, and recurrent patterns of meaning—indicates something about her writings that I have been taking for granted, and
that is their repetitiousness. Anyone reading an O'Connor story in an
anthology would undoubtedly be struck by the jolting power of her
narrative. Yet it must be admitted that the reader who goes through
her works from end to end becomes accustomed to the characteristic
surprise of her conclusions and begins to find a different surprise (perhaps even some disappointment) in those stories that do not conform
to the usual pattern of violence and death. Of course the stories are
interesting beyond these first impressions, but the almost ritualistic
patterns of action in O'Connor do point to a genuine feature of her
art. As Richard Poirier has observed, O'Connor's recurrent situations
are "an indication of how serious a writer she is. As against what
might be called writers by occupation . . . she was obsessed by
arrangements of life and language in which she saw some almost
eschatological possibilities."[1] If this is so—if a powerful religious com-

mitment shapes her fiction—does it not place unusual demands upon the reader? After all, it is harder to accept predictable intrusions of the supernatural upon life than it is to accept an occasional intrusion.

Belief and Fiction

Even for the tales in isolation, the question might arise for the reader lacking a religious commitment, of whether he can experience the full meaning of O'Connor's work. In some of the stories, surely her Catholicism works with our common human feelings: I think one has no trouble, for example, reading of the little girl's initiation into misery in the impressive "A Circle in the Fire"—no theological implications are needed to support the structure. Similarly, we can understand the experiences of old Fortune in "A View of the Woods," of Julian in "Everything That Rises Must Converge," of Mrs. McIntyre in "The Displaced Person"—we can understand these and other images of our broken human condition without having to translate them into theological images. The presence of evil, the experience of suffering—these are as concretely visible to someone outside the Church as inside. And, conversely, the presence of something we might call grace can surely be felt in terms which do not require explicit theological translation—even when theological language is made a part of the story, as, for example, in "The Artificial Nigger" and "Judgement Day."

Yet, in other tales, O'Connor's Christian viewpoint would seem to be problematical. Thus, if we hold to our accustomed estimations of human life, Hazel Motes's death at the end of *Wise Blood*—seemingly lonely and miserable—is pitiable. But for O'Connor (and it is the business of the narrative to demonstrate this), there is something unmistakably salutary about it, for it signifies Hazel's hard-fought redemption. And too, we might say that the grandmother's death in "A Good Man Is Hard to Find" is pitiable and tragic; but for O'Connor, that too is a death unto salvation.

From another viewpoint, however, what I have called problematical in these stories can be seen—more properly, I think—as a chief source of her peculiar strength as a writer; for if our common feelings do not impede our understanding of the fiction altogether, then indeed we may find a certain effective dissonance in our response—which must be the result of the tension in O'Connor's own viewpoint between the austerely Christian and the failingly human. What else allows her to treat death *at once* tragically and comically?

Perhaps the more demonstrable problems in O'Connor's fiction occur when her meaning is expressed *too clearly*. We may grant her the satirist's right to shape the reader's judgment, but still wish she would not tell him so obviously what he might otherwise be willing to infer. At other times, it is the tendentious implication itself which the reader may resist. To share a laugh, one must also share a point of view (even if momentarily), and if the assumptions of that point of view strain the reader, then his response too will be strained. Some things, to be sure, are funny regardless of what you believe: Mr. Shortley ("The Displaced Person") and his logic are funny; the grandmother's story, in "A Good Man Is Hard to Find," of someone carving his initials (E. A. T.) into the side of a proffered watermelon and finding his gift eaten shortly after—that too is funny; and many, many other examples could be adduced. Still, there are other occasions when the reader may not share a laugh precisely because of the viewpoint O'Connor assumes and the judgment she implies. I, for example, do not find it especially funny (or satirically effective) when, in "The River," little Harry's father says to the devout Mrs. Connin as she tells him of their afternoon with the healing preacher, " 'Healing by prayer is mighty inexpensive.' "[2]

Several passages in "The River" depend upon a similar use of irony and satire to make their point. There is even one passage in the story (comparable in some respects to the dinner-table scene in "A Temple of the Holy Ghost") where the question of what is funny is itself the object of O'Connor's ironic satire. Little Harry Ashfield is thinking over the discoveries he has been making as a result of his brief absence from the corrupt city and his "sophisticated" parents.

> You found out more when you left where you lived. He had found out already this morning that he had been made by a carpenter named Jesus Christ. Before he had thought it had been a doctor named Sladewall, a fat man with a yellow mustache who gave him shots and thought his name was Herbert, but this must have been a joke. They joked a lot where he lived. If he had thought about it before, he would have thought Jesus Christ was a word like "oh" or "damm" or "God," or maybe somebody who had cheated them out of something sometime. (37–38)

The humorous and satirical intentions of such a passage are too obvious, I think. Moreover, I would guess that the deadpan seriousness of

Harry's ruminations, while amusing to very few, would be a good deal more amusing to certain believers in Christ than to most non-believers. And the amusement would take the form of a "knowing" smile: the real "joke" is on his parents, on Dr. Sladewall, on those who think "Jesus Christ" is an expletive.

If I am right in assuming that such a passage is uncertainly successful for the average uncommitted reader, then how can we clarify the general relationship between a reader's beliefs and his response? Wayne Booth, in *The Rhetoric of Fiction*, states the problem clearly, I think, when he writes that "it is only when a work seems explicitly doctrinaire, or when reasonable men can be in serious disagreement about its values, that the question of belief arises for discussion." Booth goes on to say that, by contrast, "the great 'Catholic' or 'Protestant' works are not, in their essentials, Catholic or Protestant at all."[3]

If Booth's statement is compared with O'Connor's own criterion for "great fiction," the sharp difference between them becomes apparent.

> Many contend that the job of the novelist is to show us how man feels, and they say that this is an operation in which his own commitments intrude not at all. . . . Pain is pain, joy is joy, love is love, and these human emotions are stronger than any mere religious belief; they are what they are and the novelist shows them as they are. This is all well and good so far as it goes, but it just does not go as far as the novel goes. Great fiction involves the whole range of human judgment; it is not simply an imitation of feeling. The good novelist . . . tells the intelligent reader whether . . . feeling is adequate or inadequate, whether it is moral or immoral, whether it is good or evil. And his theology, even in its most remote reaches, will have a direct bearing on this.[4]

O'Connor insists on the unity of seeing and judging; for her, common feelings do not supply moral judgments, and the final concern of the novelist is with good and evil, not with love and hate.

One way of closing the distance between these two opposed views is to place them both within the schema of the reader-author relationship. Here it may be helpful to return to Booth's *Rhetoric of Fiction* and to adopt the vocabulary used there to image the relationship that obtains for every book, of whatever kind. Booth distinguishes between the author as a living human being and the "implied author" who is behind the written word; similarly, the reader is both an everyday self—he who is merely holding the book in hand—and a "mock reader" (Walker Gibson's phrase) who "become[s] the self whose beliefs must coincide with the author's" if he is to enjoy the book fully. "The author creates, in short, an image of himself and another image of his reader; he makes his reader, as he makes his second self, and the most successful reading is one in which the created selves, author and reader, can find complete agreement."[5]

We might say, then, that in the "great 'Catholic' works" Booth speaks of, the created author and the created reader meet each other on the ground of their common view of man's fate. And we might say that in the "great fiction" O'Connor speaks of, created author successfully "shows" created reader what he should be feeling and judging. Assuming, then, that we are mock readers of O'Connor, why do we feel that some of the fiction is less successful than others? Why might we accept the death of Mrs. May in "Greenleaf" but not the death of Harry Ashfield in "The River"? At what point do we refuse, as mock readers, to go along with what we are asked to feel and judge?

When we balk, as readers, at accepting the image before us, it is usually because O'Connor has violated too deeply certain ingrained assumptions about man's life in attempting to direct our judgment of a character or situation. One does not necessarily have to be an atheist to resist some of these occasions, and I will state baldly what I think are the premises underlying them: first, the belief that death can be a good thing for a person; second, the belief that a character who does not believe in Christ cannot, with any consistency, perform "good" deeds; and third, the belief that a character who believes in the devil (who accepts, in other words, the theological election, though not himself necessarily of the right party), regardless of the evil he does, still has a certain saving grace.[6] Let me add that I am positing these views not as elements of Catholic doctrine or necessarily as formal articles of O'Connor's faith but merely as inferences about her beliefs that can, I think, be drawn from the fiction.

One story that illustrates these three beliefs in a way that, it seems to me, would cause conflict within the average non-Catholic reader, is "The Lame Shall Enter First." For the various conceptions of the characters seem basically at odds with a plausible realism, and they are not made believable by the story itself. It will be remembered that Sheppard, a psychologist, brings the lame delinquent Rufus Johnson into his home in the hope of giving him the love and attention he has lacked all his life (a lack which accounts, Sheppard believes, for his evil doings). His plan backfires, however, when Rufus befriends Sheppard's own neglected son Norton and teaches him that "'you got to be dead to get [to heaven].'" (165) So Norton, who desperately longs for his dead mother, hangs himself in the attic. At last, Sheppard sees the tragic error he has made in ignoring his son Norton, just as, by implication, he has made a similar error in ignoring Christ.

The problem with the characterization of Sheppard, however, is that he is just too obtuse to represent the "intellectual" or "rational" point of view. He jeers repeatedly at Norton's obvious signs of grief and need; he is tactless and bumbling in his attempts to win Rufus's confidence. The point is not that such people never have existed (they may, even as psychologists)—but, as characters in a work of fiction, they fail to attain credibility. Moreover, Sheppard's efforts at rehabilitating the nasty Rufus Johnson are portrayed as worthless not only in terms of results but (the story implies) by intention too: there is no room here for a humanism, no middle ground of common goodness, no allowance that it might be "right" to improve on the accidents of nature. Without a belief in Christ, it is implied, good deeds are misguided—often evil.

It is a point of view we saw underlying as well the problematic characterization of Rayber in The Violent Bear It Away, and it was given expression by O'Connor in a passage from her "Introduction to A Memoir of Mary Ann" that I quoted earlier in connection with "The Displaced Person." "In the absence of this faith now, we govern by tenderness. It is a tenderness which, long since cut off from the person of Christ, is wrapped in theory. When tenderness is detached from the source of tenderness, its logical outcome is terror."[7] Yet surely we know that an attachment to the "source of tenderness" —or the claim of such—is not in itself a guarantee of tenderness: the historical role of the Church, not only in its own inquisitions but in its acquiescences in countless wars and oppressive regimes, would seem to bear witness to that.

And what is further disturbing in "The Lame Shall Enter First" is the author's implied attitude toward Rufus. The lame youth is the antagonist of Sheppard in every way: he is mischievous and perversely obdurate, but he believes himself possessed by a real devil, and eats a page from the Bible to prove it. Rufus may not be the moral norm in the story, but his *standards* of right and wrong, and of what matters, are approved because based on Christ's teachings, and these standards he implants in Norton. But if, as O'Connor has written, "stories of pious children tend to be false,"[8] it seems equally true that stories of pious children masquerading as demons tend to be false. On the one hand, Rufus lacks any truly diabolical dimension, and, on the other, he is so frankly repulsive that we balk at considering him even the *misshapen* vessel of faith he is intended to be. As for Norton, his belief in Rufus's gospel rests all too palpably on his need for a mother—a situation which considerably diminishes whatever theological meaning his death should have. As with little Harry Ashfield, O'Connor fails, I think, to make Norton's dying a positive achievement.

Because "The Lame Shall Enter First" translates O'Connor's convictions so uncompromisingly into dramatic terms, it can only make us uneasy, I think, as moral drama. One may feel a slightly different discomfort, perhaps, at the implications of the moral process in the two novels. Both Hazel Motes and Tarwater, it is easy to forget, commit murders on the way to their salvation, and, in each case, O'Connor subordinates these acts to the larger spiritual drama that results after the deaths of Solace Layfield (*Wise Blood*) and Bishop (*The Violent Bear It Away*); in neither case is a recognition of guilt of great importance to the conversion process. I do not think these are faults in either of the novels (Layfield isn't a sufficiently developed character to warrant our real concern; Bishop seems to ask for his own death), but I can see how they might puzzle the reader with the usual moral expectations.

Yet given the demands she placed upon herself as a Catholic writer, what is remarkable is not that Flannery O'Connor occasionally failed or faltered in her fiction but that she succeeded as often as she did—succeeded where one would not have thought possible. As Orwell has written, "the novel is practically a Protestant form of art; it is a product of the free mind, of the autonomous individual."[9] While O'Connor's orthodoxy did indeed at times prevail over the exigencies of psychic realism, her faith must also, one imagines, have given a confidence, boldness, and insight to her imaginings.

For most of her work, O'Connor's reader need not share all of her premises; nor must he feel obliged to accept the stricter implications of her fiction. He must, however, be interested in what has always been the basic province of the romance in America: an exploration of the more extreme states of feeling and being and an effort to get beneath the surface of our lives. He may enjoy the tales otherwise— for the pleasures of style, of humor, of plot—but he will not appreciate their larger intentions.

When she is at her best, Flannery O'Connor achieves that balance between the demands of a plausible realism—the demands of fiction—and those of her belief that permits the reader to glimpse the paradox and mystery of "our position on earth," as she termed it. When that balance is achieved, the form is not overly contrived, the irony is not overly obvious, the satire is not overly strident. The best fiction, as Frank Kermode has said, must not falsify reality "with patterns too neat, too inclusive." And he quotes Iris Murdoch's statement that "literature must always represent a battle between real people and images."[10] It is certainly the case that O'Connor's best fiction springs from that same battle—but, we might add, in such a way as to conceal the tactics; what must be avoided, and what she usually did avoid, is a field littered with dead characters.

From The Geranium to Judgment Day

It is surely more than a coincidence that the last story in Flannery O'Connor's posthumously published collection, *Everything That Rises Must Converge*, should be a reworking of her very first story, "The Geranium" (1946). With what seems rather to have been conscious design, O'Connor placed at the end of that volume a story— "Judgement Day"—that not only fulfills eschatologically her Christian vision, but, in looking back to her first publication, seems to complete the design of her career as well. A comparison of these first and last works—"The Geranium" and "Judgement Day"—thus offers a final perspective from which to view the continuities and changes in O'Connor's writing.

Both stories are set in New York City, and, by placing her main character—a diehard rural Southerner—farther from the South than any other of her heroes, O'Connor generates the central emotional situation of the story: the misery of an exile who is longing for home.

It is the clearest and starkest image she would devise for the situation of the displaced person that occurs so regularly in her fiction.

In the first version, "The Geranium," Old Dudley lives with his daughter in her small apartment, and so great are the pressures upon him of the unfamiliar city that he recurs to the safer dreams of home. His only tangible consolation in the city is the geranium plant that sits in the window opposite his own, and he spends much time contemplating it—for it has come to mean, for Old Dudley, the complex of associations and memories that compose for him "the South." The story ends when Dudley discovers that the geranium is no longer in the window opposite (it has fallen into the alley), and the Southerner is left confronting the unpleasant man who owns the plant— and who dares him to go down into the alley to retrieve it. Dudley, who fears another terrible confrontation with "the Negro" (he has already been unsettled by their friendliness and lack of docility), prefers to stay put, and our final image is of a man pathetically entrapped in a living hell.

In the later "Judgement Day," O'Connor keeps this basic situation, but Tanner (Dudley's successor) is significantly different from the earlier protagonist in being unwilling to endure that hell; instead, he contrives to get back home at any cost—if need be, in a coffin, when he will astonish his friends by resurrecting himself before their eyes and crying, " 'Judgement Day! Judgement Day!' " (265) What has been added, then, to the later story is precisely a "judgement day." For Tanner's drive is given what one might call a supernatural dimension, and Tanner himself, in the tradition of O'Connor's spiritually obsessed characters, is made slightly "mad." It is a change analogous to the heightening of theological overtones observed in the completed novel *Wise Blood*, when compared with the chapters published earlier; and it is indicative not only of the evolution of O'Connor's thematic concerns as a writer but of the very nature of her characteristic mode of perception, whereby a spiritual significance emerges from the naturalistic level of a situation and a sense of entelechy is discovered in the present moment.

With the change from a main character who passively endures his exile to one who actively pursues his deliverance comes an interesting realignment of the relationships between that character and the other figures in the story. Thus, for example, in "Judgement Day" Tanner

evinces a more hostile attitude toward his daughter than does Old
Dudley in "The Geranium"; one that hinges on his command, in the
later story, that she make sure he is buried in the South (compare old
Tarwater's command in *The Violent Bear It Away* that he be buried
in a Christian manner)—the fulfillment of which command he has
good reason to doubt.

Another change is visible in the increased warmth with which
Tanner regards his friendship with his Negro companion in the
South. Old Dudley, in "The Geranium," also had such a friendship,
but in the earlier story, the Negro, Rabie, is remembered mainly as
an essential ingredient to Dudley's sense of security in the South (his
own superiority to the black was unquestioned): thus he imagines
assuaging his feelings of anxiety and confusion in the face of the
"swishing and jamming . . . dirty and dead" Northern city by thinking how even more afraid Rabie would be. Old Dudley would say to
his friend, if he were with him: " 'It ain't so big. . . . Don't let it get
you down, Rabie. It's just like any other city and cities ain't all that
complicated.' "[11] But the affecting relationship of Tanner and the
Negro, Coleman, in "Judgement Day," goes beyond this: the two
lived together in the South in a friendship that was somewhere between that of two brothers and that of a lord and his liege man. And
this felt bond between them is brought out by O'Connor in her
depiction of their very first meeting, when Tanner, then foreman at
a sawmill, sees Coleman lounging around near his working men and
thus setting a bad example for them. Tanner goes over to him—unde-
cided whether to threaten or to con the Negro into removing himself; unable to do either, he gratuitously offers Coleman a pair of
eyeglasses he has just whittled out of wood.

> The Negro reached for the glasses. He attached the bows carefully
> behind his ears and looked forth. He peered this way and that with
> exaggerated solemnity. And then he looked directly at Tanner and
> grinned, or grimaced, Tanner could not tell which, but he had an
> instant's sensation of seeing before him a negative image of himself,
> as if clownishness and captivity had been their common lot. (255)

It is a striking scene, and one that bears comparison with an earlier
scene in O'Connor's fiction. The doubled image of white man and
black man, the grin that is a grimace, the recognition of a common
fate in the confrontation—these things are present too at the conclu-

sion of "The Artificial Nigger," when Nelson and Mr. Head face the plaster statue; in the later "Judgement Day," however, the tone is less austere, the moment dramatically an anticlimax. Yet in the different context of O'Connor's earlier satirical treatment of white-black relations, the scene is indeed a climax and most revealing. Thus, for example, compared with Asbury Fox's attempted secular communion with the black workers on his mother's farm, this meeting between Tanner and Coleman is spontaneous, uncalculated, undemeaning, a surprising discovery of their consanguinity rather than a forced charade. What it implies is consistent with O'Connor's whole outlook—that the coming together of black and white, when it happens, is a gift and not a contrivance, and that it is based on a shared sense of human limitations or, if you will, poverty.

Now separated from Coleman in the North, Tanner dreams of arriving home in a coffin; and the imagined scene, when he is greeted at the railway station by his faithful friend and by a white friend, Hooten, is a remarkable vision of reunion in the end that is at once deeply moving and hilariously funny. For the familiarity, warmth, and comic spontaneity of their relationship are marvelously evoked by the toughly colloquial language.

In his dreams he could feel the cold early morning air of home coming in through the cracks of the pine box. He could see Coleman waiting, red-eyed, on the station platform and Hooten standing there with his green eyeshade and black alpaca sleeves. If the old fool had stayed at home where he belonged, Hooten would be thinking, he wouldn't be arriving on the 6:03 in no box. Coleman had turned the borrowed mule and cart so that they could slide the box off the platform onto the open end of the wagon. Everything was ready and the two of them, shut-mouthed, inched the loaded coffin toward the wagon. From inside he began to scratch on the wood. They let go as if it had caught fire.

They stood looking at each other, then at the box.
"That him," Coleman said. "He in there his self."
"Naw," Hooten said, "must be a rat got in there with him."
"That him. This here one of his tricks."
"If it's a rat he might as well stay."
"That him. Git a crowbar."
Hooten went grumbling off and got the crowbar and came back and began to pry open the lid. Even before he had the upper end pried open, Coleman was jumping up and down, wheezing and panting from excitement. Tanner gave a thrust upward with both hands

and sprang up in the box. "Judgement Day! Judgement Day!" he cried. "Don't you two fools know it's Judgement Day?" (264–65)

We shall have occasion to recall this focal scene later.

But there is another crucial Negro character in both stories, and the change in his depiction is equally indicative of the change from "The Geranium" to "Judgement Day." For if the heightened intensity of Tanner's relationship with Coleman is reflected in the dream of deliverance we have just quoted, the heightened animosity between Tanner and the Negro neighbor in the city apartment house is reflected in the nightmarish scenes between them. In fact, the neighbor in the earlier "Geranium" is very friendly toward Old Dudley: he tries to strike up a friendship with the Southerner, and at one point gently helps him up the stairs. (Compare the final scene on the stairs in "Judgement Day.") When Dudley discovers that the fellow is no servant of a neighboring family but the neighbor himself, however, the Southerner responds with astonished hostility to his advances. But in "Judgement Day," the order of hostilities is reversed: now it is Tanner who makes advances. Taking the Negro as a fellow exile from the South, he condescendingly, but warmly, calls him "Preacher," and proposes they go fishing together. After several such attempts to establish rapport with the Negro (who is an actor), the latter responds at last with untoward outrage.

> A tremor racked him from his head to his crotch. . . . he lunged and grasped Tanner by both shoulders. "I don't take no crap," he whispered, "off no wool-hat red-neck·son-of-a-bitch peckerwood old bastard like you." He caught his breath. And then his voice came out in the sound of an exasperation so profound that it rocked on the verge of a laugh. It was high and piercing and weak. "And I'm not no preacher! I'm not even no Christian. I don't believe that crap. There ain't no Jesus and there ain't no God." (263)

The deepened hostility of the Negro, together with the blasphemous retort he makes to Tanner, alters his role in the story from that of a merely irritating presence (as he was for Old Dudley) to the stature of a spiritual antagonist, a veritable anti-Christ. (It is a change analogous to that which occurred in the portrayal of the Negro porter on the train in the two versions of the first chapter of *Wise Blood*.)

All of the changes O'Connor wrought in the character relationships from "The Geranium" to "Judgement Day" thus conspire to increase the isolation of the old man and to provide the dramatic context for his apocalyptic dream of a judgment day that will return him to the warm embrace of the South. What is equally striking in the later version is the heightened dramatic action, for, properly speaking, "The Geranium" has no dramatic action at all, or only a bare minimum. The earlier tale is more simply a portrait of a man in a hostile environment, and its chief structural device is the symbol of the geranium plant that stands on the windowsill across from Old Dudley's window. Replacing the loosely symbolic structure of "The Geranium" is a drama that, beginning with the same image of an old man looking out his window, takes us to a stark conclusion. More particularly, Tanner's successive confrontations with his Negro neighbor give narrative shape to "Judgement Day" and culminate in the final terrible scene on the stairway. (The change in structure is typical of O'Connor's development from mostly static, psychologically focused sketches to the more startling dramatizations that seem effortlessly to embody her point.)

We arrive at that scene when Tanner acts at last to emancipate himself from the North: he has prepared a note to be attached to his person to ensure his arrival in the South—dead or alive. Wonderfully evocative of the character of the old man and his feelings for his friend, it reads: "IF FOUND DEAD SHIP EXPRESS COLLECT TO COLEMAN PARRUM, CORINTH, GEORGIA. . . . COLEMAN SELL MY BELONGINGS AND PAY THE FREIGHT ON ME & THE UNDERTAKER. ANYTHING LEFT OVER YOU CAN KEEP. YOURS TRULY T. C. TANNER. P.S. STAY WHERE YOU ARE. DON'T LET THEM TALK YOU INTO COMING UP HERE. ITS NO KIND OF PLACE." (246) As he leaves his daughter's apartment, he is "as confident as if the woods of home lay at the bottom of the stairs." (267) And that's as far as he gets: pitching forward suddenly, he lands "upsidedown in the middle of the flight." (268) The geranium, bottom up in the alley, has become, in the later story, the man himself.

Once again he dreams of arriving home in a coffin—but the triumphant glory of his former imaginings is now altered to an eerie "greenish light"; and the vigor of his rejuvenated cry changed to a weak voice, murmuring, "'Coleman?'" (268) Now, Tanner awakens from his psychopannychistic state to be answered harshly by the suddenly appearing Negro actor: "'Ain't any coal man, either.' . . .

'Judgement day,' he said in a mocking voice. 'Ain't no judgement day, old man. Cept this. Maybe this here judgement day for you.'" (268) And Tanner's last confident and bewildered words, as the "Nigger actor" grabs hold of him are: "'Hep me up, Preacher. I'm on my way home!'" (269)

The final image of the old man is narrated in the author's flatly descriptive tone, deliberately understated in order to heighten, by contrast, the nightmare horror and grotesqueness of his actual fate at the hands of the Negro. "His daughter found him when she came in from the grocery store. His hat had been pulled down over his face and his head and arms thrust between the spokes of the banister; his feet dangled over the stairwell like those of a man in the stocks." (269) But the concluding paragraph, sustaining the same matter-of-fact tone, is a sardonic comment on the daughter: "She buried him in New York City, but after she had done it she could not sleep at night. Night after night she turned and tossed and very definite lines began to appear in her face, so she had him dug up and shipped the body to Corinth. Now she rests well at night and her good looks have mostly returned." (269) Thus O'Connor judges at once the vanity of the daughter and the perseverance of old Tanner: he does, at last, make it South. And more than South: "'Hep me up, Preacher. I'm on my way home!'"

In certain respects, the pattern of experience in "Judgement Day" most nearly resembles "A Good Man Is Hard to Find." Grandmother Bailey's dream of the Southern mansion is comparable to Tanner's dream of Corinth. And both the old lady and Tanner die while seeking an escape from the shabby present and a return to these idealized images of the past—though, in the case of Tanner, the point is far more forcefully made. And too, both make graceful gestures to their brutal deliverers—the grandmother in offering her maternal love to The Misfit, and Tanner in offering his friendship to the Negro.

One must say, however, that The Misfit is a subtler diabolical figure than his counterpart in "Judgement Day": the Negro actor is an unmitigatedly mean fellow, a gross caricature, and possibly symptomatic of O'Connor's pessimistic view of the progress of race relations in America—a character comparable, in some ways, to the equally distorted mirror image of the atrocious white man in James Baldwin's Blues for Mister Charley, written about the same time.

But O'Connor's figure, unlike Baldwin's, does not serve a political or social end but, rather, plays a demonic role in a theological drama. Moreover, he is balanced by the equally distorted image of the loyal Negro Coleman; these figures seem to function in O'Connor almost as dream images of extreme emotional states, and may find their aesthetic justification as projections of Tanner, and hence as ways of heightening the meaning of the tale.

One does not need to rehearse the fiction O'Connor wrote between 1952 and 1964, however, to realize that "Judgement Day" is merely an intensification and a polarization of elements in her redemptive vision that informed her work throughout those years: the sense of evil was never far from her hard view of reality, but neither was a sense of grace. In "Judgement Day," evil has lost the polite veneer it had in, say, The Misfit or Manley Pointer: the city (always a place of evil in O'Connor) was never as hostile as it appears in this last tale; and at times the intensity of satiric rage takes on an ugliness and incongruity not often seen in the earlier fiction ("At the Negro's side was another face, a woman's—pale, topped with a pile of copper-glinting hair and twisted as if she had just stepped in a pile of dung" [268]). But then the opposite pole of her vision, the redemptive pole, was never so unequivocally portrayed as in the image of Tanner—confident, as O'Connor is confident, that he is indeed on his way home.

One cannot neglect the probability that Flannery O'Connor also knew, in her last year, that she too was on her way home. Placed at the end of her last collection of fiction, "Judgement Day" stands unequivocally as a conclusion in which everything is concluded. Written in the winter of her own life, it is the only one of her works to be set in the season of winter ("The Geranium" was in summer). It is a kind of last testament of the author—a story whose manner progresses through comedy to horror, to redemption, presenting, finally, a vision of life and death that turns an ironic eye upon the whole scene. It is an irony that is the privilege of the Christian vision, an irony whose expression in her fiction was the imaginative fulfillment of her faith.

The relevance of that faith, one must admit, has been questioned in the twentieth century. I do not think one can question, however, the relevance of her imagination. And one catches an odd glimpse of its peculiar contemporaneity in "Judgement Day." In one respect, at least, the effect of that story strikingly resembles that achieved by the slow-motion convention in two films that appeared shortly after O'Connor's death—*The Shop on Main Street* (directed by Jan Kadar, 1965) and *The Pawnbroker* (directed by Sidney Lumet, 1965)—both of which movingly portray the impersonal horror that can so easily break upon our lives in the twentieth century. The strangely lyric, grimly comic dream image of Tanner's return home in a coffin shouting, "Judgement Day!" seems to me quite close in its imaginative force to certain images in these films—the graceful movement of human bodies across a field at the beginning of *The Pawnbroker*; the similarly slow-motion lyric image of graceful dancing at the end of *The Shop on Main Street*. Of course in neither of these films is the moment sustained for very long, but that is just the point: in the films, as in the story by O'Connor, these dream images function as moments out of time, recollected or imagined, moments that stand in the sharpest possible contrast to the terror of real life in the works.

It is true that O'Connor's materials seem wholesome in comparison with the Nazi holocaust or its aftermath. But it is precisely O'Connor's genius to start with such material as an apartment in New York City or life on the farm and to pierce through the mundane surface to reveal the evils of the heart. The scale is different, admittedly; but the source of evil is the same. And built into the structure of O'Connor's fiction, as it is built into the structure of such films, is an image outside time, of redeeming escape or nostalgia, born from the gravid horrors of the present.

When she died in 1964, Flannery O'Connor had published two novels and slightly more than twenty short stories. It is not a large corpus, but it is, in a sense, fully achieved. She knew, by and large, just what she wanted to do, and how to go about doing it; for one is repeatedly struck by the congruity of the critical standards of her "theoretical" intellect and the performance of her "practical" intellect. It is of course impossible to say what she might have written had she lived longer, but one feels that in essence her vision had found something like complete expression in the works she has left. She herself, in responding to an interviewer, declared:

> I'm afraid it is possible to exhaust your material. What you exhaust are those things that you are capable of bringing alive. I mean if you've done it once, you don't want to do the same thing over again. The longer you write the more conscious you are of what you can and cannot make live. What you have to do is try to deepen your penetration of these things.[12]

She was at work, at the time of her death, on a third novel, and a very small portion of it had already been published. It seems to have for its protagonist a type of character she had treated in her later stories with verve—but a certain sameness: the would-be intellectual, the young man incapable of acting, yet full of a self-assured awareness of what he takes to be the nature of reality. And the plot seems put in motion with the death of the hero's father (as *The Violent Bear It Away* had begun with the death of Tarwater's spiritual father). One might infer from this portion that it would have been the business of the narrative to transform the limited awareness of the protagonist, Walter, into a deeper awareness (compare "Everything That Rises Must Converge," "The Comforts of Home," "The Enduring Chill") through the intrusion of a sense of mystery upon his life, and thus to liberate him for some action. He does not, significantly, resemble the heroes of her two previous novels—no backwoods prophet freak, this Walter—and one must probably exclude the vocation of prophecy as a future active calling. And yet, in essence, the novel would seem to deal, as the earlier ones had, with the general subject of spiritual vocation.

O'Connor wrote about a year before her death, to a close friend, saying, "I've been writing eighteen years and I've reached the point where I can't do again what I know I can do well, and the larger things that I need to do now, I doubt my capacity for doing."[13] Whatever those "larger things" would have been, or whether, indeed, they would have materialized, one simply cannot say. One can say, however, that she had already made for herself a place uniquely her own in American fiction; a small place, perhaps, but undoubtedly a secure one.

APPENDIXES

1

CHRONOLOGICAL
LIST OF FICTION

NOTE: The following list may give some idea of the overall progress of O'Connor's career; it includes the place where she first published each piece, together with an indication of whether the tale was later included in a collection, or was incorporated into one of the novels.

1946. "The Geranium." *Accent* (Summer). Later included in *The Complete Stories*.

1947. University of Iowa Master's thesis, containing: "The Barber" (see 1970), "Wildcat" (see 1970), "The Crop" (see 1971), "The Turkey" (revised as "The Capture" [see 1948]), "The Geranium" (see 1946), and "The Train" (see 1948). All included in *Complete Stories*.

1948. "The Train." *Sewanee Review* (April). Revised as chapter one of *Wise Blood*. Original version included in *Complete Stories*.

"The Capture." *Mademoiselle* (November). A revision of "The Turkey" (see 1947).

1949. "The Heart of the Park." *Partisan Review* (February). Revised as chapter five of *Wise Blood*. Included in *Complete Stories*.

"The Woman on the Stairs." *Tomorrow* (August). Revised as "A Stroke of Good Fortune" (see 1953).

"The Peeler." *Partisan Review* (December). Revised as chapter three of *Wise Blood*. Included in *Complete Stories*.

1952. "Enoch and the Gorilla." *New World Writing* 1 (April). Revised for chapters eleven and twelve of *Wise Blood*. Included in *Complete Stories*.

Wise Blood.

1953. "A Good Man Is Hard to Find." *The Berkeley Book of Modern Writing* 1 (ed. William Phillips and Philip Rahv). Included in *A Good Man Is Hard to Find* and in *Complete Stories*.

"The Life You Save May Be Your Own." *Kenyon Review* (Spring). Included in *A Good Man Is Hard to Find* and in *Complete Stories*.

"A Stroke of Good Fortune." *Shenandoah* (Spring). Included in *A Good Man Is Hard to Find* and in *Complete Stories*.

"The River." *Sewanee Review* (Summer). Included in *A Good Man Is Hard to Find* and in *Complete Stories*.

"A Late Encounter with the Enemy." *Harper's Bazaar* (September). Included in *A Good Man Is Hard to Find* and in *Complete Stories*.

1954. "A Circle in the Fire." *Kenyon Review* (Spring). Included in *A Good Man Is Hard to Find* and in *Complete Stories*.

"A Temple of the Holy Ghost." *Harper's Bazaar* (May). Included in *A Good Man Is Hard to Find* and in *Complete Stories*.

"The Displaced Person." *Sewanee Review* (October). Enlarged and included in *A Good Man Is Hard to Find* and in *Complete Stories*.

1955. "The Artificial Nigger." *Kenyon Review* (Spring). Included in *A Good Man Is Hard to Find* and in *Complete Stories*.

"Good Country People." *Harper's Bazaar* (June). Included in *A Good Man Is Hard to Find* and in *Complete Stories*.

"You Can't Be Any Poorer Than Dead." *New World Writing* 8 (October). Revised as chapter one of *The Violent Bear it Away*.

A Good Man Is Hard to Find.

1956. "Greenleaf." Kenyon Review (Summer). Included in Everything That Rises Must Converge and in Complete Stories.

1957. "A View of the Woods." Partisan Review (Fall). Included in Everything That Rises Must Converge and in Complete Stories.

1958. "The Enduring Chill." Harper's Bazaar (July). Included in Everything That Rises Must Converge and in Complete Stories.

1960. "The Comforts of Home." Kenyon Review (Fall). Included in Everything That Rises Must Converge and in Complete Stories.

The Violent Bear It Away.

1961. "Everything That Rises Must Converge." New World Writing 19. Included in Everything That Rises Must Converge and in Complete Stories.

"The Partridge Festival." Critic (February–March). Included in Complete Stories.

1962. "The Lame Shall Enter First." Sewanee Review (Summer). Included in Everything That Rises Must Converge and in Complete Stories.

1963. "Why Do the Heathen Rage?" Esquire (July). Beginning of unfinished third novel. Included in Complete Stories.

1964. "Revelation." Sewanee Review (Spring). Included in Everything That Rises Must Converge and in Complete Stories.

1965. "Parker's Back." Esquire (April). Included in Everything That Rises Must Converge and in Complete Stories.

"Judgement Day." Included in Everything That Rises Must Converge and in Complete Stories.

Everything That Rises Must Converge.

1970. "Wildcat." North American Review (Spring). Included in Complete Stories.

"The Barber." Atlantic (October). Included in Complete Stories.

1971. "The Crop." Mademoiselle (April). Included in Complete Stories.

Flannery O'Connor: The Complete Stories.

2

BOOK REVIEWS BY
FLANNERY O'CONNOR

NOTE: Following is a list of the major books O'Connor reviewed for *The Bulletin of the Catholic Laymen's Association of Georgia* (later shortened to *The Bulletin*). In January, 1963 *The Bulletin* split into *The Georgia Bulletin* (serving the Archdiocese of Atlanta) and *The Southern Cross* (serving the Diocese of Savannah). O'Connor's reviews appeared in the latter only.

31 March 1956.   *The Presence of Grace*, J. F. Powers

31 March 1956.   *The Malefactors*, Caroline Gordon

26 May 1956.   *Two Portraits of St. Therese of Lisieux*, Etienne Robo

6 June 1956.   *Humble Powers* (Three Novelettes), Paul Horgan

23 June 1956.   *Letters from Baron Friedrich von Hügel to a Niece*, ed. Gwendolen Greene

21 July 1956.   *Beyond the Dreams of Avarice*, Russell Kirk

1 September 1956. *The Catholic Companion to the Bible*, Ralph L. Woods

24 November 1956. *Meditations before Mass*, Romano Guardini

5 January 1957. *The Metamorphic Tradition in Modern Poetry*, Sister Bernetta Quinn

2 March 1957. *Writings of Edith Stein*, Edith Stein

11 May 1957. *Criticism and Censorship*, Walter F. Kerr

3 May 1958. *The Transgressor*, Julian Greene

12 July 1958. *Patterns in Comparative Religion*, Mircea Eliade

1 November 1958. *American Classics Reconsidered*, H. C. Gardiner, S.J.

15 November 1958. *Israel and Revelation*, Eric Voegelin

29 November 1958. *Late Dawn*, Elizabeth Vandon

10 January 1959. *Freud and Religion*, Gregory Zilboorg

10 January 1959. *Temporal and Eternal*, Charles Péguy

7 March 1959. *Harry Vernon at Prep*, Frank Smith

1 October 1960. *The Science of the Cross*, Edith Stein

1 October 1960. *Beat on a Damask Drum*, T. K. Martin

15 October 1960. *Pierre Teilhard de Chardin*, Nicolas Corte

29 October 1960. *Soul and Psyche*, Victor White, O.P.

12 November 1960. *Christian Initiation*, Louis Bouyer

24 December 1960. *Modern Catholic Thinkers*, ed. A. Robert Capronegri

4 February 1961. *The Divine Milieu*, Pierre Teilhard de Chardin

18 March 1961.   *The Life of St. Catherine of Siena*, Raymond of
                  Capua

27 May 1961.   *The Conversion of Augustine*, Romano Guardini

24 June 1961.   *Life's Long Journey*, Kenneth Walker

5 August 1961.   *Selected Letters of Stephen Vincent Benet*, ed.
                  Charles Fenton

16 September 1961. *Themes of the Bible*, J. Guillet, S.J.

16 September 1961. *The Resurrection*, F. X. Durrwell, C.S.S.R.

30 September 1961. *The Mediaeval Mystics of England*, ed. Eric Colledge

28 October 1961. *Freedom, Grace, and Destiny*, Romano Guardini

25 November 1961. *The Range of Reason*, Jacques Maritain

9 December 1961. *The Bible and the Ancient Near East*, ed. G. E.
                  Wright

9 December 1961. *The Old Testament and Modern Study*, ed. H. H.
                  Rowley

23 December 1961. *The Novelist and the Passion Story*, F. W. Dillistone

23 December 1961. *Teilhard de Chardin*, Oliver Rabut, O.P.

6 January 1962.   *Conversations with Cassandra*, Sister M. Madeleva

17 February 1962. *Christian Faith and Man's Religion*, Marc C. Eber-
                  sole

17 February 1962. *Christianity Divided*, ed. Daniel J. Callahan, Heiko
                  A. Oberman, and Daniel J. O'Hanlon

2 March 1962.   *Evidence of Satan in the Modern World*, Leon
                  Christiani

2 March 1962.   *The Georgia Review*, quarterly, University of Georgia
                  Press

17 March 1962.   *The Conscience of Israel*, Bruce Vawter, C. M.

31 March 1962.   *The Victorian Vision*, Margaret M. Maison

12 May 1962.   *Toward the Knowledge of God*, Claude Tresmontant

4 August 1962.   *The Cardinal Spellman Story*, Robert I. Gannon, S.J.

4 August 1962.   *The Council, Reform, and Reunion*, Hans Kung

4 August 1962.   *The Integrating Mind*, William F. Lynch, S.J.

2 March 1963.   *The Bible*: Word of God in Words of Men, Jean
                     Levie

9 March 1963.   *Frontiers in American Catholicism*, Walter J. Ong,
                     S.J.

16 March 1963.   *New Men for New Times*, Beatrice Avalos

16 March 1963.   *Seeds of Hope in the Modern World*, Barry Ulanov

23 March 1963.   *The Wide World, My Parish*, Yves Congar, O.P.

27 April 1963.   *Letters from a Traveler*, Pierre Teilhard de Chardin

26 September 1963.   *Image of America*, Norman Foerster

26 September 1963.   *The Modern God*, Gustave Weigel, S.J.

24 October 1963.   *Evangelical Theology: An Introduction*, Karl Barth

29 November 1963.   *Morte D'Urban*, J. F. Powers

29 November 1963.   *What is the Bible?* Henri Daniel-Rops

29 November 1963.   *Faith, Reason, and the Gospels*, ed. John J. Heaney,
                     S.J.

9 January 1964.   *Prince of Democracy: James Cardinal Gibbons*, Arline
                     Boucher and John Tehan

9 January 1964.   *The Kingdom of God: A Short Bible*, ed. Louis J.
                     Putz, C.S.C.

NOTES

NOTES

PREFACE

1. "Catholic Novelists and Their Readers," *Mystery and Manners*, ed. Sally and Robert Fitzgerald, pp. 187–88 (hereinafter cited as *Mystery*).
2. Edwin Honig, *Dark Conceit*, p. 74.
3. See O'Connor, "The Nature and Aim of Fiction," *Mystery*, pp. 70–71.
4. "The Teaching of Literature," *Mystery*, p. 129.
5. "The Regional Writer," *Mystery*, p. 55.

CHAPTER 1

1. "Everything That Rises Must Converge," in *Everything That Rises Must Converge*, p. 20 (hereinafter cited as *Everything*).
2. "The Nature and Aim of Fiction," *Mystery*, p. 66.
3. "The Catholic Novelist in the Protestant South," *Mystery*, p. 200.
4. Ibid., p. 198.
5. "The Barber," *Atlantic*, October 1970, p. 112. (*Complete Stories*, pp. 16–17.)
6. James Dickey, "Notes on the Decline of Outrage," in *South: Modern Southern Literature in Its Cultural Setting*, ed. Louis D. Rubin, Jr., and Robert D. Jacobs, pp. 78–79.

7. James P. Degnan, review of *Everything That Rises Must Converge*, *Commonweal*, 9 July 1965, p. 511.

8. Alfred Kazin, "The Alone Generation," *Contemporaries* (Boston: Atlantic-Little, Brown & Co., 1962), p. 215.

9. "A Late Encounter with the Enemy," in *A Good Man Is Hard to Find*, p. 155 (hereinafter cited as *Good Man*).

10. "The Regional Writer," *Mystery*, p. 59.

11. Andrew Lytle, "How Many Miles to Babylon," in *Southern Renascence*, ed. Louis D. Rubin, Jr., and Robert D. Jacobs, p. 34.

12. Quoted by Louis D. Rubin, Jr., in "Southern Literature: The Historical Image," in *South*, ed. Rubin and Jacobs, pp. 36–37. Tate's remark is from "The New Provincialism," *On the Limits of Poetry* (New York: Swallow Press, 1948), p. 292.

13. Ibid., p. 47.

14. Up to this point, the tale would seem to illustrate perfectly Frederick J. Hoffman's observation that in Southern fiction the moral center of a work will often reside in a place where "humanity is a concern, and its formal, even ceremonial, values are treasured." Often opposed to this is the threat of an "inhuman, impersonal agent which exploits and destroys nature without love of it" ("Sense of Place," in *South*, ed. Rubin and Jacobs, p. 66).

15. See Stanley Edgar Hyman, *Flannery O'Connor*, p. 28.

16. "A View of the Woods," *Everything*, p. 70.

17. "The Fiction Writer and His Country," *Mystery*, pp. 28–29.

18. "The Regional Writer," *Mystery*, pp. 53–54.

19. Ibid., p. 59.

20. "The Fiction Writer and His Country," *Mystery*, p. 27.

21. Gore Vidal, "Ladders to Heaven," in *On Contemporary Literature*, ed. Richard Kostelanetz (New York: Avon, Discus, 1964), pp. 30–31. Originally published in *New World Writing #4* (New York: New American Library, 1954).

22. "The Fiction Writer and His Country," *Mystery*, p. 32.

23. "Catholic Novelists and Their Readers," *Mystery*, p. 184.

24. Ibid.

25. Collected in *Mystery*.

26. Her reviews first appeared in *The Bulletin*, which stopped publication in December, 1962; subsequent reviews appeared in the newly founded *Southern Cross* (serving the Diocese of Savannah). See Appendix 2 for listing of books reviewed.

27. *Bulletin*, 25 November 1961.

28. Review of *Letters from a Traveler*, by Pierre Teilhard de Chardin, *Southern Cross*, 27 April 1963.

29. Review of *The Divine Milieu*, by Pierre Teilhard de Chardin, *Bulletin*, 4 February 1961.

30. Review of *Teilhard de Chardin*, by Oliver Rabut, O.P., *Bulletin*, 23 December 1961.

31. *Bulletin,* 23 June 1956.

32. *Bulletin,* 28 October 1961.

33. *Bulletin,* 26 May 1956.

34. Review of *Soul and Psyche,* by Victor White, O.P., *Bulletin,* 29 October 1960. Compare Nathanael West's earlier description of Christ as "a maiden surrounded by maidens," *Complete Works of Nathanael West,* ed. Alan Ross, *Day of the Locust,* p. 348.

35. "The Role of the Catholic Novelist," *Greyfriar, Siena Studies in Literature* 7 (1964): 12.

36. *The Violent Bear It Away,* p. 60.

37. *Bulletin,* 18 March 1961.

38. *New Catholic Encyclopedia,* s.v. "Jansenistic Piety."

39. "Greenleaf" in *Everything,* p. 30.

40. "Writing Short Stories," *Mystery,* pp. 98–99.

41. "The Nature and Aim of Fiction," *Mystery,* p. 68.

42. Thomas M. Lorch raises a similar objection in his interesting article, "Flannery O'Connor: Christian Allegorist" (*Critique* 10 [1968]: 69–80); I cannot, however, agree with his contention that O'Connor wanted to write allegories. See Chapter 5 of the present study.

43. Romano Guardini, *Meditations before Mass,* p. 36.

44. "The Enduring Chill," *Everything,* p. 114.

45. O'Connor to William Sessions, 8 July 1956, in *The Added Dimension: The Art and Mind of Flannery O'Connor,* ed. Melvin J. Friedman and Lewis A. Lawson, p. 213 (hereinafter cited as *Added Dimension*).

46. Conor Cruise O'Brien [pseud. Donat O'Donnell], *Maria Cross,* p. 258.

47. Ibid., p. 227. See also John Hawkes, "Flannery O'Connor's Devil," *Sewanee Review* 70 (Summer 1962): 395–407.

48. *Added Dimension,* p. 228 (from C. Ross Mullins, "Flannery O'Connor, An Interview," *Jubilee,* June 1963).

49. "The Catholic Novelist in the Protestant South," *Mystery,* p. 195.

50. "Catholic Novelists and Their Readers," *Mystery,* p. 178.

51. "Novelist and Believer," *Mystery,* p. 158.

52. "Some Aspects of the Grotesque in Southern Fiction," *Mystery,* p. 38.

53. *Wise Blood,* 2d ed., p. 148.

54. "Novelist and Believer," *Mystery,* p. 159. Compare Hawthorne on Melville: "He can neither believe, nor be comfortable in his unbelief; and he is too honest and courageous not to try to do one or the other" (*The English Notebooks,* ed. Randall Stewart [New York: Modern Language Association of America, 1941], p. 433 [20 November 1856]).

55. *Added Dimension,* p. 240 (from Gerard E. Sherry, "An Interview with Flannery O'Connor," *Critic,* June–July 1963).

56. *The Complete Works of Nathaniel Hawthorne,* ed. George Parsons Lathrop, 6:191–92 (from chapter eighteen, "On the Edge of a Precipice";

subsequent references are to this edition and will be incorporated in the text).

57. "Revelation," *Everything*, p. 217.

58. My discussion of the structure of Poe's imagination derives in part from Richard Wilbur's valuable analysis of "Ligeia" in his introduction to the selection of Poe's works in *Major Writers of America*, ed. Perry Miller (New York: Harcourt, Brace & World, Inc., 1962), esp. pp. 374–79. Unfortunately, Daniel Hoffman's *Poe Poe Poe Poe Poe Poe Poe* (New York: Doubleday, 1972) appeared too late for me to use.

59. *The Complete Works of Edgar Allan Poe*, ed. James A. Harrison, 3: 242 (subsequent references are to this edition and will be incorporated in the text).

60. "On Her Own Work," *Mystery*, p. 109.

61. W. H. Auden, "Postscript: Christianity and Art," *The Dyer's Hand and Other Essays*, p. 457.

62. O'Connor to Leo Zuber, 1 April 1963.

63. Review of *The Conscience of Israel*, by Bruce Vawter, C. M., *Bulletin*, 17 March 1962.

64. "Talk Delivered at GSCW [Georgia State College for Women]," 7 January 1960, p. 5.

65. O'Connor to Sister Mariella Gable, O.S.B., 4 May 1963, *Esprit* 8 (Winter 1964): 26–27.

66. Ibid., p. 27.

67. Alexis de Tocqueville, *Democracy in America*, trans. Henry Reeve, rev. Francis Bowen, ed. Phillips Bradley (New York: Alfred A. Knopf, 1945) 2:134.

68. Sherwood Anderson to Kenneth Davenport, 1937, *Letters of Sherwood Anderson*, ed. Howard Mumford Jones and Walter B. Rideout (Boston: Little, Brown & Co., 1953), p. 375.

69. "Some Aspects of the Grotesque in Southern Fiction," *Mystery*, p. 43.

70. "A Temple of the Holy Ghost," *Good Man*, pp. 97–98. Compare Hulga on her own deformity in "Good Country People."

71. "The King of the Birds," *Mystery*, p. 4.

72. *Added Dimension*, p. 251 (from Frank Daniel, "Flannery O'Connor Shapes Own Capital," *Atlanta Journal and Constitution*, 22 July 1962).

73. "The Partridge Festival," *Critic*, February–March 1961, p. 22. (*Complete Stories*, pp. 426–27.)

74. See James Tate, "An O'Connor Remembrance." Typescript in the O'Connor Collection, Georgia State College at Milledgeville.

75. "The Displaced Person," *Good Man*, p. 205.

76. Nathanael West, *Complete Works, Day of the Locust*, p. 262.

77. Cartoons from school publications form part of the O'Connor Collection at Georgia State College at Milledgeville.

78. Robert Fitzgerald, Introduction to *Everything*, p. xii.

79. Thomas Chandler Haliburton, "Natur," from *The Attaché; or Sam Slick in England* (1843); reprinted in *Native American Humor*, ed. Walter Blair, pp. 235–36.

80. See "Some Aspects of the Grotesque in Southern Fiction," *Mystery*, p. 46.

81. "In nineteenth-century American writing," O'Connor wrote, "there was a good deal of grotesque literature which came from the frontier and was supposed to be funny; but our present grotesque characters, comic though they may be, are at least not primarily so." ("Some Aspects of the Grotesque in Southern Fiction," *Mystery*, p. 44.)

82. Augustus Baldwin Longstreet, *Georgia Scenes*, p. 51.

83. See Kenneth S. Lynn's interesting note to the Longstreet selection in *The Comic Tradition in America*, pp. 64–65.

84. "Judgement Day," *Everything*, p. 246.

85. Nathanael West, *Complete Works*, p. 320.

86. See Eleanor Prosser, *Drama and Religion in the English Mystery Plays*, pp. 83–84, for discussion of the mixture of comic brutality and serious suffering in medieval art. See also Ernst Curtius, *European Literature and the Latin Middle Ages*, trans. Willard Trask (New York: Harper & Row, Harper Torchbook, 1963; originally published in 1953), p. 424.

87. J. L. Styan, *The Dark Comedy*, p. 11.

88. Allen Tate, *Esprit* 8 (Winter 1964):48. See also Warren Coffey's excellent article on O'Connor's Jansenism in *Commentary*, November 1965, pp. 93–99.

89. Quoted by Paul Levine, *Jubilee*, December 1961, p. 51.

90. "The Turkey," Master's thesis, University of Iowa (1947), pp. 78–79. (This passage is reprinted in *Complete Stories*, p. 49, which follows the original thesis text of the story.)

91. "Wildcat," *North American Review* 255 (Spring 1970):68. (*Complete Stories*, p. 32.)

92. "On Her Own Work," *Mystery*, p. 111.

93. "The Crop," *Mademoiselle*, April 1971, p. 217. (*Complete Stories*, p. 35.)

94. Allen Tate, *Esprit* 8 (Winter 1964):48.

95. "A Circle in the Fire," *Good Man*, p. 135.

96. "The King of the Birds," *Mystery*, pp. 14–15.

CHAPTER 2

1. Pierre Teilhard de Chardin, *The Divine Milieu*, 2d ed., p. 47.

2. "The Capture," *Mademoiselle*, November 1948, p. 198. ("The Turkey," *Complete Stories*, p. 49.)

3. "A Stroke of Good Fortune," *Good Man*, p. 70.

4. Nathanael West, *Complete Works*, ed. Alan Ross, p. 365. See also Shrike's mocking speech to Miss Lonelyhearts: "The church is our only hope, the First Church of Christ Dentist, where He is worshiped as Pre-

venter of Decay. The Church whose symbol is the trinity new-style: Father, Son, and Wirehaired Fox Terrier." (*Complete Works*, p. 110.)

5. As Frederick Asals remarks, "O'Connor's hero became, in a sense, Miss Lonelyhearts in reverse" ("The Road to *Wise Blood*," *Renascence* 21 [1969]:193).

6. Besides the hat, other "talismanic objects" are Hazel's Bible and his mother's eyeglasses, the latter playing a crucial role in the mummy-smashing scene in chapter eleven. See Edwin Honig on the physical signs of allegorical heroes, *Dark Conceit*, p. 81.

7. "Train," *Sewanee Review* 56 (April 1948):262. (*Complete Stories*, p. 55.)

8. Ibid., p. 271. (*Complete Stories*, p. 62.)

9. Gaston Bachelard, *The Poetics of Space*, p. 99.

10. In an earlier version of part of the novel, "The Heart of the Park" (*Partisan Review*, February 1949), Hawks is known as Asa Moats [sic], while Hazel's last name is Weaver; the name changes in another episode, "The Peeler" (*Partisan Review*, December 1949), to Asa Shrike (compare the ad hoc "preacher" Shrike in West's *Miss Lonelyhearts*). In 1949, interestingly, Hawks [Moats] is not portrayed as a fraud; and neither was Hazel preaching his own anti-Gospel. The change in Hazel must have necessitated changing Hawks for purposes of contrast.

11. The nighttime confrontation between the two may have been inspired by the scene in Poe's "The Tell-Tale Heart," where an Evil Eye fascinates the narrator, until he at last shines a lantern on it.

12. Jonathan Baumbach, *The Landscape of Nightmare*, p. 95.

13. Frank Kermode suggests the archetypal quality of such a moment when he uses the words *kairos* and *chronos* to distinguish "what we *feel* is happening in a fiction when mere successiveness, which we *feel* to be the chief characteristic in the ordinary going-on of time, is purged by the establishment of a significant relation between the moment and a remote origin and end, a concord of past, present, and future" (Kermode's italics: *The Sense of an Ending*, p. 50).

14. Introduction to *Everything*, p. xvi.

15. For example, Stanley Edgar Hyman says, ". . . the whole episode of Enoch and the gorilla suit is unrelated to Haze, and Enoch simply falls out of the book dressed as a gorilla." *Flannery O'Connor*, pp. 13–14.

16. See reviews of *Wise Blood*: by R. W. B. Lewis, *Hudson Review* 6 (Spring 1953): 144–50, and by Isaac Rosenfeld, *New Republic*, 7 July 1952, p. 19. See also Louis D. Rubin, Jr., "Flannery O'Connor and the Bible Belt," in *Added Dimension*, p. 68.

CHAPTER 3

1. G. Ernest Wright and Reginald H. Fuller, *The Book of the Acts of God*, p. 142.

2. Thus, in addition to the white light resting upon Bishop's head and

the baptismal lake which is set before him, as if by "four strapping angels" (167), Tarwater sees, after he first sets fire to the house, "two bulging silver eyes that grew in immense astonishment in the center of the fire behind him. He could hear it moving up through the black night like a whirling chariot." (50)

3. O'Connor's conception of Rayber may have been influenced by Hawthorne's nosology, especially as illustrated in Chillingworth (*The Scarlet Letter*).

4. Compare the description of Bishop as "dim and ancient, like a child who had been a child for centuries." (91) Bishop is outside time, and is therefore unlike another aged child, Hardy's Father Time (*Jude the Obscure*), who is ravaged by it.

5. O'Connor wrote, "In my stories a reader will find that the devil accomplishes a good deal of groundwork that seems to be necessary before grace is effective." "On Her Own Work," *Mystery*, p. 117.

6. It is possible O'Connor is echoing here the call of Whitman's "gray-brown" thrush ("When Lilacs Last in the Dooryard Bloom'd"), possibly too Eliot's thrush in the garden scene of *Burnt Norton*.

7. The sun has been, at crucial moments in the narrative, "like a furious white blister in the sky" (25), "holding its breath" (42), furiously "edging its way secretly behind the tops of the trees" (44), resting benignly, "like a hand on Bishop's white head" (164), and, in the last chapter, setting "red and mammoth." (235)

8. Thomas Mann, "Freud and the Future," *Essays of Three Decades*, p. 422.

9. Ibid., p. 423.

10. Ibid.

11. The difference in tone between the conclusion of the narrative and the treatment of old Tarwater is roughly analogous to the tonal difference between the approach to mystery in Eliot's *Four Quartets* (with its similar distinction between redeemed time and historical time) and the more confident perspective of *The Cocktail Party*, where the mood is that of drawing room farce, including the festive figure of Reilly.

12. O'Connor to William Sessions, 13 September 1960, in *Added Dimension*, pp. 222–23.

13. *Added Dimension*, p. 258 (from an interview with Joel Wells, "Off the Cuff," *Critic*, August–September 1962).

14. "On Her Own Work," *Mystery*, p. 116.

CHAPTER 4

1. "The Nature and Aim of Fiction," *Mystery*, p. 77.
2. "Writing Short Stories," *Mystery*, p. 93.
3. "On Her Own Work," *Mystery*, p. 118.
4. "Novelist and Believer," *Mystery*, p. 159.

5. "The Artificial Nigger," *Good Man*, pp. 128–29; Samuel Beckett, *Waiting for Godot*, translated from the original French by the author (New York: Grove Press, 1954), p. 29.

6. "The Nature and Aim of Fiction," *Mystery*, p. 76.

7. Added after the original Harcourt, Brace & Co. edition (1955).

8. The plot and principal characters of "A Good Man Is Hard to Find" bear an eerie resemblance to the following encounter, reported by the *New York Times* (27 March 1969, p. 49). "A 60-year-old retired school principal who was held hostage for three hours this morning by an armed soldier on medical leave was released unharmed after she had persuaded the intruder to surrender to the police. . . . Mrs. Georgette Gardner of Tampa, Fla., calmly told the gunman 'You don't look like the type of person who would kill me.' . . . The intruder told her he was a soldier waiting for his medical discharge after being wounded in Vietnam and 'didn't have anything to live for and wanted to die.'"

9. "A Good Man Is Hard to Find," *Good Man*, p. 10.

10. "On Her Own Work," *Mystery*, pp. 112–13. See also pp. 110–12.

11. Elizabeth Hardwick, *Esprit* 8(Winter 1964):28.

12. O'Connor remarked once in an interview: "It always amuses me when people say 'brutality.' People keep referring to the brutality in the stories, but even 'A Good Man Is Hard to Find' is, in a way, a comic, stylized thing. It is not naturalistic writing and so you can't really call it brutal." Katherine Fugin, Faye Rivard, and Margaret Sieh, "An Interview with Flannery O'Connor," *Censer*, Fall 1960; reprint, Summer 1965, p. 53.

Compare J. L. Styan's description of the Duke of Guise's murders in Marlowe's *Massacre at Paris*: "Each killing is conducted with a grim mockery of the victim and a short parody of his belief. Thus he mimics a Protestant preacher with 'Dearly beloved brother—thus 'tis written' as he thrusts his dagger home." *The Dark Comedy*, p. 13.

13. "The Life You Save May Be Your Own," *Good Man*, p. 54.

14. Robert Fitzgerald, "The Countryside and the True Country," *Flannery O'Connor*, Christian Critics Series, ed. Robert E. Reiter, pp. 78–79.

15. "The Teaching of Literature," *Mystery*, p. 132.

16. Compare O'Connor's article on raising peacocks, in which she wrote of her own first reaction to the fowl: "As soon as the birds were out of the crate, I sat down on it and began to look at them. I have been looking at them ever since, from one station or another, and always with the same awe as on that first occasion. . . . When I first uncrated these birds, in my frenzy I said, 'I want so many of them that every time I go out the door, I'll run into one.' Now every time I go out the door, four or five run into me—and give me only the faintest recognition." ("The King of the Birds," *Mystery*, pp. 6–7.)

17. "Introduction to *A Memoir of Mary Ann*," *Mystery*, p. 227.

18. Ibid.

19. This second basic pattern can be found as well in "A View of the Woods" (with old Fortune and Mary Pitts as the key figures), "Everything That Rises Must Converge" (with Julian and his mother), "The Partridge Festival" (with Calhoun and Mary Elizabeth), and "The Lame Shall Enter First" (with Sheppard and Norton). All were written after "The Artificial Nigger."

20. Katherine Fugin, "An Interview with Flannery O'Connor," Censer, p. 55.

21. "The Nature and Aim of Fiction," Mystery, pp. 75–76.

22. "The Comforts of Home," Everything, p. 115.

23. "Some Aspects of the Grotesque in Southern Fiction," Mystery, p. 43.

24. An earlier use of the pistol's bawdy connotation, in "A Stroke of Good Fortune," was remarked by Stuart L. Burns in "Flannery O'Connor's Literary Apprenticeship," Renascence 22 (Autumn 1969): 16.

25. "The Nature and Aim of Fiction," Mystery, p. 64.

26. "Parker's Back," Everything, pp. 222–23.

27. Edwin Honig, Dark Conceit, p. 125.

28. Theodore Gaster, Customs and Folkways of Jewish Life (New York: Apollo Editions, 1955), pp. 51–52.

29. Caroline Gordon, "Heresy in Dixie," Sewanee Review, 76 (Spring 1968):266.

Chapter 5

1. Richard Poirier, review of Everything That Rises Must Converge, New York Times Book Review, 30 May 1965, p. 6.

2. "The River," Good Man, p. 47.

3. Wayne Booth, Rhetoric of Fiction, p. 142. Compare George Orwell's less optimistic view that "the atmosphere of orthodoxy is always damaging to prose, and above all to the novel, the most anarchical of all forms of literature. How many Roman Catholics have been good novelists? Even the handful one could name have usually been bad Catholics." Inside the Whale, p. 173.

4. "Novelist and Believer," Mystery, p. 156.

5. Wayne Booth, Rhetoric of Fiction, p. 138.

6. Compare Martha Stephens's discussion, from a sympathetic viewpoint, of "Flannery O'Connor and the Sanctified-Sinner Tradition," Arizona Quarterly 24 (1968):223–39. See also Morton Dauwen Zabel's more critical discussion of this lineage in his chapter on Graham Greene in Craft and Character, pp. 276–96.

7. "Introduction to A Memoir of Mary Ann," Mystery, p. 227.

8. Ibid., p. 213.

9. George Orwell, Inside the Whale, p. 173.

10. Frank Kermode, The Sense of an Ending, p. 130.

11. "The Geranium," *Accent* 6 (Summer 1946): p. 247. (*Complete Stories*, p. 6.)

12. *Added Dimension*, p. 260 (from an interview with C. Ross Mullins, *Jubilee*, June 1963).

13. O'Connor to Sister Mariella Gable, O.S.B., *Esprit* 8(Winter 1964):27.

BIBLIOGRAPHY

BIBLIOGRAPHY

Adams, Robert M. Review of *A Good Man Is Hard to Find*. *Hudson Review* 7 (Winter 1956): 630.

Alice, Sister Rose, S.S.J. "Flannery O'Connor: Poet to the Outcast." *Renascence* 16 (Spring 1964): 126–32.

Asals, Frederick. "The Road to *Wise Blood*." *Renascence* 21 (1969): 181–94.

Auden, W. H. "Postscript: Christianity and Art." *The Dyer's Hand and Other Essays*. New York: Random House, 1962.

Bachelard, Gaston. *The Poetics of Space*. Translated by Maria Jolas. New York: Orion Press, 1964.

Ballif, Algene. Review of *The Violent Bear It Away*. *Commentary* 30 (October 1960): 358–62.

Barrett, William. Review of *Everything That Rises Must Converge*. *Atlantic Monthly*, July 1965, p. 139.

Bartlett, C. Jones. "Depth Psychology and Literary Study." *Mid Continent American Studies Journal* 5 (Fall 1964): 50–56.

Bassan, Maurice. "Flannery O'Connor's Way: Shock, with Moral Intent." *Renascence* 15 (Summer 1963): 195–99, 211.

Baumbach, Jonathan. *The Landscape of Nightmare*. New York: New York University Press, 1965.

Bier, Jesse. *The Rise and Fall of American Humor*. New York: Holt, Rinehart & Winston, 1968.

Blair, Walter. *Native American Humor* [1937]. San Francisco: Chandler, 1960.

Bliven, Naomi. Review of *Everything That Rises Must Converge*. *New Yorker*, 11 September 1952, pp. 220–21.

Booth, Wayne. *The Rhetoric of Fiction*. Chicago: University of Chicago Press, 1961.

Bornhauser, Fred. Review of *A Good Man Is Hard to Find. Shenandoah* 7 (Autumn 1955): 71–81.

Bowen, Robert O. "Hope vs. Despair in the New Gothic Novel." *Renascence* 13 (Spring 1961): 147–52.

Brittain, Joan T., and Driskell, Leon V. "O'Connor and the Eternal Crossroads." *Renascence* 22 (1969): 49–55.

Brunini, John Gilland, and Connolly, Francis X., eds. *Stories of Our Century by Catholic Authors*. Rev. ed. Garden City: Image Books, 1955.

Burns, Stuart L. "Flannery O'Connor's Literary Apprenticeship." *Renascence* 22 (1969): 3–16.

———. "Flannery O'Connor's *The Violent Bear It Away*: Apotheosis in Failure." *Sewanee Review* 76 (Spring 1968): 319–36.

———. "Structural Patterns in *Wise Blood*." *Xavier University Studies* 8 (1969): 32–43.

———. " 'Torn by the Lord's Eye': Flannery O'Connor's Use of Sun Imagery." *Twentieth Century Literature* 13 (October 1967):154–66.

Burns, Thomas Shannon. "Southern Evangelism and Flannery O'Connor." Master's thesis, University of Georgia, 1967.

Canfield, Francis X. Review of *The Violent Bear It Away. Critic*, May 1960, p. 45.

Carlson, Thomas M. "Flannery O'Connor: The Manichean Dilemma." *Sewanee Review* 77 (1969): 254–76.

Carter, Thomas H. Review of *A Good Man Is Hard to Find. Accent* 15 (Autumn 1955): 293–97.

Clarke, John J. "The Achievement of Flannery O'Connor." *Esprit* 8 (Winter 1964): 6–9.

Coffey, Warren. "Flannery O'Connor." *Commentary* 40 (November 1965): 93–99.

Coleman, Richard. "Flannery O'Connor: A Scrutiny of Two Forms of Her Many-Leveled Art." *Phoenix* [College of Charleston] First Semester, 1965–66.

Colledge, Eric, ed. *Mediaeval Mystics of England*. New York: Scribners, 1961.

Coulbourn, Mildred Elizabeth. "Flannery O'Connor's 'Displaced Persons': An Interpretive Study of a Motif in Selected Works." Master's thesis, Duke University, 1965.

Creekmore, Hubert. Review of *The Violent Bear It Away. New Leader*, 30 May 1960, pp. 20–21.

Cruttwell, Pat. Review of *Everything That Rises Must Converge*. *Hudson Review* 18 (Autumn 1965): 444.

Davenport, Guy. Review of *Everything That Rises Must Converge*. *National Review*, 27 July 1965, p. 658.

Davidson, Donald. Review of *The Violent Bear It Away*. *New York Times Book Review*, 28 February 1960, p. 4.

―――. *Southern Writers in the Modern World*. Athens: University of Georgia Press, 1958.

Davis, Barnabas. "Flannery O'Connor: Christian Belief in Recent Fiction." *Listening*, Autumn 1965, pp. 5–21.

Degnan, James P. Review of *Everything That Rises Must Converge*. *Commonweal*, 9 July 1965, pp. 510–11.

Dickey, James. "Notes on the Decline of Outrage." In *South*, edited by Louis D. Rubin, Jr., and Robert D. Jacobs. Garden City: Doubleday, Anchor, 1961.

Didion, Joan. Review of *The Violent Bear It Away*. *National Review*, 9 April 1960, pp. 240–41.

Doornik, Dr. N. G. M. Van; Jelsma, Rev. S.; and de Lisdonk, Rev. A. Van. *A Handbook of the Catholic Faith*. Translated from the Dutch. Edited by Rev. John Greenwood. Garden City: Doubleday, Image, 1956.

Dowell, Bob. "Grace in the Fiction of Flannery O'Connor." *College English* 27 (December 1965): 235–39.

Drake, Robert. *Flannery O'Connor*. Contemporary Writers in Christian Perspective Series. Grand Rapids, Mich.: Wm. B. Eerdmans, 1966.

Dupray, R. A. Review of *Everything That Rises Must Converge*. *Catholic World* 202 (October 1965): 54.

Eggenschwiler, David. "Flannery O'Connor's True and False Prophets." *Renascence* 21 (1969): 151–61, 167.

Elder, Walter. Review of *A Good Man Is Hard to Find*. *Kenyon Review* 17 (Autumn 1955): 661–70.

Emerson, Donald C. Review of *The Violent Bear It Away*. *Arizona Quarterly Review* 16 (Autumn 1960): 284–86.

Engle, Paul. Review of *The Violent Bear It Away*. *Chicago Sunday Tribune Magazine of Books*, 6 March 1960, p. 4.

Esprit [University of Scranton] 8 (Winter 1964). Flannery O'Connor memorial issue.

Esty, William. "In America, Intellectual Bomb Shelters." *Commonweal*, 7 March 1958, pp. 586–88.

Feeley, Sister M. Kathleen, S.S.N.D. "Thematic Imagery in the Fiction of Flannery O'Connor." *Southern Humanities Review* 3 (1968): 14–32.

Ferris, Sumner J. "The Outside and the Inside: Flannery O'Connor's *The Violent Bear It Away*." *Critique* 3 (Winter–Spring 1960): 11–19.

Fitzgerald, Robert. "The Countryside and The True Country." *Sewanee Review* 70 (Summer 1962): 380–94. Reprinted in *Flannery O'Connor*, edited by Robert Reiter. St. Louis: B. Herder, 1968.

———. Introduction to *Everything That Rises Must Converge*, by Flannery O'Connor. New York: Farrar, Straus & Giroux, 1965.

Fitzgerald, Sally, and Fitzgerald, Robert, eds. *Mystery and Manners: Occasional Prose* [by Flannery O'Connor]. New York: Farrar, Straus & Giroux, 1969.

Flint, R. W. Review of *The Violent Bear It Away*. *Partisan Review* 77 (Spring 1960): 378.

Friedman, Melvin J., and Lawson, Lewis A., eds. *The Added Dimension: The Art and Mind of Flannery O'Connor*. New York: Fordham University Press, 1966.

Frohock, W. M. *The Novel of Violence in America*. 2d ed. Boston: Beacon Press, 1957.

Fugin, Katherine; Rivard, Faye; and Sieh, Margaret. "An Interview with Flannery O'Connor." *Censer* [College of Saint Teresa, Winona, Minnesota], Fall 1960; reprint, Summer 1965, pp. 53–56.

Gable, Sister Mariella, O.S.B. "The Ecumenic Core in the Fiction of Flannery O'Connor." *American Benedictine Review* 15 (June 1964): 127–43.

———. Review of *Everything That Rises Must Converge*. *Critic*, June–July 1965, pp. 58–60.

Gafford, Charlotte Kelly. "The Fiction of Flannery O'Connor: A Mission of Gratuitous Grace." Master's thesis, Birmingham-Southern College, 1962.

Gardiner, Harold C., S. J. Review of *The Violent Bear It Away*. *America*, 5 March 1960, pp. 682–83.

Geismar, Maxwell. *American Moderns*. New York: Hill & Wang, American Century Series, 1958.

Gerda, Charles. Review of *The Violent Bear It Away*. *New Statesman*, 24 September 1969, pp. 445–46.

Gordon, Caroline. "Heresy in Dixie." *Sewanee Review* 76 (Spring 1968): 263–97.

———. *How to Read a Novel*. New York: Viking, Compass, 1953.

———. *The Malefactors*. New York: Harcourt, Brace & Co., 1956.

———. Review of *A Good Man Is Hard to Find*. *New York Times Book Review*, 12 June 1955, p. 5.

Gossett, Louise Y. *Violence in Recent Southern Fiction*. Durham: Duke University Press, 1965.

Gossett, Thomas F. Review of *The Violent Bear It Away*. *Southwest Review* 46 (Winter 1961): 86–87.

Goyen, William. Review of *Wise Blood*. *New York Times Book Review*, 18 May 1952, p. 4.

Green, Martin. *Yeats's Blessings on von Hügel: Essays on Literature and Religion*. New York: W. W. Norton & Co., 1967.

Greene, James. Review of *A Good Man Is Hard to Find*. *Commonweal*, 22 July 1955, p. 404.

————. Review of *The Violent Bear It Away*. *Commonweal*, 15 April 1960, pp. 67–68.

Gresset, Michel. "Le Petit Monde de Flannery O'Connor." *Mercure de France*, No. 1203 (January 1964): 141–43.

Griffith, Albert. "Flannery O'Connor." *America*, 27 November 1965, pp. 674–75.

————. "Flannery O'Connor's Salvation Road." *Studies in Short Fiction* 3 (Spring 1966): 329–33.

Guardini, Romano. *Meditations before Mass*. Translated by Elinor Castendyk Briefs. Westminster, Md.: Newman Paperback, 1964.

Halverson, Marvin, and Cohen, Arthur A., eds. *A Handbook of Christian Theology*. Cleveland: World, Living Age (Meridian), 1958.

Hawkes, John. "Flannery O'Connor's Devil." *Sewanee Review* 70 (Summer 1962): 395–407. Reprinted in *Flannery O'Connor*, edited by Robert Reiter. St. Louis: B. Herder, 1968.

————. "Notes on the Wild Goose Chase." *Massachusetts Review* 3 (Summer 1962): 784–88.

Hawthorne, Nathaniel. *The Complete Works of Nathaniel Hawthorne*, edited by George Parsons Lathrop. Boston: Houghton Mifflin, Riverside Edition, 1883.

Hays, Peter L. "Dante, Tobit, and 'The Artificial Nigger.'" *Studies in Short Fiction* 5 (1968): 263–68.

Hoffman, F. J. "Sense of Place." In *South*, edited by Louis D. Rubin, Jr., and Robert D. Jacobs. Garden City: Doubleday, Anchor, 1961.

Holman, C. Hugh. *Three Modes of Modern Southern Fiction*. Mercer University Lamar Series, No. 9. Athens: University of Georgia Press, 1966.

Honig, Edwin. *Dark Conceit*. New York: Oxford University Press, Galaxy, 1966.

Hood, Edward M. Review of *The Violent Bear It Away*. *Kenyon Review* 23 (Winter 1961): 170–72.

Howe, Irving. Review of *Everything That Rises Must Converge*. *New York Review of Books*, 30 September 1965, p. 16.

Hubbell, Jay B. *Southern Life in Fiction*. Mercer University Lamar Series, No. 3. Athens: University of Georgia Press, 1960.

Hyman, Stanley Edgar. Review of *Everything That Rises Must Converge*. *New Leader*, 10 May 1965, pp. 9–10.

————. *Flannery O'Connor*. University of Minnesota pamphlet No. 54. Minneapolis: University of Minnesota Press, 1966.

Jackson, Katherine Gauss. Review of *Everything That Rises Must Converge*. *Harper's*, July 1965, p. 112.

Kane, Patricia. Review of *Everything That Rises Must Converge*. *Critique* 8 (Fall 1965): 85–91.

Kayser, Wolfgang. *The Grotesque in Art and Literature.* New York: McGraw-Hill Paperback, 1966.

Kazin, Alfred. "Our Middle Class Storytellers." *Atlantic Monthly,* August 1968, pp. 51–55.

Kermode, Frank. *The Sense of an Ending.* New York: Oxford University Press, Galaxy, 1967.

Kieft, Ruth M. Vande. "Judgment in the Fiction of Flannery O'Connor." *Sewanee Review* 76 (Spring 1968): 337–56.

Kiely, Robert. Review of *Everything That Rises Must Converge. Christian Science Monitor,* 17 June 1965, p. 7.

Lensing, George. "De Chardin's Ideas in Flannery O'Connor." *Renascence* 18 (Summer 1966): 171–75.

Levine, Paul. Review of *The Violent Bear It Away. Jubilee,* May 1960, p. 52.

———. "The Violent Art." *Jubilee,* December 1961, pp. 50–52.

Lewis, R. W. B. Review of *Wise Blood. Hudson Review* 6 (Spring 1953): 144–50.

Lockridge, Betsy. "An Afternoon with Flannery O'Connor." *Atlanta Journal and Constitution Magazine,* 1 November 1959.

Longstreet, Augustus Baldwin. *Georgia Scenes* [1835]. New York: Sagamore Press, American Century Series, 1957.

Lorch, Thomas M. "Flannery O'Connor: Christian Allegorist." *Critique* 10 (1968): 69–80.

Lynn, Kenneth S. *The Comic Tradition in America.* Garden City: Doubleday, Anchor, 1958.

Lytle, Andrew. "How Many Miles to Babylon," in *Southern Renascence,* edited by Louis D. Rubin, Jr., and Robert D. Jacobs. Baltimore: Johns Hopkins Press, 1966.

McCarthy, John F. "Human Intelligence Versus Divine Truth: The Intellectual in Flannery O'Connor's Works." *English Journal* 55 (December 1966): 1143 ff.

McCown, Robert M. "The Education of a Prophet: A Study of Flannery O'Connor's *The Violent Bear It Away.*" *Kansas Magazine,* 1962, pp. 73–78.

———. "Flannery O'Connor and the Reality of Sin." *Catholic World* 188 (January 1959): 285–91.

McLoughlin, William G., Jr. *Modern Revivalism: Charles Grandison Finney to Billy Graham.* New York: Ronald Press, 1959.

Mann, Thomas. "Freud and the Future." *Essays of Three Decades.* Translated by H. T. Lowe-Porter. New York: Alfred A. Knopf, 1947.

Martin, Carter W. *The True Country: Themes in the Fiction of Flannery O'Connor.* Nashville: Vanderbilt University Press, 1968.

Meaders, Margaret. "Flannery O'Connor: Literary Witch." *Colorado Quarterly* 10 (Spring 1962): 377–86.

Mercier, Vivian. Review of *The Violent Bear It Away. Hudson Review* 13 (Autumn 1960): 449–56.

Merton, Thomas. "Flannery O'Connor." *Jubilee* 12 (November 1964):
49–53.

Meyers, Sister Bertrande, D.C. "Four Stories of Flannery O'Connor."
Thought 37 (Autumn 1962): 410–26.

Mizener, Arthur. Review of *The Violent Bear It Away*. *Sewanee Review*
69 (Winter 1961): 161–63.

Montgomery, Marion. "Beyond Symbol and Surface: the Fiction of Flannery O'Connor." *Georgia Review* 22 (Summer 1968): 188–93.

———. "Miss O'Connor and the Christ-Haunted." *Southern Review* 4
[new series] (Summer 1968): 665–72.

———. "O'Connor and Teilhard de Chardin: The Problem of Evil."
Renascence 22 (1969): 34–42.

———. "The Sense of Violation: Notes Toward a Definition of 'Southern' Fiction." *Georgia Review* 19 (Fall 1965): 278–87.

Mooney, Harry J., Jr. "Moments of Eternity: A Study in the Short
Stories of Flannery O'Connor." In *The Shapeless God*, edited by Harry
J. Mooney, Jr., and Thomas F. Staley. Pittsburgh: University of Pitts-
burgh Press, 1968.

"Motley Special: An Interview with Flannery O'Connor," *Motley*
[Spring Hill College, Mobile, Alabama], Spring 1959, pp. 29–31.

Mueller, William R. *The Prophetic Voice in Modern Fiction*. Garden
City: Doubleday, Anchor, 1966.

Muggeridge, Malcolm. Review of *Everything That Rises Must Converge*.
Esquire, May 1965, pp. 46, 48.

Muller, Gilbert H. "The City of Woe: Flannery O'Connor's Dantean
Vision." *Georgia Review* 23 (1969): 206–13.

———. "*The Violent Bear It Away*: Moral and Dramatic Sense." *Renascence* 22 (1969): 17–25.

Mullins, C. Ross. "Flannery O'Connor, An Interview." *Jubilee*, June
1963, pp. 32–35.

Murray, James G. "Southland à la Russe." *Critic*, June-July 1963, pp.
26–28.

Nolde, Sister M. Simon, O.S.B. "*The Violent Bear It Away*: A Study in
Imagery." *Xavier University Studies* 1 (Spring 1962): 180–94.

O'Brien, Conor Cruise [Donat O'Donnell]. *Maria Cross: Imaginative
Patterns in a Group of Modern Catholic Writers*. London: Chatto &
Windus, 1953.

O'Connor, Flannery. "The Barber." *Atlantic*, October 1970, pp. 111–18.

———. "The Capture." (s.v. "The Turkey" in *Complete Stories*.) *Mademoiselle*, November 1948, p. 148.

———. *The Complete Stories*. (Including the following short stories
listed in this bibliography—"The Barber," "The Capture" [s.v. "The
Turkey"], "The Crop," "Enoch and the Gorilla," "The Geranium,"
"The Heart of the Park," "The Partridge Festival," "The Peeler,"
"The Train," "Why Do the Heathen Rage?", "Wildcat," "The
Woman on the Stairs" [s.v. "A Stroke of Good Fortune"], "You Can't

Be Any Poorer Than Dead.") New York: Farrar, Straus & Giroux, 1971.

————. "The Crop." *Mademoiselle*, April 1971, p. 217.

————. "Enoch and the Gorilla." *New World Writing* No. 1 (April 1952), pp. 67–74.

————. *Everything That Rises Must Converge.* New York: Farrar, Straus & Giroux, 1965.

————. "The Geranium." *Accent* 6 (Summer 1946): 245–53.

————. *A Good Man Is Hard to Find and Other Stories.* New York: Harcourt, Brace & Co., 1955.

————. "The Heart of the Park." *Partisan Review* 16 (February 1949): 138–51.

————. Master's thesis, University of Iowa, 1947.

————. *Mystery and Manners: Occasional Prose.* Edited by Sally and Robert Fitzgerald, New York: Farrar, Straus & Giroux, 1969.

————. "The Partridge Festival." *Critic*, February-March 1961, pp. 20–23, 82–85.

————. "The Peeler." *Partisan Review* 16 (December 1949): 1189–1206.

————. "Talk Delivered at GSCW [Georgia State College for Women]," 7 January 1960. Typescript in O'Connor Collection, Georgia State College at Milledgeville.

————. "The Train." *Sewanee Review* 56 (April 1948): 261–71.

————. *The Violent Bear It Away.* New York: Farrar, Straus & Cudahy, 1960.

————. "Why Do the Heathen Rage?" *Esquire*, July 1963, pp. 60–61.

————. "Wildcat," *North American Review* 255, n.s. 7 (Spring 1970): 66–68.

————. *Wise Blood.* 2d ed. With an Introduction by the Author. New York: Farrar, Straus & Cudahy, 1962.

————. "The Woman on the Stairs." (*s.v.* "A Stroke of Good Fortune" in *Complete Stories.*) *Tomorrow* 8 (August 1949): 40.

————. "You Can't Be Any Poorer Than Dead." *New World Writing* No. 8 (October 1955), pp. 81–97.

O'Connor, Frank. *The Lonely Voice: A Study of the Short Story.* Cleveland: Meridian, 1965.

O'Connor, William Van. *The Grotesque: An American Genre.* Carbondale: Southern Illinois University Press, Crosscurrents, 1962.

Orwell, George. *Inside the Whale and Other Essays.* London: Victor Gollancz, 1940.

Pickrel, Paul. Review of *The Violent Bear It Away. Harper's*, April 1960, p. 114.

Poe, Edgar Allan. *The Complete Works of Edgar Allan Poe*, edited by James A. Harrison. 1902. Reprint, New York: AMS Press, 1965.

Poirier, Richard. Review of *Everything That Rises Must Converge. New York Times Book Review*, 30 May 1965, p. 6.

Price, George. *George Price's Characters: More Than 200 of His Best Cartoons.* New York: Simon & Schuster, 1955.

————. *My Dear 500 Friends, Embalmed and Treasured Up by George Price.* New York: Simon & Schuster, 1963.

Pritchett, V. S. "Satan Comes to Georgia." *New Statesman,* 11 April 1966, pp. 469–72.

Prosser, Eleanor. *Drama and Religion in the English Mystery Plays: A Re-evaluation.* Stanford: Stanford University Press, 1961.

"Recent Southern Fiction: A Panel Discussion." [Katherine Anne Porter, Flannery O'Connor, Caroline Gordon, Madison Jones, Louis D. Rubin, Jr.; October 28, 1960 at Wesleyan College, Macon, Georgia.] *Bulletin of Wesleyan College.* Vol. 41, No. 1 (January 1961).

Rechnitz, Robert M. "Passionate Pilgrim: Flannery O'Connor's *Wise Blood.*" *Georgia Review* 19 (Fall 1965): 310–16.

Reiter, Robert, ed. *Flannery O'Connor.* St. Louis: B. Herder, A Christian Critic Book, 1968.

Rosenberger, Coleman. Review of *The Violent Bear It Away. New York Herald Tribune Book Review,* 28 February 1960, p. 13.

Rosenfeld, Isaac. Review of *Wise Blood. New Republic,* 7 July 1952, p. 19.

Rourke, Constance. *American Humor* [1931]. Garden City: Doubleday, Anchor, 1953.

Rubin, Louis D., Jr. "Flannery O'Connor and the Bible Belt." In *Added Dimension: The Art and Mind of Flannery O'Connor,* edited by Melvin J. Friedman and Lewis A. Lawson. New York: Fordham University Press, 1966.

————. "Southern Literature: The Historical Image." In *South,* edited by Louis D. Rubin, Jr., and Robert D. Jacobs. Garden City: Doubleday, Anchor, 1961.

————. "Two Ladies of the South." *Sewanee Review* 63 (Autumn 1955): 67–81.

Rubin, Louis D., Jr., and Jacobs, Robert D., eds. *South: Modern Southern Literature in Its Cultural Setting.* Garden City: Doubleday, Anchor, 1961.

————. *Southern Renascence* (1953). Baltimore: Johns Hopkins Press, 1966.

Rupp, Richard. "Fact and Mystery: Flannery O'Connor." *Commonweal,* 6 December 1963, pp. 304–7.

Schott, Webster. Review of *Everything That Rises Must Converge. Nation,* 13 September 1965, pp. 142–44.

Sessions, William. "Correspondence." In *Added Dimension: The Art and Mind of Flannery O'Connor,* edited by Melvin J. Friedman and Lewis A. Lawson. New York: Fordham University Press, 1966.

Shear, Walter. "Flannery O'Connor: Character and Characterization." *Renascence* 20 (1968): 140–46.

Sherry, Gerard E. "An Interview with Flannery O'Connor." *Critic*, June-July 1963, pp. 29–31.

Simons, J. W. Review of *Wise Blood*. *Commonweal*, 27 June 1952, pp. 297–98.

Smith, Francis J., S.J. "O'Connor's Religious Viewpoint in *The Violent Bear It Away*." *Renascence* 22 (1970): 108–12.

Smith, J. Oates. "Ritual and Violence in Flannery O'Connor." *Thought* 41 (1966): 545–60.

Smith, Lillian. Review of *Everything That Rises Must Converge*. *Chicago Sunday Tribune Magazine of Books*, 6 June 1965, p. 5.

Snow, Ollye Tine. "The Functional Gothic of Flannery O'Connor." *Southwest Review* 50 (Summer 1965): 286–99.

Solotaroff, Theodore. Review of *Everything That Rises Must Converge*. *New York Herald Tribune Book Week*, 30 May 1965, p. 1.

Stallings, Sylvia. Review of *Wise Blood*. *New York Herald Tribune Book Review*, 18 May 1952, p. 3.

———. Review of *A Good Man Is Hard to Find*. *New York Herald Tribune Book Review*, 5 June 1955, p. 1.

Stelzmann, Rainulf. "Shock and Orthodoxy: An Interpretation of Flannery O'Connor's Novels and Short Stories." *Xavier University Studies* 2 (March 1963): 4–21.

Stephens, Martha. "Flannery O'Connor and the Sanctified-Sinner Tradition." *Arizona Quarterly* 24 (1968): 223–39.

Stern, Richard. "Flannery O'Connor: A Remembrance and Some Letters." *Shenandoah* 16 (Winter 1965): 5–10.

Styan, J. L. *The Dark Comedy*. 2d ed. Cambridge: At the University Press, 1968.

Tate, James. "An O'Connor Remembrance." Typescript in O'Connor Collection, Georgia State College at Milledgeville.

Tate, Mary Barbara. "Flannery O'Connor: A Reminiscence." *Columns* [Georgia State College at Milledgeville], 2 (Fall 1964).

Taylor, Henry. "The Halt Shall be Gathered Together: Physical Deformity in the Fiction of Flannery O'Connor." *Western Humanities Review* 22 (1968): 325–38.

Teilhard de Chardin, Pierre. *The Divine Milieu* [1957]. Translated by Bernard Wall. New York: Harper & Row, Harper Torchbook, 1965.

———. *The Phenomenon of Man* [1955]. Translated by Bernard Wall. 2d ed. New York: Harper & Row, Harper Torchbook, 1965.

Thorp, Willard. "Suggs and Sut in Modern Dress." *Mississippi Quarterly* 13 (Fall 1960): 169–75.

Trachtenberg, S. Review of *Everything That Rises Must Converge*. *Yale Review* 55 (Autumn 1965): 144.

Trowbridge, Clinton W. "The Symbolic Vision of Flannery O'Connor: Patterns of Imagery in *The Violent Bear It Away*." *Sewanee Review* 76 (Spring 1968): 298–318.

Wells, Joe. "Off the Cuff." *Critic*, August-September 1962, pp. 4–5, 71–72.

West, Nathanael. *The Complete Works of Nathanael West*, edited by Alan Ross. New York: Farrar, Straus & Cudahy, 1957.

Wilder, Amos. *Theology and Modern Literature*. Cambridge: Harvard University Press, 1967.

Wright, G. Ernest, and Fuller, Reginald H. *The Book of the Acts of God*. Garden City: Doubleday, Anchor, 1960.

Zabel, Morton Dauwen. *Craft and Character: Texts, Method, and Vocation in Modern Fiction*. New York: Viking, 1957.

INDEX